MW01256843

A CHOSEN PEOPLE, A PROMISED LAND

A CHOSEN PEOPLE, A PROMISED LAND

Mormonism and Race in Hawai'i

HOKULANI K. AIKAU

FIRST PEOPLES
New Directions in Indigenous Studies

UNIVERSITY OF MINNESOTA PRESS

MINNEAPOLIS • LONDON

Publication of this book was made possible, in part, with a grant from the Andrew W. Mellon Foundation.

Portions of chapter 2 were previously published as "Resisting Exile in the Promised Land: He Moʻolelo no Lāʻie," *American Indian Quarterly* 32, no. 1 (2008): 70–95; reprinted with permission of the University of Nebraska Press.

Published by the University of Minnesota Press
111 Third Avenue South, Suite 290
Minneapolis, MN 55401–2520
http://www.upress.umn.edu

Library of Congress Cataloging-in-Publication Data

Aikau, Hokulani K., author.
A chosen people, a promised land : Mormonism and race in Hawaiʻi /
Hokulani K. Aikau.
(First peoples, new directions in indigenous studies)
Includes bibliographical references and index.
ISBN 978-0-8166-7461-9 (hc : alk. paper) — ISBN 978-0-8166-7462-6 (pb : alk. paper)
1. Polynesians—Relations with Mormons. 2. Mormon Church—Hawaii.
3. Mormons—Hawaii. 4. Race relations—Religious aspects—Church of Jesus Christ of Latter-day Saints. 5. Race relations—Religious aspects—Mormon Church.
6. Polynesian Cultural Center (Laie, Hawaii). I. Title. II. Series: First peoples (2010).
BX8643.P635A35 2012
289.3′969089—dc23
2011031740

Printed in the United States of America on acid-free paper

The University of Minnesota is an equal-opportunity educator and employer.

18 17 16 15 14 13 12   10 9 8 7 6 5 4 3 2 1

This book is dedicated to the loving memory of my father, Ned Kaili Aikau,
with whom I struggled along this path of understanding,
and to the memory of my kūkū kāne, Thomas Hewahewa Aikau,
who always wanted to see an Aikau publish a book

Contents

Preface / ix

INTRODUCTION Negotiating Faithfulness / 1

1 Mormonism, Race, and Lineage: The Making of a Chosen People / 31

2 Lāʻie, a Promised Land, and Puʻuhonua: Spatial Struggles for Land and Identity / 55

3 Called to Serve: Labor Missionary Work and Modernity / 91

4 In the Service of the Lord: Religion, Race, and the Polynesian Cultural Center / 123

5 Voyages of Faith: Contemporary Kanaka Maoli Struggles for Sustainable Self-Determination / 157

CONCLUSION Holomua, Moving Forward / 185

Acknowledgments / 189
Notes / 193
Glossary / 211
Bibliography / 215
Index / 223

Preface

As a child growing up in Utah I attended church with my family every Sunday. Our Sunday school lessons were filled with stories of the prophet Joseph Smith Jr. whose faith and dedication established the Church of Jesus Christ of Latter-day Saints. We also learned about how Brigham Young, the second prophet of the church, led the Mormon pioneers out of Illinois and away from persecution to Utah where they built the Kingdom of God on earth. My child's imagination was filled with stories of pioneers pulling and pushing handcarts across the dry plains and over the Rocky Mountains. At church, the perseverance of these pioneers was echoed in the songs we sang:

> When pioneers moved to the West,
> With courage strong they met the test.
> They pushed their handcarts all day long.
> And as they pushed they sang this song.
> For some must push and some must pull as we go marching up the hill.
> So merrily on our way we go until we reach the valley, O.[1]

For a Mormon child who was raised within the embrace of the Wasatch Mountains, the songs and stories about pioneers settling in the Salt Lake and Utah valleys were narratives that provided a collective origin story, an explanation and rationale of how we, the Mormons, came to be in Utah and how Utah came to be figured as a Mormon place.

As a Hawaiian child, church was not the only site for my religious education. At home, when our Polynesian family friends came to visit, we also learned another origin story about how Polynesians were a chosen people descended from Israel. The central figure of these stories was George Q. Cannon, one of the first Mormon missionaries to Hawai'i, who had a vision that Polynesians were one of the Lost Tribes of Israel and to whom the Mormon missionaries had an obligation to return the gospel of Christ. According to this story, we were one of God's chosen people who had, at one time, the fullness of His gospel. The conversations we had in my family home, which were reinforced once we started attending a Polynesian branch of the church, focused on how Polynesians readily accepted the gospel because it resonated with something deep inside us and touched a part of us that had been dormant for so long.[2] The stories told at home and at the Polynesian branch reiterated a collective understanding that the Mormon missionaries returned our heritage to us. As a chosen people, we were the original Mormons.

These two narratives provided me with a genealogy story that was figured bilaterally through mainline Mormon religious orthodoxy and through a distinctive Polynesian Mormon historical articulation. The Hawaiian Mormon

The author with her father at her baptism in the Church of Jesus Christ of Latter-day Saints, 1978. Photograph courtesy of the Aikau family.

identity nurtured by stories of missionaries and visions was further consolidated with the knowledge that my tūtū wahine, my Hawaiian grandmother, and her family from Molokaʻi had been members of the church since the turn of the twentieth century. As a young child I was comforted in this knowledge of my origins, however as I grew up and became more aware of the racial dynamics in the white Mormon community where we lived and learned of the racism that has plagued the Mormon church, I began to question what it meant that Polynesians were a chosen people.

The identity-affirming stories about Polynesians in the church began to lose their luster when my Hawaiian father told stories about being an undergraduate student at the Church College of Hawaiʻi, a small private college owned and operated by the Mormon church in Lāʻie, Hawaiʻi, where a haole (white) American Mormon professor told him to drop out of college and pursue a career in entertainment since Hawaiians were good at making people laugh and he wasn't going to amount to anything anyway.[3] This professor's words left a trace on my father's life as well as on the lives of his children who shouldered the pain of this man's racist attitude about Hawaiians. From my vantage point, Polynesians were a racial minority marginalized by the dominant haole Mormon population in Utah. It did not appear to me that Polynesians were venerated; on the contrary, it looked as though we were at best an exotic novelty who could perform hula and play music at church social functions, and at worst troublemakers who could not get along with haole coreligionists. As such, it appeared that a separate Polynesian congregation was a necessary solution to the Polynesian problem.

By the time I began college, I no longer experienced the articulation of my ethnic and religious identity as a synergistic, natural pairing. Rather, I was frustrated by the tension I saw and experienced between the notion that Polynesians were a chosen people and the way that Polynesians were marginalized in separate ethnic congregations and belittled by some haole Latter-day Saints. The stories of nineteenth-century Mormon missionaries restoring our connection to *The Book of Mormon* and stories of ancient shipbuilders from the Americas voyaging across the vast Pacific to settle the Polynesian islands lost its charm once I learned more about the racial policies that excluded blacks from full membership in the church. By the time I started college I had a crisis of faith and found that I was unable to negotiate these contradictory messages. I have since become an inactive member of the church.[4] This book was inspired by my personal challenge to understand how my Native Hawaiian ethnic identity came to be "naturally" linked to my religious identity as a Latter-day Saint and to understand the racial politics that position Polynesians as a chosen people in this predominantly white religious organization. My determination to understand these articulations required that I return to Hawai'i, the place of my birth, where the Mormon church has had a visible presence for over one hundred and fifty years.

In attending to the fraught and revealing episodes in Hawaiian Mormon history, *A Chosen People, a Promised Land: Mormonism and Race in Hawai'i* is more than a personal journey. In this book I open up new terrain for historical and discursive analyses of racial politics, colonization, Americanization, tourism, and struggles for Native Hawaiian self-determination. Grounded in the lives and stories of Latter-day Saints differentially situated within the church, I set out to understand how it is that colonial religious traditions such as Mormonism can be lived and inhabited as sites and sources of indigenous cultural vitality. When I started this project, my perspective was that Mormon missionaries and settlers, although marginalized in various ways, played a role in the colonization of Hawai'i by the United States. From this standpoint, Mormonism appeared to be wholly incompatible with indigenous cultural rejuvenation projects. Over the course of research, writing, and thinking about the relationship between Christianity, specifically Mormonism, and Hawaiian cultural politics I have struggled to understand how these social forces came to be conjoined and the meanings that people bring to them. Today, I understand the story of the Mormon church in a much more complicated and nuanced way. People speak about their membership in the church with great love and affection for the promises the gospel holds for them. But these promises are not solely about eternal salvation; indeed, in the stories I heard and read there was also a tremendous amount of aloha for the opportunities afforded Polynesian Latter-day Saints to reconnect with a way of life that has been threatened and a subjectivity that has been devalued.[5]

In 2001, I attended the launching of the wa'a kaulua 'o *Iosepa*, the double-hulled voyaging canoe named after Joseph F. Smith, a nineteenth-century Mormon missionary and former president of the church. On that sunny day in November I found myself looking out onto a sea of people whose faith, hard work, and determination brought this vessel to life. The salt from our tears of joy at seeing the launch and the sweat from the brows of those doing the launching mingled with the sea at the same moment that the wa'a, caressed by the ocean waves, broke free from its terrestrial tethers and undulated in the rise and fall of the kai (sea).

The waʻa was the physical manifestation of the Hawaiian Mormon identity I set out to understand. The visionaries who saw the waʻa in the giant logs before a single cut was made drew on many sources to maintain their dedication to this project; they had faith that the knowledge of their ancestors was true and accurate and faith that the Lord would be a solace to them during difficult times. Their faith was infectious and spread to everyone whose hands became callused by the work of honing wood into waʻa. My faith was restored, if only for a moment, as I stood on a sandy hill and watched hundreds of people emerge from the kai, reborn. I have had a tortured experience with Mormonism, but on that day I believed.

Introduction:
Negotiating Faithfulness

HAWAIIANNESS AND MORMONISM CAME TO BE FUSED THROUGH A religious invention initiated by the Mormon missionary George Q. Cannon who had a vision in 1851 that traced Polynesian lineage to *The Book of Mormon* and to Israel. This articulation expanded the racial and religious boundaries of the Church of Jesus Christ of Latter-day Saints (the LDS church) at a time when those boundaries were being codified and constrained. A central question of this book concerns the fusion of Hawaiianness and Mormonism.[1] Once they were fused, what was the impact of this articulation for Hawaiian and, later, Polynesian converts to the LDS church? How did they negotiate this new Hawaiian Mormon identity?[2]

Over the course of researching and writing this book I learned that the fusion of Mormon theology with Polynesian lineage was experienced by Native Hawaiian and, later, Polynesian Latter-day Saints as spiritually affirming—it brought them personal comfort and joy. I also came to learn that this identity provided Polynesian Latter-day Saints with a political tool of leverage that they could use during times of struggle and conflict.[3] As I document in the chapters to follow, the making and remaking of Mormonism in Hawai'i was a political enterprise initiated by church leadership and enacted by proselytizing missionaries. But religion is more than an institution with the power to transmit and transform society and identities; the devotees themselves also have the power to transform religion. How was Mormonism transformed when it crossed the ocean and landed on Hawai'i's shores? What new practices, beliefs, and tropes emerged alongside this new Hawaiian Mormon identity?

When I began this project, I could not understand how Polynesians, in general, and my family, in particular, could remain faithful to Mormonism given the racial tensions and contradictions I observed. I left the church as a young adult disillusioned by what I saw as an irresolvable contradiction between Polynesians as a chosen people and the racially discriminatory practices I experienced and witnessed. In the course of doing the research for this project, I learned there are many reasons why Polynesians maintain their faithfulness to the church—not the least of which are the spiritual rewards promised to the truly faithful. By keeping to the faith they will receive salvation. My research kept returning me to the question of faith, but I was at a loss for making sense of it. While teaching feminist theory I had an "aha" moment after rereading a piece by M. Jacqui Alexander in which she describes how an ideology of faithfulness operated in the Bahamas. In this piece she explores how a state-managed semiotic system functions to differentially position tourists, Bahamians, sex workers, and women within the tourist economy by relying on "an ideology that premises faithful Bahamian citizenship upon a faithfulness to tourism."[4] The notion of an ideology of faithfulness opened up a new way for me to understand how I saw faith deployed both at the institutional and the individual levels. In my adoption of this concept, an ideology of faithfulness is not about one's active membership in the church; rather, it is a way to leverage faith in order to solicit community consent to church projects, even when they are in the interests of the church and not the community.

Alexander's notion of ideologies of faithfulness helps to explain how LDS church leaders use faithfulness, which is an ideology of blind obedience to the gospel and the priesthood, as a regime of truth in the maintenance of power. As the cultural theorist Stuart Hall instructs, ideology has the power to "unite the group from the inside and maintain its dominance and leadership over society as a whole."[5] Throughout the history of the LDS church in Hawai'i I mark those moments when ideologies of faithfulness unite members of the church in common cause and when faith is used as a tool to maintain dominance and exert order over the community to ensure faithfulness. For example, in the nineteenth century the Hawaiian mission president allocated parcels of land along the stream where Hawaiian Latter-day Saints could grow kalo (taro). He was motivated by faith: namely, faith that if he provided Hawaiians with land they would gather in Lā'ie and create a strong religious foundation for the mission; faith in the gospel and its plan of salvation; and faith that his actions were guided by the Holy Spirit and were in the service of the Lord. The Hawaiian Latter-day Saints were also motivated by faith: faith that through the gospel many blessings would come to them; and faith that by returning to the land they would be nourished physically by the life-sustaining kalo and spiritually by reestablishing their cosmological connection to the 'āina (land).

The allocation of land for kalo production drew upon various ideologies of faithfulness to unite the mission community and to further consolidate a Hawaiian Mormon identity. But I also mark the ways in which faith was used as a form of coercion, when an ideology of faithfulness became hegemonic. Land was available to the Saints only when it was economically beneficial to the mission and as long as they faithfully obeyed the rules established by the mission president. During times of conflict or struggle, the interests of the church superseded the desires of the Saints. As I also note, the situation was not fixed but dynamic. When the mission president asserted a position contrary to the interests of the Saints, they pushed back. They drew upon rearticulated ideologies of faithfulness to assert their claim that the land was not given by the church but by God as part of His covenant to His chosen people. By drawing on Mormon rhetoric and discourses of lineage, namely Cannon's vision that linked Hawaiians to Mormonism, they were able to stay on the land and maintain their indigenous land use practices, at least for a time. At the turn of the twentieth century, as the economic needs of the mission increased and Hawai'i's economy became more dependent on sugar production, I document how the subversive ideologies of faithfulness used to challenge the mission president weakened as more lo'i kalo (water garden area) was transformed into rice paddies or cleared for sugar cultivation. Although not always successful, Native Hawaiian and other Polynesian Latter-day Saints used their status in the church to push back and assert their own desires and vision for Lā'ie.

AMERICAN NATIONALISM AND MORMONISM'S UNIVERSAL MESSAGE

The history of the LDS church is mired in various internal and external tensions, two of which inform the parameters of this project. First, I engage the tension between the universal message of missionary work and racial discourses that in the 1850s drew a bold line between those souls who were worthy of salvation and those who were beyond redemption. Second, I employ the ongoing tension between the issue of Mormonism as a quintessentially

American religion that is also persecuted and marginalized. I argue that an ambiguous relationship between the LDS church and the U.S. government and American nationalism continues to inform how nonmembers understand and relate to the church and how Latter-day Saints understand and relate to American nationalist discourses. These tensions not only have been negotiated within the church by way of debates and policies that have attempted to resolve these contradictions but also have been played out on the ground as people of color, who were differentially included in the church, have negotiated their place in the racial hierarchy.

In 1820 Joseph Smith Jr. knelt in prayer to ask for guidance in his quest to find the true church of Christ. He was merely fourteen years old at the time, and he was surrounded by the religious fervor of the Second Great Awakening in upstate New York. As Smith fervently prayed, he was visited by two personages believed to be God the Father and His son, Jesus Christ. He was instructed not to join any of the churches vying for his soul, and if patient he would be given instructions for how to return Christ's church to the earth. In response Smith rejected all other denominations, and after a series of other celestial visitations he formed the Church of Jesus Christ of Latter-day Saints. One of the visitations provided Smith with the location of plates or tablets made of gold, which held the story of an ancient peoples as well as instructions and tools for their subsequent translation. Smith completed the translation of what came to be known as *The Book of Mormon,* canonized as Holy Scripture, and then officially established the church based on the same organizational structure and principles as Christ's original church.

Since the late 1860s, the small town of Lāʻie has become a central gathering place for Saints from around the world. When an LDS temple was built in the town in the early twentieth century, Lāʻie was elevated to a Promised Land in the Pacific that drew waves of Polynesian Latter-day Saints eager to participate in the sacred ordinances performed only in an LDS temple. New waves of migration would transform the community again as students from around the world attended school at the Church College of Hawaiʻi (renamed Brigham Young University–Hawaiʻi in 1974). Today, the Polynesian Cultural Center is one of the major tourist facilities on Oʻahu island despite being an hour drive from Honolulu and Waikīkī, the fulcrum of tourism in Hawaiʻi. However, in spite of the changes over the years Lāʻie has adapted to the changing tides while holding firm to its Hawaiian and religious roots. For people whose popular image of Mormonism conjures images of a clean-cut, blond-haired and blue-eyed young white man wearing a dark suit, white shirt, and narrow tie, Lā'ie with its national and racial diversity may be unrecognizable as a Mormon community. However, in contrast to Salt Lake City, the world headquarters of the LDS church, Lā'ie more accurately represents the global face of contemporary Mormonism. Today the worldwide membership of the church is fourteen million souls, "a majority of whom live outside the United States."[6] In many ways the story of the church in Hawai'i is anomalous. The missionaries were relatively successful in Hawai'i at a time in church history when missionaries to other nonwhite countries had little or no success in sharing their message. This trend would take nearly a century to be overturned, yet what it highlights is a conflict between the universalistic message of missionary work—namely that all people regardless of race or nationality need to hear the word of God—and the racial hierarchies of white racial superiority embedded in the belief system. The tension is most evident in the "ethnic-geographic" focus of Mormon missionary work.

As the LDS historian Newell G. Bringhurst describes, between 1830 and 1850 missionary efforts were focused on the New England and New York areas. These efforts were most successful in small to midsized communities among lower-middle-class and working-class white Americans.[7] At this same time, missionaries were also dispatched to preach to Native Americans; however, these efforts did not garner the same outcomes as only a small number of Native Americans were baptized, after which they joined the Mormon settlers in Nauvoo, Illinois, and migrated to Utah.[8] Renewed interest in and commitment to preaching to Native Americans would not resurface until the mid-twentieth century. In 1846, the church's missionary work went international, and missionaries saw their highest success in Britain and in the Scandinavian countries. Scholars of LDS immigration history suggest that it is this influx of converts from England, Denmark, Sweden, and Norway that produced the "'decidedly Anglo-Scandinavian' or 'Nordic Cast'" of Utah's Mormons.[9] While Mormonism was gaining momentum in Western Europe, in 1843 missionary work in Polynesia began in the Society Islands. This work did not, however, produce the kind of stronghold that was able to be generated in Hawai'i.[10] In the 1850s, at the same time that missionaries began preaching to Native Hawaiians, the church sent missionaries to India, Thailand, and Hong Kong. In India, Jessie Embry notes, "the missionaries had some success teaching and baptizing British soldiers."[11] But they had next to no success elsewhere in Asia. It was not until the 1920s that missionary work would resume in Asia, primarily in Japan, but efforts would be stalled again during World War II and not recommence until after the war.

According to Armand Mauss, missionaries were sent to Africa in the mid-nineteenth century, but with no success these missions were closed. Over a century later missionary efforts were once again attempted, but they failed in no small part because of church policy that denied black African men from holding the priesthood. Their efforts in Africa would not resume until 1978 when the ban that denied black men the priesthood was lifted.[12] Despite the lifting of the ban and the global success of its missionary efforts, the LDS church continues to negotiate a tension between its universal message and racial ideologies. The racial discourses that continue to haunt the LDS church are not distinct from those that continue to wreak havoc in the United States at large.

As I argue, the LDS church is simultaneously quintessentially American and yet continues to be marginalized and seen as a threat to American values. Thomas F. O'Dea, one of the first non-Mormons to write a history of the LDS church without unduly criticizing it, is a leading proponent of the thesis that Mormons are quintessentially American, and despite some peculiar beliefs the church is far more mainstream than most Americans realize. O'Dea begins his history of the Mormons by yoking the American ideologies of westward expansion and patriotism to church history. He recounts scenes of manifest destiny across the North American continent where Mormon settlers tamed the savage frontier first in Utah and later in Idaho, Oregon, Wyoming, Colorado, Arizona, Nevada, and New Mexico. He tells stories of American patriotism when he writes, "a battalion of Mormons, five hundred strong, recruited under orders from President Polk, marched through what is now Arizona and New Mexico and arrive[d] in California in January, 1847, thereby playing a major role in incorporating that area into the United States."[13] His use of these particular examples emphatically places Mormons squarely within a discourse of American nationalism, while also eliding the legacy of conquest that underlies this history. In this way, Mormons become typically "American"; "Mormons," O'Dea declares, "feel themselves very much to be Americans. Patriotism and American institutions have been greatly emphasized by the church in recent decades."[14] Just as the American frontier myth fails to account for the removal of Native peoples from their land in order to make way for "American" settlers, the history of settlement that I learned in school and at church celebrated Mormon history as an extension of American history; the settlement of Utah by Mormon pioneers was, after all, a manifestation of divine prophesy from God to the second prophet of the church, Brigham Young.

This articulation of American nationalism with Mormon history is best expressed in a tiled mural placed above the entrance to Brigham Young University–Hawaiʻi that depicts an American flag-raising ceremony performed by three boys—one Hawaiian, one haole (Caucasian), and one Japanese American—attending Lāʻie Elementary School. David O. McKay, who at the time was a high-ranking leader in the church and would become its prophet and president, witnessed the flag ceremony while visiting Lāʻie in 1921. About this event McKay wrote:

> As I looked at the motley group of youngsters, and realized how far apart their parents are in hopes, aspirations, and ideals, and then thought of these boys and girls, the first generation of their children, all thrown into what Israel Zangwell has aptly called the "Melting Pot" and coming out Americans, my bosom swelled with emotion and tears came to my eyes and I felt like bowing in prayer and thanksgiving for the glorious country which is doing so much for all these nationalities. But more than that, when I realize that these same boys and girls have the opportunity of participating in all the blessings of the Gospel which will transform the American into a real citizen of the Kingdom of God, I feel to praise His name for the glorious privileges vouchsafed to this generation. We held short services in the school room in which all—American, Hawaiian, Japanese, Chinese, Filipino—participated as though they had belonged to one nation, one country, one tongue.
>
> America and the Church of Christ will truly make of all nations one blood. May God hasten the day when this is accomplished.[15]

With this act of remembering, McKay seamlessly draws the notion of America as a melting pot into the strong proselytizing rhetoric of the LDS church and then grounds both in Hawaiʻi. From its origins in upstate New York, the church has held a fundamental belief that through missionary work it will bring all the people of the earth—past, present, and future—into salvation through the teaching and acceptance of the gospel.

Contemporary scholars of LDS history have become more attentive to the particularity and peculiarity of the Mormon context while not losing sight of how it converges with and diverges from the American religious mainstream.[16] Laurie Maffley-Kipp minimizes the potential conflict between Mormonism and American patriotism by suggesting that most Mormons draw a distinction between the U.S. government, which in the nineteenth and early twentieth century used military force to suppress their religious

The mosaic of the flag-raising ceremony adorns the entrance to the David O. McKay Building, one of the original buildings of the Church College of Hawaiʻi. Photograph courtesy of Brigham Young University–Hawaiʻi Archives.

freedom, and the sacredness of the American continent within its theology. She claims that although the history of persecution of Mormonism by the U.S. government is codified in religious texts, anti-American sentiment is mediated by the geographic significance of North America as the site for the second coming of Christ. She alleviates any concern that non-Mormon Americans may have of the church by reiterating that since Mormon theology is linked to the land and not the government, concerns about LDS political dominance can be quelled.[17]

John Heineman and Anson Shupe, by contrast, suggest that missionary work is more than a means to spread the word of God. Indeed, they contend that the LDS church is a corporate empire committed to nothing short of "political and economic control of the United States," and they note that "the Church is still engaged in a crusade to bring about theocracy in the United States."[18] For Heinerman and Shupe, the mission of the church has always included global religious supremacy. Unlike Mauffly-Kipp who minimizes the political significance of restoring the gospel in the United States, Heineman and Shupe make the connection explicit. During the early years of the church, leaders spoke openly about their belief that Joseph Smith restored the true church of Christ to the world so a new Zion could be built in the United States. The hinge that connects the restoration of Christ's church to American nationalism (not just the American landscape) is freedom of religion codified by the U.S. Constitution.

The significance of the U.S. Constitution was highlighted during my interview with Ron and Wendy Sing, who are strong supporters of Hawai'i's current relationship with the United States as they do not support the contemporary sovereignty movement. I interviewed Uncle Ron and Aunty Wendy (the monikers they use in the Hawaiian tradition) in May 2002 in their home in Orem, Utah.[19] I grew up across the street from the Sing family and attended school and church with their daughters. I was not surprised when Aunty Wendy stated, "I am not for the Hawaiian movement, for the Hawaiians to have their own kingdom back again." In many ways her perspective reflects the teleological perspective of American historians who have narrated the incorporation of Hawai'i into the United States as inevitable. In fact, this teleological history becomes part of a larger story about the restoration of the gospel to the Hawaiians. As she stated further, "I feel that the reason why we were, had to have one kingdom [was] so that we could be part of the United States. Only in freedom can you have the true religion restored. And that [was] the basis that was preparation for the missionaries coming to Hawai'i."[20] For Aunty Wendy, the unification of the Hawaiian Islands by Kamehameha I was significant because it was the necessary precondition for the establishment and growth of the church. Thus, not only is Hawai'i history teleologically connected to the United States but the church's very existence in Hawai'i was made possible by the United States through the freedom of religion.

I contend that Mauffly-Kipp is able to draw a line between an ambivalent American patriotism and an unambiguous religious relationship to the American landscape because she disavows the narratives and practices of conquest that underscore Mormon history. It is this same history of colonization that is elided in Aunty Wendy's statement and grouted over in the tile mural depicting President McKay at the multicultural flag-raising ceremony. Despite the insights that O'Dea brings to the history of the LDS church, his account reinforces the "natural" connection between whiteness and the church while also reinforcing the articulation of whiteness with Americanness. For example, he mentions that the church has a history of missionary work in foreign countries, but these are primarily European nations whose citizens migrated to the United States and, presumably, became American. As such, within the racial lexicon of the United States they became white. What is missing from his historical record is the fact that the first LDS missions were to Native American communities. When the Native Americans became members of the church they neither became "American" nor were racialized as "white." As Craig Prentiss argues, unlike their Anglo co-religionists, Native Americans are interpellated by the doctrine of the church as a loathsome people.[21] This example challenges notions of the LDS church as white while also exposing the politics of race embedded in its very origins. My focus on the history of the church in Hawai'i expands O'Dea's contention that the church espouses American nationalist principles by tracing how these principles and beliefs travel beyond the boundaries of the nation and how this legacy of conquest was also a racial project that interpreted, represented, and explained racial dynamics in order to justify the establishment of a mission in the islands.[22] In Hawai'i, the inclusion of Hawaiians into the religious racial matrix of the church exposed the contradictions between the universal message of missionary work and the racial ideologies that determined the differential inclusion of people of color in the church. I argue that the categories of race and ethnicity and notions of whiteness were not disrupted by this redrawing of the racial lines of the church but instead reiterate them.

Religious Sitings

For its first one hundred years in Hawai'i the LDS church was considered a Hawaiian church by local church leaders, and this fact was evidenced by its membership.[23] Except for a small number of American missionaries and leaders, and a group of about twenty Sāmoans who immigrated to Lā'ie in the 1920s, the church membership was almost entirely comprised of Native Hawaiians.[24] According to Max Stanton, only about 10 percent of the Hawaiian Mormon population lived in Lā'ie, with the remainder of the membership spread out across the pae 'āina (archipelago). Given that Hawaiian Mormons could be found in most Hawaiian communities, one option for my project in this book would be to focus broadly on how Hawaiians made use of their status in the church and how they maintained cultural practices and beliefs while also being faithful Latter-day Saints. Indeed, future research could focus on how Native Hawaiian Mormon activists and cultural practitioners make sense of their political and cultural kuleana (responsibilities) and their religious identities. However, I limit my focus to Lā'ie, a town located on the northeastern shore of O'ahu island, because indigenous relationships to place are central to how we understand the past, the present, the future, and ourselves. Lā'ie is a place deep with indigenous and Mormon meaning. By limiting my focus to one place I illuminate the institutional motivations of LDS church leaders while also paying attention to the experiences of individual members. Within an indigenous Hawaiian religious-political context, Lā'ie was a pu'uhonua (a place of refuge) where a person charged with a crime could flee and thus be saved from a punishment of death.[25] This indigenous understanding of place articulated with an LDS ideology of gathering came to be imagined as a Zion in the Pacific. Lā'ie was the headquarters of the church in the Pacific from 1865 to 1919; it became an educational center with the opening of the Church College of Hawai'i in the 1950s; and it was made a site for global tourism when the Polynesian Cultural Center was opened in the 1960s. These divergent understandings of place serve to illustrate how Lā'ie became a place of contestation, negotiation, and cultural survivance.[26]

Religions are also sites of contestation, negotiation and survivance. For the purposes of this book I define religion provisionally as an institution with an organizational and bureaucratic structure that can transmit and transform traditions through the establishment and manipulation of, in the words of Thomas Tweed, "tropes, values, emotions, and beliefs."[27] By drawing upon oral histories, interviews, and the journals of missionaries, I explore how broader social and historical forces and processes such as racialization, colonialism, assimilation to American culture, and touristification shape Hawaiian members of the church.[28] Additionally, I explore how Native Hawaiian Latter-day Saints in turn shape the church. This dual approach to the study of religion is resonant with a theoretical tradition in sociology that recognizes and examines the dialogic intersection of social forces at the macro level and processes of everyday life at the micro level. The extended case method, the methodological approach that informs this research, is attentive to how historical context shapes everyday lived experiences and, in the words of Michael Burawoy, "the multiple dimensions of power" that come from reflexive ethnography.[29] This approach, Burawoy further writes, enables "the exploration of broad historical patterns and macrostructure *without* relinquishing either ethnography or science."[30] I am interested in the dynamic relationship between institutions and individuals—namely, how institutions shape individuals and how individuals transform institutions.

This perspective allows me to be attentive to the constraints as well as the prospects of religious hegemonies.

For nearly three decades contemporary Native Hawaiian scholars have challenged prior research that distorted our past and our people. These works produced and continue to reproduce a central narrative of American domination as inevitable and justified. They also represent Hawaiians as powerless children in need of the benevolences of the United States and its representatives. These narratives assumed that Hawaiians did not have anything of worth to contribute to history, politics, and our understanding of the various social formations in Hawai'i nei. This book is part of a growing body of scholarship by Hawaiian scholars who use the words and worldviews of our kūpuna (elders and ancestors) as an archive that can inform how we see the past as well as the possibilities for an alternative future. Works such as Lilikalā Kame'eleihiwa's *Native Land and Foreign Desires: Pehea Lā E Pono Ai?* Haunani-Kay Trask's *From a Native Daughter,* Jonathan Kay Kamakawiwo'ole Osorio's *Dismembering Lāhui,* and Noenoe Silva's *Aloha Betrayed* rewrite and recover Hawaiian history from the perspective of Native Hawaiians and challenge previous research that describes Hawaiians as passive victims of Christianity, capitalism, and American colonialism. A new generation of Kanaka scholars such as Ty Kāwika Tengan and J. Kēhaulani Kauanui have used the momentum and new intellectual space generated by these foundational texts to expand the boundaries of Hawaiian studies into new areas.[31] My book is part of this new wave of research and expands the discussion beyond a focus on Protestant and Catholic missionaries as part of the colonial legacy in Hawai'i by exploring how Native Hawaiian members of the LDS church negotiated their membership in this marginal yet American religion while struggling to maintain their connection to place as well as to their distinct ethnic identity.

Although Christianity has played a central role in Hawai'i's culture and politics since Protestant missionaries arrived in the islands in 1820, few books have focused exclusively on the interplay between this colonial imposition and the way that Native Hawaiians took it and used it toward their own objectives.[32] Whereas Kame'eleihiwa and Osorio attend to the impact that Christianity and missionaries from the American Board of Commissioners for Foreign Missions had on Hawaiian sovereignty, my work takes the discussion of American colonialism in a new direction by looking at the specific context of LDS missionary work in Hawai'i.[33] I am interested in the particular strategies the Mormon missionaries used to further the cause of American colonialism while also attempting to preserve various Native

Hawaiian cultural practices. Conversely, I am interested in how Native Hawaiian and other Polynesian Latter-day Saints used their faith toward their own goals of cultural perpetuation and regeneration. Indeed, I interrogate what is at times a fraught relationship between indigeneity and Christianity, as Christianity has historically been implicated in legacies of imperialism, colonialism, and cultural genocide. While I am interested in how a unique Hawaiian Mormon identity emerged out of an ambivalent colonial relationship between the LDS church and its Polynesian membership, I maintain a tension between the church as a colonial agent of U.S. imperialism and its efforts to preserve Polynesian culture. For example, in addition to being attentive to how the church enabled expressions of self-determination in the nineteenth century by providing landless Hawaiians with a place to grow kalo, I also trace how by the mid-twentieth century the church's interests and those of Native Hawaiians came into conflict as areas of lo'i kalo were removed in order to build the Polynesian Cultural Center. Finally, I situate the establishment of a Hawaiian Mormon identity within a larger struggle between indigenous self-determination and Christianity.[34]

As Native Hawaiians continue in the work of our kūpuna to strive for our sovereignty as a nation and for expressions of self-determination, it is imperative to understand what is at stake when indigenous people embrace Christianity.[35] As my research demonstrates, since the establishment of the LDS church in Hawai'i some Native Hawaiians have embraced the gospel of the church as an essential part of their identity. The oral histories archived at Brigham Young University–Hawai'i and the interviews I conducted serve as a testament to the belief held by many members of the church that their religious experiences enrich their cultural understanding and in turn perpetuate traditional cultural practices. My research also documents a darker side to this story as I expose how various church practices and business ventures benefited the organization at the expense of the Polynesian membership, a perspective that is conspicuously absent in the archive. I learned that explicitly critical perspectives have existed but were silenced out of fear of recrimination that criticism of church practices could place one's status in the church in jeopardy. The religion scholar James Treat suggests that indigenous people need to "work together to make sense of the problem [of indigeneity and Christianity] in order to arrive at a reasonable accommodation that will facilitate personal and communal survival."[36] As Hawai'i's history illustrates, we have not always agreed upon the appropriate path that would lead to our personal and communal survival, but the actions of our kūpuna were guided by a sense of kuleana to imagine and articulate an alternative future for generations to come.

<h2 style="text-align:center">THEORETICAL SIGHTINGS</h2>

My research took me on a personal huakaʻi (journey) back and forth between Utah and Hawaiʻi and set me on an intellectual path with many detours, danger zones, and diversions. Despite being physically and firmly planted in frigid archives as I read the oral histories and journals of people who were long since gone, I was transported to the nineteenth century when Cannon and his fellow missionaries disembarked on these shores; I stood with Polynesian farmers when they saw visions of angels above their fields; and I could hear the songs of joyful music floating on the wind coming from Sunday services at the old chapel. On this journey I have crossed physical, disciplinary, theoretical, and emotional boundaries, all of which inform how this book came to be.

My emphasis on movement, travel, wayfaring, voyaging is important for two reasons. First, I want the reader to come on this journey with me. Huakaʻi are important because they allow us to see things in a new light. I want readers to go on their own journey, be it intellectual, temporal, or spatial, and to see how the Mormon church in Hawaiʻi was shaped by Native Hawaiians and how the church was also transformed. Second, I want to emphasize the theoretical importance of movement, transformation, and change. Thomas Tweed writes that "theories, in the first sense of the word, are travels." In conceptualizing theory as travel, he figures "theory as movements across space (and time)." He explains further that it is "useful to understand theory as travel—but not as the displacement of voluntary migrants who seek settlement, tourists who chase pleasure on round-trip journeys, or pilgrims who depart only to return home after venerating a sacred site. *Theory is purposeful wandering*" (emphasis added).[37] Tweed's metaphor of the research process as a journey describes scholars who lean on "staffs" "bestowed by others as [we] set out in one direction on a journey of uncertain duration towards sites unseen and vaguely imagined, and [we] negotiate the trail by what illumination [we] can find along the way." While on this journey, he writes, "theorists in motion offer partial views of shifting terrain." There are blind spots, things we cannot see from the place from which we are positioned, thus, "theories . . . are *sightings* from sites. They are positioned representations of a changing terrain by an itinerant cartographer."[38]

The notion of travel as theory is not new in the context of the Pacific. Vicente Diaz and J. Kēhaulani Kauanui theorize a Native Pacific cultural studies by first establishing that the Pacific is literally on the move. The shifting of the tectonic plates and the addition of new land by volcanic flow challenges any notion of fixed terrestrial groundings. Pacific Islanders, they argue, have known for centuries what contemporary theorists only recently started to understand, namely that islands move and that our theories reflect that movement. Diaz and Kauanui's evocation of the Carolinian navigational theory of etak (moving islands) provides a useful illustration of a traveling theory. Etak, they write, "involves reckoning the distance traveled and one's location at sea calculating the rate at which one's island of departure moves away from the traveling canoe and the rate at which a second reference island moves along another prescribed star course."[39] Navigators and voyagers describe their experience of etak as the canoe being fixed in place while the islands and stars move around them. The canoe as the fixed point of the triangulation resonates with my experience of doing research. Although I was firmly situated in a particular time and space the stories and people came and went along the horizon, thereby allowing me to orient myself to the social processes I encountered.

Tweed's focus on movement and travel is also evident in his theory of religion because he incorporates spatial and aquatic metaphors: "Spatial metaphors (*dwelling* and *crossing*) signal that religion is about finding a place and moving across space, and aquatic metaphors (*confluences* and *flows*) signal that religions are not reified substances but complex processes."[40] It is not only religions that are dynamic and fluid but also people as they cross boundaries, strive to find their place in changing historical contexts, and use whatever means available to them to navigate complex economic, political, and social processes.

A second theoretical sighting is Stuart Hall's theory of articulation, a staff upon which Tweed also relies. Articulation is the linking of ideology with social forces, and it provides another way to understand the making and remaking of a Hawaiian Mormon identity. By the term ideology Hall means "the mental frameworks—the languages, the concepts, categories, imagery of thought, and the systems of representation—which different classes and social groups deploy in order to make sense of, define, figure out and render intelligible the way society works."[41] Hall explains his usage of articulation as a theory that helps us understand how certain terms and meanings come to be linked by larger historical forces: "An articulation is thus the form of the connection that *can* make a unity of two different elements, under certain conditions. It is a linkage, which is not necessary, determined, absolute and essential for all time. You have to ask, under what circumstances *can* a connection be forged or made?"[42] As he argues, the articulation or linkage between ideology and social forces is not natural or normal but occurs under certain historical circumstances.

Chapter 1 offers my explanation of the historical circumstances that produced the connection between Hawaiians and LDS doctrine. The identification of Polynesians as being derived from the Lost Tribes of Israel was not the only outcome that could have been expected. As I describe in more detail later in this introduction, when Mormon missionaries first arrived in Hawai'i they were not interested in preaching the gospel to the Natives. At that moment in time Hawaiians were not a part of the missionaries' racial social imaginary of the church. In fact, had only a few historical events been different—had Cannon not had a vision and had he capitulated to his mission president and agreed to leave Hawai'i—it is likely the church would not have returned until World War II to provide religious support to the American soldiers who were members of the church. Had this been the case, the history of the church in Hawai'i would be quite different. Rather than taking the link between Hawaiianness and Mormonism as natural and normal, as I had done as a child, I explore the circumstances by which they came to be linked. What initially started as a way for Mormon missionaries to make sense of their interest in preaching to Native Hawaiians instead of haole residents was transformed and became the foundation for the religious belief that Polynesians are a chosen people. This revelation has since been taken up by church leaders and historians as proof of the validity of *The Book of Mormon* and the restoration of Christ's true church on earth. I contend that the political implication of the articulated identity was a racial formation that hails Polynesians as a chosen people whose culture must be preserved while simultaneously reproducing dominant racial hierarchies that situate American (read white) Mormons as saviors of this Lost Tribe of Israel.

Articulations, Hall argues, also produce new social and political actors. Once Cannon made the initial connection between Polynesians and *The Book of Mormon* he was compelled to act in particular ways in accordance with this new understanding. The revelation transformed Hawaiians from a people ineligible to hear the gospel to a people who needed the gospel "returned" to them. According to Mormon ideology, it was Cannon's obligation as a missionary to stay in Hawai'i even when his fellow missionaries lost their faith and made plans to return home. In his instructional manual for other missionaries, Cannon shared his decision to remain in Hawai'i:

> For my part I felt it to be clearly my duty to warn all men, white and red; and no sooner did I learn the condition of the population than I made up my mind to acquire the language, preach the gospel to the natives and to the whites whenever I could obtain an opportunity, and thus fill my mission. I felt resolved to stay there, master the language and warn the people of those islands, if I had to do it alone; for I felt that I could not do otherwise and be free from condemnation; the spirit was upon me.[43]

The articulation of *The Book of Mormon* and Hawaiians was a powerful rationale that inspired a firm commitment to remain in Hawai'i, learn the language, and preach the gospel to the natives. Cannon's vision in its immediate historical context provided him and his fellow missionaries with an explanation for the new relationship between them and the Native Hawaiians they found themselves drawn to. By drawing upon religious doctrine and emerging debates in the church about the Lost Tribes of Israel and connecting these religious ideologies to Hawaiians, Cannon and those missionaries who opted to remain in Hawai'i were able to express this relationship within an ideological frame that made sense.

But as Hall explains, an ideological conception, such as the Hawaiian-Israelite lineage, cannot "become materially effective unless and until it *can* be articulated to the field of political and social forces and to the struggles between different forces at stake."[44] Although Cannon's vision inspired him and a few other missionaries, the Hawaiian-Israelite lineage took time to take hold and to produce a material effect on a larger scale. As I illustrate in chapter 1, although the Polynesian-Israelite connection has been incorporated into the larger religious doctrine, it has not produced the same kind of material effect on mainline Mormonism as it has had in Hawai'i and across Oceania where it is a central organizing principle for a Polynesian Mormon identity. Despite the uneven receptivity of the revelation, what remains clear is that the consolidation of a Polynesian Mormon identity emerged in concert with other ideological formations occurring in mainline Mormonism, not tangential to it.

But these categories—Hawaiian and Mormon—were not empty signifiers prior to their articulation. The articulation of ideology is not something totally new, Hall explains: "It is not something which has a straight, unbroken line of continuity from the past." Instead, it is a reorganization of already existing ideological elements, "which do not in themselves have any necessary political connection." Over time they become consolidated, material, and adhere together to produce a "new discursive formation."[45] Mormonism was already articulated with American nationalism in complicated and sometimes contradictory ways. As a marginal and persecuted religion, Mormonism was often seen as a threat to American nationalism. And yet, the LDS church was a homegrown religion that incorporated many American nationalist discourses of freedom, private property, individualism, a Protestant work ethic, and a belief in manifest destiny that God provided them with land that would become His Kingdom on earth. By exploring how particular meanings come to adhere to certain concepts, for example how Mormonism can simultaneously be a persecuted religion and a vehicle for transmitting American nationalist and racial discourses, I expand current theories and understandings of Christianity's role in colonial projects. I argue that even a marginal religion such as the LDS church can reiterate colonial projects of exploitation, expropriation, and dispossession because it is seeped in American ideologies of land acquisition and settlement.

Once we understand that the Hawaiian Mormon articulation is not natural but historically contingent then we can also see the potential for other articulations—that ideology and social forces can be disarticulated and rearticulated in other ways. Because the initial articulations, Hall explains, "are not inevitable, not necessary, they can potentially be transformed, so that religion can be articulated in more than one way." Hall cautions by clarifying that locating religion as a site for social change is challenging because, "historically, it has been inserted into particular cultures in a particular way over a long period of time, and this constitutes the magnetic lines of tendency which are very difficult to disrupt."[46] In order for social change to happen, social activists must engage with the dominant religious articulation. A social movement cannot succeed without this engagement. In the conclusion I discuss how Christianity continues to be a force with which Native Hawaiian activists are engaged and must engage even as we rearticulate a vision for an alternative future of sustainable self-determination.

POLITICAL IN(TER)VENTIONS

Throughout this book my focus is on the political—that is, the relative power of different regimes of truth in Lāʻie at various historical moments and social contexts. These power struggles and contestations over meaning and the distribution of material goods have certain consequences for the maintenance of power in the community. Derek Peterson and Darren Walhof's theory of the invention of religion challenges notions that consider religion to be apolitical and a personal essence. Although they do not deny that religious belief has a personal component and that one's spiritual beliefs can be detached from the political, their point is to show how the separation of religion from secular matters such as politics is a historical invention. As Peterson and Walhof write, "Thinking of religion as a historical invention helps us see religion not as a prior category organic to human experience nor as a past bound to be superseded by the secular future. Studying religion in its creation links the study of ontology and ritual to politics and helps trace out the struggles involved in the constitution of modernity."[47] The relationship between politics and religion is a complicated one to tease out in Hawai'i.

As Lilikalā Kame'eleihiwa writes, "In traditional times, the Hawaiian polity was religious and Hawaiian religion, at the level of the Chiefs, was political. The two were inseparably entwined and their purpose was to keep the universe in a state of *pono*, or 'perfect equilibrium.'"[48] Although the Kingdom of Hawai'i incorporated Western law as part of the process of becoming recognized by the international community of nations, Sally Engle Merry posits that Western law had already been articulated with Christianity, thereby becoming the twin markers of civilization. Merry explains that "it was Massachusetts prototypes that formed the basis of Hawaiian criminal law, for example, because these law books happened to be in Honolulu."[49] Additionally, the Protestant New England missionaries saw law as necessary to control native bodies and their excesses. Whereas some scholars mark the end of the kapu system (the indigenous political-religious system) and the formation of a nation-state as a critical secular shift in Hawai'i politics, for Kame'eleihiwa the transformation of the political structure of the kingdom was religiously motivated albeit informed by Christianity through the actions of the missionaries from the American Board of Commissioners for Foreign Missions. Merry supports this claim and argues that a new regime of truth, "a Protestant Christian one premised on the authority of Jehovah," merely replaced the "Hawaiian legal order [which was] premised on divine authority."[50] Thus politics and religion were again fused.

The fusion of politics and religion, Juri Mykkanen argues, posed an ideological problem for Protestant missionaries whose explicit dictate was "to abstain . . . from the interference with the *political* and party concerns of the nation."[51] In the process of what Mykkanen calls "cross-cultural invention," Protestant missionaries became enmeshed in the political affairs of the kingdom in large part because politics was already a part of the public discourse. As Jonathan Osorio contends, once these missionaries entered in the political affairs of the kingdom they actively worked within the system in self-serving as well as self-sacrificing ways.[52]

Managing a distinction between politics and religion, however, was less of a concern for the Mormon missionaries. The principle of gathering to Zion created what Jan Shipps calls "LDS cultural islands, where religion, economics, politics, and other dimensions of life were thoroughly intertwined."[53] Within these "autonomous cultural enclaves," LDS communities functioned as quasi theocracies where high-ranking leaders served in both secular and religious capacities. For example, Brigham Young, the second prophet of the church, was the highest-ranking spiritual leader, the president of the institution, and the governor of Utah. This practice was also evident in Hawai'i where it took on a racial hue. Up until the 1960s, the highest-ranking leaders of the church in Hawai'i—mission president, stake president, and Lā'ie plantation manager—were often the same person, a haole settler from Utah. It was also true that local leadership positions were filled by Native Hawaiian male converts who were deemed worthy of the priesthood.

The Sandwich Islands Mission

The story of the Sandwich Islands mission begins in winter 1850 when a group of ten young men were called by Brigham Young to serve as missionaries to the Sandwich Islands. These men were originally called to serve as labor missionaries in the gold mines in California, but with the slow winter months approaching they were ordered to sail to Hawai'i where they would attempt to establish a presence among the haole population there. Hawai'i was a logical site for these missionaries; travel between California and Hawai'i was common, so they could easily sail to the islands and then return to San Francisco in the spring to resume mining for gold. The first ten missionaries were Henry William Bigler, George Q. Cannon, John Dixon, William Farrer, James Hawkins, James Keeler, Thomas Morris, Thomas Whittle, Hiram Blackwell, and Hiram Clark, the eldest in the group who was appointed as mission president. The men departed San Francisco on November 15, 1850, and arrived in Honolulu on December 12, 1850. Although travel between the continent and Hawai'i was a routine event, it was a long, arduous trip for the missionaries. They were no doubt relieved when they disembarked in Honolulu and eager to begin their service to the Lord.

The Mormon missionaries were belated travelers to Hawai'i.[54] They arrived on the scene thirty years after the first New England missionaries of the American Board of Commissioners for Foreign Missions formally brought Jehovah to Hawai'i.[55] As Ali Behdad writes about other belated travelers who arrived in European colonies after the Orient had been transformed from an exotic other "into the familiar sign of Western hegemony," Mormon missionaries found Honolulu to be a bustling port town.[56] For nearly forty years it had been a center for commerce beginning with the sandalwood trade in the 1810s, and by the 1830s it had become a mercantile town that provisioned and refitted ships and provided various services to crew members. Cannon described Honolulu as a "pretty" town that "wears a tropical look." From the waterfront, Honolulu probably looked a lot like a New England harbor town with warehouses, storehouses, hotels, and sailing vessels docked in the harbor. But the tropical was still evident in the "canoes, containing natives of the islands, who were out fishing."[57] Indeed, the Mormons arrived to a place that was uncannily familiar yet quite foreign as well.

These belated missionaries arrived to find that the Hawaiian population had already heard the message of Jehovah and had become Christian, either Protestant or Catholic. The sign of Western hegemony was also notable in the recognition of the kingdom as a Christian constitutional monarchy that was in the final phases of transforming the indigenous land tenure system into a capitalist system of private property ownership, about which I will say more in chapter 2. But there were also many things the Mormon missionaries experienced that produced what Behdad calls "a sense of displacement in time and space." The anxiety of the unfamiliar would within a few short months inspire half of these missionaries to return to the United States, while simultaneously producing "an obsessive urge to discover an 'authentic' Other" in those who remained.[58]

The missionaries' first task, once lodging was secured, was to mark the beginning of their service with the familiar act of prayer. The Sandwich Islands mission was officially opened on the following morning when the missionaries hiked to a nearby hill where they consecrated the land for the service of the Lord. Twenty-five years later Cannon describes the impact of the dedicatory prayer to his readers:

The spirit of the Lord rested powerfully upon us, and we were filled with exceeding great joy. I had the satisfaction, afterwards of witnessing the fulfillment of the promise made on that occasion. The sun was sinking low in the heavens when we got through. Our descent was quickly made, for we felt joyful, and when men are joyful and the spirit of God rests upon them, they feel lithe and active. We had been in the presence of the Lord, and had felt His power, and why should we not be happy.[59]

With the mission officially open, the elders devised a plan for preaching the gospel. Since they all shared the assumption that they were to preach to the haole, white Euro-American, residents, and considering how small their numbers were in Honolulu, President Clark decided to split the group up and send pairs of missionaries to each of the outer islands.

Although each of the missionary groups serving on different islands found small numbers of haole residents with whom they intended to share their message, those they did encounter were hostile to them. For example, Cannon recounts one Protestant minister in Wailuku, Maui, who threatened Native Hawaiians who showed any kindness to the Mormons, let alone interest in their message. The missionaries on Oʻahu found few haole who were interested in their message, despite their efforts to advertise in the *Polynesian,* a local English-language newspaper, and to secure a site for church services in town. The missionaries on Kauaʻi did not fare much better. When

The consecration of Hawaiʻi by the first ten missionaries is represented in a dramatic mural painted above the internal doors of the David O. McKay Building. Photograph courtesy of Brigham Young University–Hawaiʻi Archives.

they arrived in Nāwiliwili Harbor they preached to a small group of haole, but when they sailed on to Kōloa, a sugar plantation, they experienced antagonism from the haole there. After three weeks of trying to generate interest on Kauaʻi, Farrer and Dixon decided to send Farrer back to Honolulu to check on the progress of the others. Hawkins and Blackwell were not faring much better on Hawaiʻi island. They began their efforts in Hilo but were unable to generate measurable interest among the small haole population there, so they moved up the coast to Kohala where they continued to have little success. The report from the Oʻahu missionaries reinforced a growing sentiment that there was little need to remain in Hawaiʻi. The ambivalent relationship the missionaries had toward the Hawaiians was evident in this crisis of faith. Since they understood their task to be to preach the gospel to the haole people, most of the missionaries did not pay much attention to the Hawaiians. The only exception to this was the attitude of Bigler, Cannon, and Keeler on Maui.

Given the difficulties they were having on Oʻahu and the discouraging reports from the missionaries on Hawaiʻi island and on Kauaʻi, President Clark sent a letter to Cannon on Maui and to Dixon on Kauaʻi to return to Honolulu for reassignment. He intended to dissolve the mission and send the missionaries home. However, when Cannon arrived in Honolulu and heard the plan, he protested. He believed they would be negligent in their duty to the Lord if they left Hawaiʻi without sharing the gospel with both native and haole alike. His assertion was based on the unexpected developments that had been unfolding on Maui during their first three weeks of preaching.

When the missionaries assigned to Maui island arrived in the port town of Lahaina, their first task was to secure lodging and identify a location for church services. Their attempt to rent the unused royal palace resulted in failure, and their subsequent attempt to use the Bethel Chapel proved hopeless as few haole appeared interested in their message. The hostility that the Maui missionaries experienced from haole residents was contrasted by the openness and generosity from the Native Hawaiians they met. One of the first acts of generosity toward the missionaries came from a Native Hawaiian woman named Nālimanui who offered the young men her room in her family home so they could be together. Nālimanui was also instrumental in helping Cannon learn the Hawaiian language. Cannon, like his fellow missionaries, shared the initial assumption that their purpose was to preach the gospel to the haole population. But within a month he felt it necessary to preach to

Native Hawaiians as well. It was during his stay with Nālimanui that he knelt in prayer asking the Lord to provide him with guidance and direction during these early weeks. As Cannon recorded in his journal fifty years later,

> He [the Lord] condescended to commune with me, for I heard His voice more than once as one man speaks with another, encouraging me and showing me the work which should be done among this people if I would follow the dictates of His spirit, Glory to God in the highest that He has permitted me to live to behold the fulfillment of His words.[60]

It was also at this time that Cannon had his vision that Native Hawaiians were the posterity of Abraham and descended from the House of Israel. According to the LDS historian R. Lanier Britsch, "while at Lahaina, Maui, [Cannon] had a revelation in which the Lord spoke to him telling him that the Hawaiians were of the House of Israel. From this time on, Cannon and his associates began to preach that the Hawaiian people were an offshoot branch of Israel through the posterity of Lehi, a *Book of Mormon* prophet."[61] Armed with a new conviction to share the gospel with the native population, Cannon, Bigler, and Keeler committed themselves to learning the Hawaiian language and shifted their focus to work diligently among Native Hawaiians.

With these deeply spiritual experiences freshly imprinted on Cannon's soul, it is no wonder that he was taken aback when Hiram Clark informed him of the plan to begin closing the mission by first sending Whittle home. For Cannon their work had just begun, and according to his interpretation of their objective the missionaries were to stay at least through the winter months and longer if the work was going well and they were so moved by the Holy Spirit. Cannon's conviction was expressed years later when he wrote, "I felt resolved to stay there, master the language and warn the people of those islands, if I had to do it alone; for I felt that I could not do otherwise and be free from condemnation; the spirit of it was upon me. Elders Bigler and Keeler felt the same."[62] Competing ideologies of faithfulness were at work in this exchange. According to LDS notions of authority, Cannon should have supported Clark's decision since he was the mission president, the highest-ranking priesthood holder in the mission. However, Cannon's position held legitimacy because his vision was innovative and drew upon the tradition of leaders receiving visions and revelations that were meant to add clarity and purpose to this young organization. Visions and revelation were thought to be necessary because one of the foundational tenets of Mormonism is the claim that prior to Joseph Smith's actions, "the true Church had been absent from the earth from the time of a 'Great Apostasy' at the end of the Apostolic era until its restoration in 1830."[63] Mormons fundamentally believe that Smith and other high-ranking leaders in the church received revelation from God that restored the true Church of Christ to earth in its fullness.[64] They also believe that individuals can communicate with God through prayer, and conversely that God will "condescend to commune" with those who have a sincere desire to know the truth. In this instance, Cannon's vision so powerfully represented his faith and that of the church that Clark opted not to close the entire mission but to leave the decision to each individual missionary.

Despite Cannon's assertion of faith three missionaries left immediately, and by the end of February President Clark would leave his post on Oʻahu to sail to Tahiti. From Tahiti he intended to proceed to the Marquesas Islands to work with missionaries there, but his plans changed and he ended up in Tubuai. In April, Morris would lose hope and return to California, and thus in five short months the number of missionaries was reduced by half. Cannon's faith never waned, however; in fact, he retells the story of the missionaries who left Hawaiʻi in his book *My First Mission* and adds that Dixon, who

George Q. Cannon overlooks ʻĪao Valley, Maui, during his first mission to Hawaiʻi. Photograph courtesy of Brigham Young University–Hawaiʻi Archives.

was stationed on Kauaʻi, was killed shortly after returning home. Not only does Cannon's action affirm the power of faith, it also serves as an object lesson for other missionaries that they should not lose their faith lest they experience a similar tragic fate.

With only five missionaries remaining, the elders divided themselves again: Cannon and Keeler remained on Maui; Bigler and Farrer returned to Oʻahu; and Hawkins continued to work alone on Hawaiʻi island. Their new approach would be to increase their fluency in the Hawaiian language and spread their message to the more open Native Hawaiians. The progress on Maui was greatly enhanced by Cannon's friendship with Jonathan H. Nāpela, one of the first Native Hawaiian converts to the church and an important political leader in the Wailuku district of the island. Nāpela was instrumental in helping to spread the gospel on Maui, and he played a key role in securing an LDS presence in the islands more generally. He introduced Cannon to other Native Hawaiians with whom he could share his message, and he made it possible for Cannon to begin proselytizing in the Kula area. Nāpela also initiated the construction of a hale pili, a Hawaiian-style building that would be used for church services. Nāpela's position as a secular judge elevated the status of Cannon and the other missionaries in the Hawaiian community on Maui. Within a few short months Cannon had baptized nineteen Native Hawaiians in Kula, and by the end of July 1851 he established the first branch of the church in Hawaiʻi.[65]

Between 1851 and 1853 an additional handful of missionaries joined the remaining five in their efforts to spread the gospel. Although they experienced uneven success, the number of Hawaiian converts continued to grow, with the greatest success occurring on the islands of Maui and Oʻahu. One of the challenges they faced was to produce written material for the purpose of teaching the beliefs and tenets of the church in the Hawaiian language. In 1852, Farrer published a pamphlet in Hawaiian that described the significance of *The Book of Mormon*. Concurrently, Cannon and Nāpela worked together to translate *The Book of Mormon* into Hawaiian, and the project was finally completed in 1854.

Hawaiian members of the church remember with reverence the history of the first missionaries to Hawaiʻi. It is Cannon's prophecy of the Hawaiian people's link to *The Book of Mormon* and to Israel that is heralded as a sign of God's hand at work in returning the gospel to Hawaiians. Cannon's vision would also be used as a powerful rationale for the continued presence of the church in Hawaiʻi. Despite Cannon's leadership and determination, however, the long-term future of the Sandwich Islands mission was always precarious as missionaries continued to experience hostility and threats from Protestant and Catholic clergy. Additionally, the public announcement in 1852 of the acceptance of polygamy by the church placed the missionaries and their new members under a fog of suspicion that was not lifted until 1890 when polygamy was officially banned by the church. Finally, without a permanent settlement the mission was not financially stable; in fact, many of the missionaries were so destitute they relied heavily on the charity and goodwill of converts for their food and lodging. Economic stability would not come to the mission until the late 1860s, after the establishment of Lāʻie as a permanent gathering place for saints.

HUAKAʻI: THE JOURNEY AHEAD

Although this book is a huakaʻi, a journey with twists and turns through the history of the LDS church in Lāʻie, Hawaiʻi, it does not cover a broad geographical area. Instead it travels through time from the 1850s when the first Mormon missionaries arrived at Hawaiʻi's shores to 2001 when the Jonathan Nāpela Center for Hawaiian Language and Cultural Studies at Brigham Young University–Hawaiʻi launched the waʻa kaulua ʻo *Iosepa*, a double-hulled open ocean voyaging canoe. Chapter 1 provides a historical grounding in how in the nineteenth century Hawaiians came to be incorporated into the larger cosmology of the Mormon church through notions of lineage. From this point of departure, each chapter offers examples of how Hawaiians made sense of this connection and used it to meet their own spiritual, cultural, economic, and political needs. The first layover, chapter 2, is in the late nineteenth century as I examine how Hawaiian Latter-day Saints sought refuge in Lāʻie from landlessness due to the privatization of land along with its consolidation for sugar cultivation. During this time of dispossession by degrees, some Hawaiian Latter-day Saints were able to use their status in the church to restore their connection to the ʻāina (land) and the subsistence lifestyle that nourished them physically, psychically, and spiritually. In chapter 3, the next layover is in the mid-twentieth century during a time in Lāʻie history when LDS leaders transformed Lāʻie from a Polynesian village to modern town. There I focus on several development projects including the construction of the permanent buildings for the Church College of Hawaiʻi and the Polynesian Cultural Center, which were built by labor missionaries from Hawaiʻi, Tonga, and Sāmoa. I examine the various articulations of modernity circulating during this time by reading and comparing the narratives of Polynesian labor missionaries, American supervisors, and church leaders.

Chapter 4 arrives at the Polynesian Cultural Center during the period of the 1960s through the 1980s. This was an important time in Hawai'i history as the cultural nationalist movement was beginning to emerge out of the global anticolonial struggles around the U.S. war in Vietnam, decolonization projects in colonial Africa, and student organizing on college campuses throughout Europe and the United States. As these anticolonial sentiments started to arrive on Hawai'i's shores, Native Hawaiians took them up and used them to challenge the U.S. empire in the Pacific and militarization and land evictions for urbanization in Hawai'i. Out of these struggles emerged renewed interest and pride in things Hawaiian. The Polynesian Cultural Center opened in 1963 during the height of development for the emerging tourism economy. As a facility that sells to tourists a particular racialized representation of Polynesian people and culture, workers at the Polynesian Cultural Center described it as more than just a place for a job. Instead, it provided some with a cultural education with kūpuna (elders) who were key sources of knowledge as well as giving them a reaffirmation of their religious faith.

The final stop on this huaka'i, chapter 5, is in 2001 with the launching of the wa'a kaulua 'o *Iosepa*. This event represents a culmination of the themes traced throughout the book. The wa'a kaulua 'o *Iosepa* and the stories told by those associated with it reiterate the naturalness of the Hawaiian Mormon identity that emerged in the 1850s. It is also a symbol of the contemporary moment as Kānaka look to the past and our kūpuna as we navigate our way forward toward an alternative future yet to be fully realized. For many affiliated with the wa'a 'o *Iosepa*, George Q. Cannon, Joseph F. Smith, and other nineteenth-century LDS leaders were counted among the kūpuna who provided the knowledge needed to bring this dream to fruition.

The Hawaiian Mormon context is exceptional in many ways. However, all Native Hawaiians in the present face somewhat similar realities to those traced by this research. Questions about "pure" identities, authentic traditions, and cultural revitalization and rejuvenation are being debated and engaged on many fronts. Native Hawaiians, indeed many indigenous peoples, if in varying degrees, must find points of articulation in the world by which to construct, announce, and inhabit their identities. Sometimes these are through churches, sometimes through schools, civic organizations, museums, and sometimes activist groups. In any event, these various contexts become points of articulation that entail compromises, tensions, contradictions, negotiations, and moments of provocative cultural elaboration. This book concludes with some reflections on the intersections of religion and social activism in Hawaiʻi. I began this project with the question of how do we make sense of the articulation between Hawaiianness and Mormonism. This huakaʻi taught me that rather than rebel against this link I instead needed to recognize that they are joined. Religion is infused in all aspects of life, including politics. In order to revitalize and regenerate our people we need to start where they are at. This includes recognizing that Christianity is a part of the contemporary struggle for sustainable self-determination.

Kuleana: Responsibility and Authority

As I described in the preface, stories from my childhood and my personal quest to understand how my Hawaiian identity came to be articulated with my religious one inspired this project. While on this huakaʻi I have used the Hawaiian concept of kuleana as an ethical marker and an analytical tool. As with many Hawaiian concepts and values, kuleana has many meanings. It is often translated to mean responsibility; however, it also carries the meaning of "right, privilege, concern, . . . authority."[66] The word kuleana, when understood as both responsibility and authority, directs me, as a native scholar who conducts research in my community, to maintain a balance between my responsibility to academic research and the structures of authority legitimated by this system, and my responsibility to the people whose life stories I feature in this book and the structures of authority that operate at the interpersonal level. My understanding of kuleana thus forces me to be accountable to the rigors of academic research, my community, and to myself.[67]

As Diaz and Kauanui argue, "Central to native studies are the struggles for sovereignty and decolonization for Islanders resisting benevolent and malevolent assimilation into larger, more powerful, entities."[68] On the one hand I see this project as an expression of how islanders resist benevolent assimilation into the LDS church. On the other, nearly all of the stories I feature in the following chapters were told by Polynesian members of the church, a religious institution that in many ways was committed to a civilizing mission no different from its Protestant and Catholic predecessors. How then do I balance a critique of this imperial apparatus with people's beliefs and faith?

I answer this question by being committed to, in the words of Diaz and Kauanui, "native-based research, theory and methodology." As they further explain, "Scholarship for us involves at least two interconnected fronts: the identification and dismantling of colonial structures and discourses variously conceptualized and theorized, and cultural reclamation and stewardship."[69] Throughout this process I struggled to be attentive to what people had to say and the conceptual framework used to give their perspective meaning. When I was successful, I was able to identify those spaces where the colonial structure and discourse could not reach. For example, by paying attention to what former Polynesian Cultural Center workers got out of their jobs that exceeded the expectations of the daily grind of working at a tourist facility, I was able to understand how it was more than just a job for these workers. In the process of taking people and their stories seriously I am engaging in an act of reclamation and stewardship. Just as kuleana signals the parameters of my responsibility and authority, stewardship identifies to whom I must be accountable.

Kuleana, stewardship, and a commitment to dismantle colonial structures wherever I find them are the ethical and analytical tools I carried with me when I embarked on this book project. Yet throughout this project I struggled to strike a balance between respect for belief and faith and critical engagement. Donna Haraway's "Situated Knowledges: The Science Question in Feminism and the Privilege of Partial Perspective" has been useful to me in clarifying my understanding of accountability. She contends that all knowledge is situated, partial, and connected to other knowledge. In order to challenge understandings of objectivity as a view from nowhere, she argues for, in her words, "a doctrine and practice of objectivity that privileges contestation, deconstruction, passionate connections, and hope for transformation of systems of knowledge and ways of seeing."[70] By invoking the idea of accountability I reflexively approach this project with an intention to make connections and to transform systems of knowledge while also being aware that my knowledge is partial. In so doing I may unintentionally be reproducing those structures I intend to dismantle. In addition, Haraway cautions feminist scholars and others who represent the perspective of the subjugated in research that "the standpoints of the subjugated are not 'innocent' positions. . . . 'Subjugated' standpoints," she acknowledges, "are preferred because they seem to promise more adequate, sustained, objective, transforming accounts of the world."[71] Haraway's caution pushes me to do the tough work of being attentive to how the subjugated's standpoint is also mediated, contradictory, and partial.

1 Mormonism, Race, and Lineage: The Making of a Chosen People

IN THE 1850S THE CHURCH OF JESUS CHRIST OF LATTER-DAY SAINTS, drawing upon dominant notions of race and worthiness, began to redraw the boundaries between those souls who they deemed chosen and those who were not. At that time the church reasoned that the social meanings of black skin marked sin and unworthiness. Such thinking might have positioned Polynesians as among the less desirable subjects of religious conversion, and yet in the history of Mormonism something quite the opposite happens. Instead of being seen as unworthy, Hawaiians are positioned as chosen peoples connected to Israelite lineage and thereby are desirable religious subjects. In this chapter I examine the development of a chosen people against a backdrop of the racialized logic of the 1850s. By what devices is the racialization of non-Polynesian people of color maintained while making space for Hawaiian chosenness? In what follows I examine three mechanisms for the making of a chosen people: racial discourses, ideologies of lineage, and invention of religious customs and practices.

Notions of lineage played a central role in how the church rationalized the inherent contradiction between an ideology of universalism and its policy of internal racial exclusion. By freely choosing to accept the gospel and enter the sacred waters of baptism, one could become adopted into the lineage of Abraham, one of God's chosen elect and to whom He had made a lasting covenant. Despite attempts by the LDS church to use lineage to avoid race, the two notions were articulated such that the ranked hierarchy of lineage from chosen to ineligible was always already racialized. Baptism could change one's lineage; however, it could not remove the symbolic significance of skin color.

31

The church did not create these linkages but rather transformed ideas, debates, and understandings of the time to serve its own religious and political interests. Although the Mormon missionaries came to Hawai'i with no intention of proselytizing to Native Hawaiians, once they arrived and began their service to the Lord they found that Native Hawaiians were receptive to their message of the gospel. For George Q. Cannon and his companions serving on the island of Maui, this turn of events inspired a spiritual awakening that could not be denied. Cannon made sense of it the only way he knew how, through religious innovation; namely, he had a vision, and this vision was part of a larger project to redefine the religious community of the church.

Cannon's vision also brought into relief the tension between an ideology of universalism, which presumed that all Latter-day Saints were equivalent in the eyes of God and the gospel, and racial assumptions about chosenness. For the LDS historian R. Lanier Britsch, universalism is founded on the belief that all people must "accept the divinity of Jesus Christ, but also . . . accept new revelation through contemporary prophets." In contrast to Britsch who contends that the universalist principle meant that missionaries made no distinction between "the Hawaiians and mainstream Christians: both required the saving ordinances of salvation as performed by men who had the authority of the priesthood, as restored through Joseph Smith," in my interpretation of Cannon's journal and publications other missionaries clearly did not share his sentiments.[1] Indeed, Cannon's perspective was in the minority, indicating that a more common understanding held by his fellow missionaries was that Hawaiians were not chosen. Focused attention on the growing debate about what should be the official status of black members of the church informs how we can understand Cannon's position in contrast to that of the other missionaries. I argue that it is through a racialized discourse of lineage that Polynesians were incorporated into the church during a time when the racial boundaries of the church were being redrawn and codified in exclusionary ways.

THE RACIALIZATION OF LINEAGE

Although much research has taken up the issue of race in LDS theology, these studies have focused primarily on blacks and Native Americans.[2] When mentioned at all, Polynesians are merely glossed over.[3] The process of inventing a genealogical and religious connection between Polynesians and the church was not innocent but rather part of a larger political project to reimagine the cultural and racial boundaries of the church. It is within the historical context of the codification of racial policies that the church received Cannon's vision. It reiterated a new narrative of the destiny of God's chosen people. How was this connection institutionalized? How did this religious invention come to be a religious innovation that positioned Polynesians as a chosen people within Mormon doctrine?

My analysis of LDS racial discourses and my exegesis of sacred texts such as the *The Book of Mormon* and *The Pearl of Great Price* suggests a trajectory parallel to those being developed and codified in the discipline of anthropology in its nascent period. The belief that Polynesians are a chosen people did not become codified as doctrine overnight. Rather it was a gradual process that initially emerged in the late nineteenth century within a moment in LDS church history when racial lines were being consolidated between whiteness, which was associated with purity, righteousness, worthiness, and redemption, and blackness, which was associated with contamination, wickedness, a lack of worthiness, and a state of being cursed or fallen. As the anthropologist Adam Kuper notes, it is during this same time period that anthropology began to seriously investigate the progression of human society as scholars actively engaged Darwin's theory of evolution. To be clear, however, anthropology's interest in primitive societies was not intended to understand the intrinsic nature of these peoples. Rather, as Kuper writes, "They looked back in order to understand the nature of the present, on the assumption that modern society had evolved from its antithesis."[4] Indeed, this process of "looking back" created a time-space divide that denied the copresence of researchers (who were modern) and their subjects (the primitive who were anachronistic), thus reinforcing the presumption that primitive societies were evidence of a linear evolution of humanity.[5]

The religious racializations of Native Americans, blacks, and Polynesians were both overt and subsumed within an ideology of lineage, an important component of LDS theology established by Joseph Smith. Lineage, in the lexicon of nineteenth-century anthropology, was used to explain the political structure of "primitive" societies that were segmented according to clan. Lineage maintains its association with descent insofar as it privileges bloodline and familial relations over political associations; it is not, however, equivalent to ancestry. Descent is more specifically associated with ancestry and genealogy. Anthropologists used lineage to describe political structures in stateless societies (i.e., primitive societies) and descent to explain how duties and resources (such as land) would be distributed. Lineage explained one's place in the social hierarchy and descent determined the material conditions of that social location. Lineage is associated with familial relationships based on kinship, bloodline, and descent; however, its meaning is not limited to these familial relationships. Rather, as Kuper notes, "the lineage principle takes the place of political allegiance, and the interrelations of territorial segments are directly co-ordinated with the interrelations of lineage segment."[6] The evolution of a primitive society toward civilization would be evidenced by the shift from kinship-based political structures (grounded in notion of blood relations and family ties) toward nonkinship-based structures grounded in private property and citizenship.

Discourses of lineage, descent, and ancestry were intimately tied up with theories of evolution. In the imperial context of late-nineteenth-century Europe, lineage became wedded to theories of scientific racism. Anne McClintock marks panoptical time and anachronistic space as emerging in this era as social evolutionists used the scientific standards of the day to visually categorize human evolution at a glance. Through a spatial logic of time and drawing up Darwinian evolution, "the taxonomic project, first applied to nature, was now applied to cultural history. Time became a geography of social power, a map from which to read a global allegory of 'natural' social difference." Social evolutionists invented "the evolutionary family Tree of Man" which served two goals. First it bridged the divide between the cosmological time of religion and the secular time of science, and second, it "offered an ancient image of a natural genealogy of power."[7] Within this framework, we can ascertain at a glance where each society ranks in the evolutionary hierarchy of progress. In the case of the LDS church, the illustration of the family tree of man printed in McClintock's book helps us see the possible pathways for racializing Polynesians as distinct from blacks and Native Americans because it shows Polynesians and Semites as part of the same branch of the family tree as Aryans. On a separate and lower branch are Americans, and near the base of the tree are Africans.[8] People borrowed from these theories wittingly or unwittingly as they were part of the cultural memory of this historical era. What is striking is that these anthropological notions resonate so strongly with how LDS leaders and writers were thinking about race, religion, and "chosenness."

These anthropological notions of race, lineage, and evolutionary hierarchy resonated with Mormon understandings of lineage. For example, the sociologist Armand Mauss argues that within LDS theology lineage comes to be racialized in particular ways in the 1850s at precisely the time when the larger narrative map of Mormonism was being reimagined. Reinterpretations of *The Book of Mormon* and *The Pearl of Great Price,* in conjunction with biblical exegesis, were used to make and remake racial policies of mainline Mormonism, which effectively banned men of black African descent from acquiring the priesthood and barred all black members of the church from attending the temple.[9] This policy stayed in effect until 1978 when President Spencer W. Kimball (1973–1985) ended this racist practice. Mauss attributes the process of remaking the racial boundaries of the church to the larger project of remaking its narrative history that was necessitated by Mormon exile from Missouri, the land Mormons believe to be chosen for them by God. This process was overseen by the second prophet of the church, Brigham Young, who, Mauss argues, assigned the task to Mormon "scribes" who came from different regions in the United States as well as from "the British Isles, Scandinavia, Germany, and other European countries." In addition to "the creation of a new people, a new *ethnos,* unified by a common understanding, explanation and vindication of their past," Mauss writes further, Mormon leaders created "the retrospective construction of Mormon *lineage.*"[10]

The historian and political scientist Newell Bringhurst agrees that the 1850s were a critical moment in LDS church history. However, he contends that these racial attitudes were merely a continuation of those already institutionalized in *The Book of Mormon,* which was written and translated by Joseph Smith in the late 1820s (albeit completed in 1830). For Bringhurst, *The Book of Mormon* is the seminal text for establishing Mormon racial hierarchies, which were then used to interpret key passages from *The Pearl of Great Price. The Book of Mormon* is significant, Bringhurst argues, because it "became an important medium for the expression of Latter-day Saint racist concepts emphasizing inherent non-white racial inferiority."[11] The attitudes of white racial superiority evident in *The Book of Mormon* were an extension of Smith's personal racial attitudes as well as larger racial attitudes in the United States in the 1820s and 1830s. In addition to delineating a racial hierarchy, Bringhurst explains that *The Book of Mormon* "also outlined several concepts emphasizing [Smith's] role as a religious leader." This text authorized his religious status by establishing him as "a member of the 'chosen race' by virtue of his 'descent' from the ancient Tribe of Joseph—one of the Chosen Tribes of Israel."[12] Specifically, Smith traced his lineage to Ephraim, the oldest son of Joseph, who was the leader of the Kingdom of Israel but whose people were scattered among the Gentile nations.[13]

LINEAGE AND *THE BOOK OF MORMON*

The Book of Mormon is the foundational scripture for the LDS church and is considered a second testament of Jesus Christ equal to the Bible. *The Book of Mormon* chronicles the rise and fall of an ancient civilization that existed on the American continent between 600 BC and 400 AD. It documents the lives of a group of Israelites who fled the Holy Land and made the American continent their home. One of the most significant aspects of *The Book of Mormon* is that Christ appeared to these people and established his church with them. Although it relies on many of the same narrative devices and organizing principles as the New Testament, various themes covered in *The Book of Mormon* have a strong resemblance to the stories in the Old Testament, and its preoccupation with Israelite lineages gives Mormonism, in Jan Shipps's terms, "a Hebraic dimension."[14]

The Book of Mormon is an epic tale of the rise and fall of two great and ancient civilizations believed to have existed in Central and South America. The majority of the volume follows the lives of the descendents of Lehi, the patriarch of these Israelites and the father of four sons, Laman, Lemuel, Sam, and Nephi, the latter of whom would become the leader of a great civilization and his people would be called Nephites. Christ established the full teachings of his church with Lehi, and his loyal son Nephi perpetuated those teachings. Laman and Lemuel were not content to follow the leadership of their younger brother, however, and they organized a rebellion against him and his religious principles. Due to their disloyalty and the actions against their brother, Laman, Lemuel, and their followers were banished to the wilderness and "cut off from the presence of the Lord."[15] The apostates were given a second punishment, a curse directly from the Lord:

> Wherefore, as they were white, and exceedingly fair and delightsome, that they might not be enticing unto my people the Lord God did cause a skin of blackness to come upon them. And thus saith the Lord God: I will cause that they shall be loathsome unto thy people, save they shall repent of their inequities.[16]

The curse of a skin of blackness was extended to all of the descendants of Laman and Lemuel, known as the Lamanites. Embedded in this scripture is both the explanation of the curse and the solution for overcoming it: through repentance the curse could be lifted and one could become "white, and exceedingly fair and delightsome" once again. The curse of blackness was both literal—a punishment exacted on Lamanites—and metaphoric: blackness became a symbol of a people's wicked actions. These passages from *The Book of Mormon* establish a racial binary whereby whiteness is a sign of all things pure and good, while blackness signifies that which is wicked and evil.

Throughout *The Book of Mormon* stories abound that chronicle many battles between the Nephites and Lamanites, but ultimately the Lamanites defeat the Nephites. Native Americans are believed to be descendants of Lamanites who, at one time, had the fullness of the gospel of Christ but rejected it.[17] For Craig Prentiss, *The Book of Mormon* uses the curse on the Lamanites to establish "a hierarchy based on color," which was then used to "enforce a social order" that situated all people with black skin as "loathsome."[18] Although the Lamanite story clearly establishes a color hierarchy, Prentiss also references passages from the book of Jacob in *The Book of Mormon* that caution the white-skinned Nephites not to judge the black-skinned Lamanites because Nephites too could be cursed if they failed to live the precepts of the gospel. What is instructive is that race is not a fixed category but instead is malleable. A literal interpretation of *The Book of Mormon* suggests that baptism was not merely a figurative process of salvation—a metaphoric process of moving from darkness to light—but that one would undergo a literal lightening of the skin.[19]

MORMON THEOLOGY AND THE ISRAELITE CONNECTION

In addition to the explicit racial language in *The Book of Mormon,* Mauss's research also suggests that Mormon ideas about the race of the Lost Tribes of Israel were constantly being adapted as missionaries traveled to different places and encountered new people and new ideas. For example, he found that missionaries called to serve in England in the 1840s and 1850s became attracted to the British Israelite theory because it supported the assertion in *The Book of Mormon* that Lehi and his descendents were white and that Laman and his followers became black only *after* their fall from grace.

British Israelism was fundamentally about providing a rationale for Anglo-Saxon superiority. According to Douglas Cowan, British Israelism emerged in the early nineteenth century and attempted to explain where the ten Lost Tribes ended up after being exiled from Israel after the death of King Solomon in 930 BCE. British Israelism postulates that the ten Lost Tribes migrated north where, Cowan writes, "they simply assimilated into their new environment, intermarrying both with their Assyrian captors and with the people of neighboring tribes, [thus] gradually losing any tribal distinction they may have carried with them into exile." Proponents of this theory presume that from Assyria the Lost Tribes migrated through Europe and settled in Britain, where, Cowan continues, "they became ancestors of various British races."[20] Mauss explains that what resonated for the Mormon missionaries was the belief that it was the descendants of the tribe of Ephraim who comprised the majority of British Israelites. As noted above, this was significant because Smith maintained that he was descended from the tribe of Ephraim.

The British Israelite connection also served to reinforce other significant religious and racial understandings of the time. Norman Douglas marks 1567 as the first time the theory that American Indians were a Lost Tribe of Israel appeared in print. He also asserts that the theory was so well established, especially among "the religiously inclined," the story told in *The Book of Mormon* would not have appeared fantastical to Smith's contemporaries.[21] It appears that the Israelite connection resonated with missionaries in other ways as well. The missionaries believed that descendents of Israel were, according to Mauss, "especially responsive to the teachings of the gospel; . . . the same peoples show a natural penchant for superior cultural traits, such as enterprise, vitality, and representative government; and . . . LDS missionary success in the British Isles and Scandinavia is a *natural* consequence of these historic developments" (emphasis added).[22] Although *The Book of Mormon* explains the whiteness of Lehi and his descendents and the curse of blackness of Native Americans, what we also learn is that although they were cursed due to their depraved, barbarous, and treacherous actions, they could be saved. Moreover, it was the duty of the Anglo missionaries to return the gospel to these lost people.

In a similar way that social evolutionists described all human societies as deriving from the same family tree, Mormonism's embrace of British Israelism provided a religious explanation of the presumed racial superiority of Joseph Smith and his Anglo contemporaries while also explaining how Native Americans could be both primitive and lineally descended from the white patriarch Lehi. The key distinction is that the LDS church used a religious notion of time to explain the reason why Mormon missionaries believed they were superior to the primitive Native Americans. Within a Mormon discourse the Native Americans were once white but were cursed;

their "barbarous and depraved" condition was the result of their rejection of Christ's gospel. Within the lexicon of late-nineteenth-century social Darwinism, they had been stalled in a primitive evolutionary state. The family metaphor is important to return to because it resonates with interpretations of *The Book of Mormon* and *The Pearl of Great Price*, which posit a premortal, spiritual family comprised of God the Father and an unnamed but assumed God the Mother.[23] It is the reinterpretation of these texts and this idea of a spirit family in a premortal existence that is used to authorize the hierarchy of lineage such that Anglo Mormons occupy the highest branches of this religious family tree.

THE PREMORTAL FAMILY, THE HIERARCHY OF LINEAGE, AND RACIAL EXCLUSION

Anthropological definitions of lineage as a political structure helps to explain how a hierarchy of lineage was used by the church to explain and justify the racial superiority of Anglo Mormons, the ambivalent position of Native Americans, and the exclusion of blacks. Interestingly, up until the 1850s a small number of blacks had joined the church, in which the men were given the priesthood and all were allowed to participate in the sacred ordinances in the temple.[24] However, it was under the direction of Brigham Young and his "scribes that new interpretations of *The Pearl of Great Price* legitimized the policy to ban black men from holding the priesthood. *The Pearl of Great Price* is a compilation of writings by Joseph Smith that were originally published in serial form. These disparate texts were compiled and bound under a single title in 1851 and became Holy Scripture in 1880.

For Latter-day Saints, the Book of Moses and Book of Abraham published in *The Pearl of Great Price* provide a detailed sketch of the premortal existence; however, the Book of Abraham includes an account of how a hierarchy of lineage originated in the premortal existence. The Book of Abraham was one of several Egyptian scrolls purchased by Smith that purportedly represented a lost biblical scripture. The scrolls chronicled Abraham's experiences as he traveled throughout Egypt. While on his journey, God appeared to him and shared many revelations with him, including the process of creating the earth. God also told him that he was chosen in a premortal life to be one of the great leaders on earth. As such, his descendents, both literal and adopted, would receive the full blessing of salvation, including the priesthood, and they would become a great nation.

Scholars agree that the notion of a premortal existence is not unique to Mormonism; however, LDS scripture provides a much more detailed explanation than is evident in other Christian denominations.[25] What God shares with Abraham is a glimpse of this premortal existence, specifically a gathering of all of God's spirit children together to hear his plan for salvation. God chose the planet earth for his children so they could have a mortal body and to prove their worthiness for eternal salvation. God explains to Abraham that in the multitude gathered there were souls with different "intelligences." Abraham was among those souls identified by God to be "the noble and great ones . . . And he said unto me: Abraham, thou art one of them; thou wast chosen before thou was born."[26] Also gathered were souls with lesser "intelligences." Abraham also learns that "there stood one among them that was like unto God, and he said unto those who were with him: We will go down, for there is space there, and we will make an earth whereon these may dwell."[27] When God asked which among them he would send to earth, "one answered like unto the Son of Man: Here I am, send me."[28] Although God chose the first son, Christ, to establish his kingdom on earth, others volunteered. One in particular, Satan, became angry, and he and his followers did not receive mortal bodies and were not allowed to join the others on earth.[29]

The story of the selection of Christ and the rejection of Satan is believed to be what ignited a great battle in heaven between good and evil. Bringhurst argues that this premortal battle was used as one rationale for why blacks were denied full membership in the faith while also providing an explanation for their dark skin color as they were cursed for the role they played in this epic battle. Interestingly, *The Pearl of Great Price* offers two additional explanations for barring blacks from full participation in the church. First was the theory that blacks were the descendents of Noah's grandson, Canaan, Son of Ham. The curse of Canaan originally appeared in the Bible but was reiterated in the Book of Moses in *The Pearl of Great Price*. Second was the theory that they were descendents of Cain, the Son of Adam, who was cursed for the murder of his brother Abel. The curse of Cain is also described in the Book of Moses. The theory of a premortal existence that determined one's eligibility for salvation gained leverage well into the twentieth century and was not curtailed until President Kimball's 1978 proclamation.[30]

The racialization of both lineage and intelligences within LDS doctrine is explained when read through the racial lens established in *The Book of Mormon*. As I reread these passages from *The Pearl of Great Price,* I fully expected to encounter clear racial language that would explain how the choices blacks made in the preexistence made them ineligible for salvation. As noted above, what I found was the vague language of intelligences and references to a premortal war of good and evil. In returning to these holy texts and in my struggle to make sense of the inconsistencies between these texts and racial meanings, what I came to realize is that it is within the binary racial logic of *The Book of Mormon* that whiteness comes to be associated with people who possess higher intelligences, who were chosen by God to be leaders, and who were given the responsibility to save the souls of the lesser intelligent, non-white peoples of the world. The category of nonwhite—read as black—was thus delineated along a ranking of lineages that distinguished between those who were chosen or were of a "favored Israelite lineage," such as American Indians and Polynesians, and those who were beyond salvation, such as people of African descent. These racial ideas were not distinct to Mormons, but as the historian Paul Harvey documents, the reliance on biblical inter-pretation for the rationalization of white superiority emerged as early as the sixteenth century and persists until today.[31] The theory of a premortal exis-tence provided a rationale for the discriminatory racial policy by attributing the curse of blackness to the will of God based on an individual's actions in the spirit world and not to any individual church leader's prejudicial or racial attitudes.

These racial ideas were not invented by Smith or Young but were part of what constituted "commonsense" understandings of race in the nineteenth century. In nineteenth-century American nationalist discourse, Natives were the tragic noble savage whose evolutionary time was nearing its end; African slaves were property permanently ineligible for citizenship; and white men were the natural benefactors of Native land and black labor. As the historian Patrick Wolfe argues, this racialization is part and parcel of a settler colonial project intent on the territorial expropriation of native land and the correl-ative need for an ever-expanding labor source.[32]

Just as the American nationalist discourse relied on a combination of reli-gious and scientific racism to expropriate land and exploit labor, the theol-ogy of the LDS church drew upon religious notions of lineage in order to rationalize a racial triangulation that figured Smith and other Anglo Mormons as the saviors of the fallen Native Americans while deflecting any respon-sibility for the disenfranchisement of blacks. Mormon leaders used their reinterpretation of Israelite lineage to "include themselves with the Jews" as Israelites in counterdistinction to Gentiles while also excluding the "lineage of Cain" from any "ecclesiastical citizenship."[33]

POLYNESIAN LINEAGE AND THE LDS FAMILY TREE

According to these dominant racial discourses, one would expect to see Polynesians positioned similarly on the family Tree of Man as Native Americans. However, as I describe above, Polynesians and Native Americans are represented as being a part of two separate branches of the family tree. Mormon doctrine imitates a similar relationship between Polynesians and Native Americans. Within the church framework Polynesians are understood as being "cousins" to Native Americans and thus descended from one of the Lost Tribes of Israel. Although the association of Polynesians with the Lost of Tribes of Israel was not a new theory, this Mormon articulation of it differed from other theories circulating in the late nineteenth century.

The historian K. R. Howe's detailed survey of theories of Oceanic origins identifies the missionary Samuel Marsden as being the first person to trace Polynesian lineage back to "Semitic" societies. "Until the 1870s," he writes, "numerous missionaries and non-missionary writers established an entrenched and now well annotated tradition of Māori as one of the Lost Tribes of Israel."[34] The haole journalist Abraham Fornander's attempt to provide a thoroughly genuine account of Polynesian origins, with a particular emphasis on Hawaiians, illustrates Howe's point. Fornander's work, published in 1878, acknowledges the theory that Polynesians were descended from one of the Lost Tribes of Israel. Indeed, he concludes that Polynesians originated either from "Aryan or Cushite sources," and that they arrived in Polynesia via Southeast Asia and the western Pacific islands of Papua and Fiji.[35] Fornander's example carries the echo of social evolutionists as his theory postulates that Polynesians descended from a branch of the family tree that presumably included Aryans and Jews. Although Mormon theories of the Polynesian-Israelite connection resonate with these dominant theories, one important distinction is that they believe that Polynesians migrated from the Americas rather than the more common theory that they migrated eastward from the western Pacific and Asia.

Mormon leaders and scholars point to four short passages in *The Book of Mormon* to connect Cannon's vision with this broader structure of the church. Alma 63: 5–8 tells the story of Hagoth, an adventurer and shipbuilder, who sailed "forth into the west sea." He did not travel alone but "there were many of the Nephites who did enter therein and did sail forth with much provisions, and also many women and children" (Alma 63: 6). A year later, Hagoth would return to build more ships, stock them with people and provisions, and would set sail again. The final verse states,

And it came to pass that they were never heard of more. And we suppose that they were drowned in the depths of the sea. And it came to pass that one other ship did sail forth; and whither she did go we know not. (Alma 63: 8)

Innovation meets invention in a brilliant move whereby Mormon leaders and scholars were able to take Cannon's vision and use it to answer the question implied above: Where did Hagoth and his fellow travelers go and what became of them? The answer is that they are the present-day Polynesian people. The question that continues to be debated, however, is whether Polynesians were originally Lamanites or Nephites. Although baptism affords Lamanites all the privileges of Nephites, the racial formation of Lamanites as cursed with "blackness" and Nephites blessed with "whiteness" persists. Indeed, the racial implication of defining Polynesians as either Nephites or Lamanites has been ongoing, and it is a topic I will return to in the next section.

An ideology of universalism assumes that whether Polynesians are descendents of Nephi or Laman is in many ways irrelevant. Instead, what is doctrinally significant is that they are descendents of Lehi and thus ancestrally connected to *The Book of Mormon* and Israel. They are a chosen people with whom God had made a covenant that included the blessings of salvation and land to build the Kingdom of God on earth. Again, it is impossible to completely ignore the racial assumptions that continue to fester under the surface of universalism. Although Native Americans also share the same connection to the House of Israel as Polynesians, there is no debate among LDS scholars that they are descendents of Laman and thus Lamanites.[36] Indeed, Mormon theology also instructs that Lamanites can recover from the curse through repentance and baptism and thus be returned to their precursed state of being white and delightsome. Herein lies the rub: a literal interpretation of the text suggests that the waters of baptism had the power to physically lighten one's skin. According to Bringhurst, the first missionaries among American Indians expected their recent converts' skin color to be transformed. When the miracle did not take place, the church adopted a figurative approach to the transformative power of baptism.[37] If taken metaphorically, as most contemporary readings suggest, the waters of baptism symbolize one's choice to repent from one's evil ways and become reborn in goodness and light. What is maintained in both interpretations is the foundational principle that lineage matters. Whether literal or metaphoric, whiteness persists as a privileged state of being and the sign of salvation.

During one of my interviews I was directed to the book *Lehi, Father of Polynesia: Polynesians are Nephites* by Bruce Sutton. Not only did the book provide insight into how the interviewee made sense of the relationship between Polynesians and the House of Israel, but Sutton seems to rely on similar methodological techniques and theories as these nineteenth-century anthropologies to make his case that Polynesians were Nephites and thus originally white. His argument is founded on the belief that Hagoth was a Nephite, therefore making all of his progeny Nephites as well. Sutton's explanation and rationale illustrate the problem of trying to overcome the racial binaries in *The Book of Mormon*. Sutton takes on the question of skin color as his first attempt to explain why Polynesians are Nephites. He explains the distinction in terms of skin color, with Nephites being blessed with light skin because they followed the cultural and religious teachings of Israel, and the Lamanites being cursed with black skin because they rejected the teachings of their forefathers. Sutton qualifies the strict racial divisions between these two groups by making clear that even in the time of *The Book of Mormon*, Nephites who "apostatized from their religion, culture, and government, and dissented over to the Lamanites, they became Lamanites."[38] Sutton attempts to remove the racial connotations from the discussion by retaining the language of genealogy and lineage. When Lamanites rejected their customs and accepted the religion and culture of the Nephites, they became Nephites. Polynesians, on the contrary, descended from Nephites, and according to Sutton's interpretation of their traditions and customs, they "maintained the worship of the Nephites' God."[39] For Polynesians, missionary work returns them to their prior belief system and baptism grants them full access to and the blessings of membership in the contemporary church.

Sutton offers two theories for how the brown-skinned people of Polynesia could in fact descend from the light-skinned Nephites. The first argument he makes is that the intermingling of Lamanites and Nephites over the thousand of years that *The Book of Mormon* chronicles produced peoples of various skin colors ranging from nearly white to dark black, with the darkest-skinned Lamanites retaining the original curse. This theory resonates with British Israelite theories of the early nineteenth century that also rely on intermarriage to explain the assimilation of the Lost Tribes into dominant society. Sutton's second theory presumes that in the beginning Hagoth and his companions were in fact white, but "in tropical climates, people exposed to the sun on a continual basis, usually acclimatize to these elements, and their skin pigmentation becomes more intensified, causing the skin to acquire a darker shade."[40] In attributing skin color to environment (the sun darkened their skin) rather than culture (a depraved state of being), Sutton bypasses the question of curse altogether together.

Whereas Sutton attempts to walk a fine line between biological determinism and lineage to make the case that Polynesians are positioned higher on the evolutionary family tree than are American Indians, the LDS church genealogists William Cole and Elwin Jensen rely on biology as well as lineage to make a slightly different claim. They use blood tests, skull measurements, and racial characteristics to argue that Polynesians are a distinct race from Melanesians, Micronesians, and Malayans. Again, this was not a new insight but merely a reiteration of imperial racial classifications of Oceania.[41] The groundwork for this argument was established long before the Mormons looked to the Pacific and, according to Howe, was well established as part of mainstream thinking by the mid-nineteenth century.[42] By the 1830s, Oceania was already divided into three distinct cultural regions, Polynesia, Melanesia, and Micronesia. These cultural regions were also deeply embedded with racial assumptions that ranked the peoples of the regions in a hierarchal relationship to each other. "Polynesians," Howe writes, "were regarded as relatively superior; Melanesians as smaller, darker, inferior; and Micronesians as not very important at all owing to the supposed minuscule size of their island homes."[43] What we see here is an intersection of racial and geographic determinism that resonated with the increasing popularity of social Darwinist theories in the mid-nineteenth century.

CONSOLIDATING THE
POLYNESIAN–ISRAELITE CONNECTION

Interestingly, although Cannon's vision is recorded as having taken place in 1851, Britsch argues that the details did not become public until Cannon's return to Hawai'i for the fiftieth anniversary of the establishment of the Hawaiian mission. While traveling on the island of Maui in search of the home of Nālimanui, the Hawaiian woman who gave the missionaries her room so they could remain together, Cannon shares with his companions the significance of this place. In his journal he writes, "I wanted to find the site of this house and the garden where I sought the Lord in secret prayer and where He condescended to commune with me, for I heard His voice more than once as one man speaks with another, encouraging me and showing me the work which should be done among this people if I would follow the dictates of his Spirit."[44] It is at this site where the Lord told him that Polynesians were descendants of Abraham.

Cannon's vision is significant, indeed, because it suggests that Polynesians have a primordial genealogical connection to the House of Israel that supersedes their inclusion through the laying on of hands by men with the proper authority. As descendants of Abraham, Polynesians were subsequently counted among those who will, as described in the Book of Abraham, "be blessed, even with the blessings of the Gospel, which are blessings of salvation even of life eternal" (2: 11). This scripture establishes that Polynesians are the "literal seed or of the seed of the body" of Abraham, and it extends the Lord's covenant with other descendents of Abraham to them. Although Polynesians, as with other people, must still undergo the process of being ordained through baptism as full members of the church, it is this ancestral connection that elevates the status of Polynesians in the eyes of the church. Within the hierarchy of lineages established in the Book of Abraham Polynesians become one of the chosen people who were among the noble and

A group of church members in Lāʻie in 1900 during the fiftieth anniversary of the Hawaiʻi mission. George Q. Cannon is seated front row center. Photograph courtesy of Brigham Young University–Hawaiʻi Archives.

elite during the premortal existence. As such, the covenant of the priesthood could and should be (re)established with them.

As described above, anthropological theories had already established a lineal connection between Polynesians and the House of Israel; however, it took time for Cannon's vision to be fully integrated into Mormon theology. Norman Douglas's research attempted to pinpoint the exact moment when the Polynesian-Israelite connection was publicly articulated. His work confirms that Cannon was one of the first Mormons to make this connection. He also notes that Louise Pratt, the wife of Addison Pratt, a missionary to Tubuai, gave a speech in October 1851 where she names Nephi as the father of Tahitians. Although Pratt's speech was concurrent with Cannon's vision, Douglas concludes that these two events occurred independently of each other. Douglas also found that the first mention of the Polynesian-Israelite connection by a high-ranking church leader was in 1865 in a letter written by Brigham Young to King Kamehameha V.[45] Well into the twentieth century church leaders continued to expand and develop this origin story by relying on scripture as much as genealogy and anthropology to confirm the connection. In echoing the methodologies of nineteenth-century anthropologists, Mormons who were keen to consolidate the Polynesian-Israelite connection relied on spiritual rituals, religious figures, cultural practices, myth, and language as evidence to support their claim. What resonates is an assumption shared by Mormons and anthropologists alike. Describing the anthropological approach, Kuper writes: "Like extinct species, these primeval institutions were preserved in fossil form, [with] ceremonies and kinship terminologies bearing witness to long-dead practices."[46]

In 1921, Elder Duncan McAllister sketched out the cultural and spiritual connections between Polynesians and Mormonism in the essay "Important Appeal to Native Hawaiians and Other Polynesians" that he wrote for the *Improvement Era,* a Mormon magazine. It was McAllister's intent to use the genealogies traced by Māori, Tahitian, and Hawaiian members of the church on the occasion of their first visit to the Lāʻie temple to show how the people of Polynesia were related to the "American aborigines, and that the ancestors of the native Americans were Israelites."[47] He begins the essay with a Māori saying about the origins of the Māori people that traces their genealogy from New Zealand to Tahiti, back to Hawaiʻi, and then further back to a place known in both Māori and Hawaiian legend as Kahiki. McAllister, relying on historians of Hawaiʻi, argues that the Kahiki of Hawaiian legend is not the island of Tahiti but rather the Americas. Once he is able to connect the

Māori to Tahitians, then to Hawaiians, and finally to the Native people of the Americas, he relies on "ancient" history by referencing *The Book of Mormon* to argue that the people of the Americas were in fact descendents of Israel who escaped persecution in Palestine and found refuge in a new land. He uses this genealogy as a call to Polynesians that they embrace this "marvelous history" as the origin story of their ancestors. He believes that this genealogy also makes the Polynesian people "the most righteous people on the face of the earth, exemplars of all that is good and great, the true nobility of the work, worthy relatives of the most sanctified Being who has ever trodden this mundane sphere, the Redeemer and Savior of all mankind." Although this genealogy is their birthright, McAllister is not keen to end there. Rather he appeals to Polynesians to "assume your part in the great work that God desires his chosen people to perform," namely, "the banishment of wickedness and strife, and the establishment of his kingdom of peace."[48] Ultimately, this is a call for more missionary work.

In 1937, Elder William M. Waddoups, former president of the Sāmoa mission and the Hawaiʻi mission, gave a short radio broadcast titled "The Gospel of Jesus Christ in Polynesia." In the broadcast he described the connection between the people of Polynesia and the Saints in Utah:

> The Church has established missions in Tahiti, Hawaii, Samoa, Tonga, and New Zealand. People of a common ancestry, all having the same physical characteristics, the same fundamentals in language, and a similar background of traditional and mythological origin, inhabit all of these island groups. It is commonly believed and acknowledged that these Polynesian groups are descendants of Israel.

He goes on to explain the connection between the Mormon church and the Polynesian people by drawing explicitly on the similarities between their religious practices and traditions and those of ancient Israel. Although Waddoups qualifies Polynesian traditions and practices as "colored and somewhat changed," he emphasizes to his listeners that despite the generations and distance that separate Polynesia from the rest of the world, the similarities between the chants of Pacific people "leave no doubt in the mind that they obtained their information from the same source as the compilers of the Bible." For example, he informs his listeners that upon contact Europeans were surprised to learn that Polynesians had chants that told of "every great event of the Old Testament." He acknowledges that the characters' names and some of the specific details were different, but that one should look to the similarities to see that Polynesians relied on the same sources as the authors of the Bible for their chants.

Waddoups draws his listeners' attention to the Hawaiian story of the creation by the Hawaiian gods Kāne, Kū, and Lono of "the first man Kumuhonua," who lived in a beautiful green garden until he was cast out for eating a forbidden fruit. Waddoups shares other equally short examples of similar Hawaiian legends and stories from the Bible. The most significant example he shares is that of Lono, who he describes as a "white skinned God . . . who visited the Hawaiian people and lived with them for some moons." Upon his departure, he promised that he would return to the Hawaiian people. As the legend goes, when Captain Cook arrived on Hawaiʻi's shores, the Hawaiians believed that he was Lono fulfilling his promise to return to the islands.[49] We know how this story ends; Cook's behavior demonstrated that he was a mere mortal and he was killed. In the remainder of the radio broadcast Waddoups shares a number of examples of sacred rites performed by Hawaiians that resemble those of ancient Israel, such as ritual sacrifice and ceremony, the separation of men and women during certain times of the month, priestly blessings, and the venerated status of kāhuna. In sum, the entire broadcast drew distinct connections between Polynesians and references to *The Book of Mormon* and the Bible that would be familiar to his Utah Mormon audience.

The LDS church genealogists Cole and Jensen draw upon Polynesian traditions and chants, language ties, genealogy, and food to make connections between Polynesians and the Americas. In an uncanny way, they echo McAllister's 1921 article when they identify the Hawaiian and Māori chants that refer to "the cradle of Polynesia" located in "kahiki ku" or "Tawhiti . . . the land beyond where the red sun comes up" in order to argue that the place these chants refer is the Americas not Tahiti.[50] As Cole and Jensen were church genealogists, they put tremendous weight in the genealogies preserved in Māori chants, and they use the significance of genealogy for Polynesian people to call for the gathering and compiling of these records for the church. They also draw heavily on connections between Mormon beliefs and Polynesian belief systems and use the same references to Hawaiian gods and Māori chants that Waddoups used in his radio broadcast, albeit delivered to a more contemporary audience. For example, Mormons believe that the Godhead is comprised of three separate entities, God the Father, His Son Jesus Christ, and the Holy Spirit. Cole and Jensen point to the Hawaiian gods Kāne, Kū, and Lono to argue that despite the time that passed between initial migrations from the American continent to the return of Christianity to the islands, these three preeminent gods are evidence that Hawaiians retained elements of their original religious understandings. This interpretation only works when the fourth major male god of the 'aikapu religion, Kanaloa, is omitted. The 'aikapu religion, Tengan writes, is "a religiopolitcal set of laws that separated men and women during eating periods [and] . . . it separated the classes of ali'i (chiefs) from maka'āinana (commoners) and imbued the class of specialists known as kāhuna with powerful ritual authority that could direct the political and spiritual course of events in the island."[51]

Another example of this connection is the Māori creation story that holds a strong resemblance to the biblical creation story. As Cole and Jensen write:

> In some Māori traditions Tane himself was known as the first man, or the Adam of the Polynesians, and he sought out and created a woman who became his wife and ancestors of the human race. In other traditions he was the creator of both man and woman. One account says that Tane made man by mixing his own blood with red clay, and forming it into a figure like himself; and by breathing into it he gave it life. Another account says that this first man was made of red clay and the center shoot of rāupo (a variety of bulrushes). He was made in the resemblance of Tane.[52]

Regardless of the various accounts of the Māori creation story, Cole and Jensen are convinced that this is "more evidence to strengthen our conviction that the Polynesians are descendents of Lehi, and that Lehi did have the scriptures and genealogies upon the gold plates, as told in the *Book of Mormon*."[53]

What these examples illustrate is how the same evidence gets reproduced over time, thus taking an innovation and overlaying it with invention to produce a belief system. But not all Mormon scholars fully accept these origin stories. The historian and political scientist Jerry Loveland argues that the Mormon version of the origin of the peopling of Polynesia coming from the Americas is still contested by Mormon scholars. Loveland's critique of the Polynesian migration narrative is more methodological than it is a complete challenge to earlier perspectives. He is far more critical than earlier Mormon missionaries regarding the accuracy of the myths, traditions, and chants of ancient Polynesia, and he cautions the reader to be skeptical of the truthfulness of the information provided by "Polynesian informants."[54] He also warns that the strikingly similar stories between Polynesian myth and the stories of the Old Testament may in fact indicate that Polynesians brought these stories with them when they settled the islands. Once again, however, he cautions the reader to be skeptical of the accuracy of the stories because they could also be embellishments intended to please the haole recorders of this history.

Whereas the accounts offered by "native informants" are to be accepted with caution, genealogy is treated as the most valid proof of the connection between Polynesians, the Americas, and *The Book of Mormon*. For Loveland, the most promising explanation of the connection between the Americas and Polynesia comes from migration stories. As he writes, "The most striking Polynesian account of a Hagoth-like voyage is that of Hawaii Loa or Hawaii-nui. Mormon tradition has it that Hawaii Loa and Hagoth are the same person, and LDS temple records show them as being the same."[55] Sutton also relies heavily on the Hawai'i Loa connection; however, he is unwilling to say whether or not they are the same person. According to Sutton's genealogical chart, "The Royal Nephite Lineage," Hawai'i Loa is descended from Nephi through his offspring Alma and Alma the Younger (both characters in *The Book of Mormon*). He concludes this genealogy by drawing a direct link from Hawai'i Loa to Papahānaumoku, she who gives birth to islands, and Wākea, sky father. Loveland finds the story of Hawai'i Loa the most convincing account to explain the connection, but once again he tempers his enthusiasm by qualifying that the story of Hawai'i Loa is charged as being an invention. Whether fabricated or doctored, the story of Hawai'i Loa continues to be central to Mormon explanations of the connection between the people of *The Book of Mormon* and Polynesians.

Racism and the LDS Church Today

Mormon leaders and scholars alike mark the lifting of the ban in 1978 that barred men of African descent from holding the priesthood as a turning point in the racial history of the church. A new racial ideology was thought to have emerged that conclusively marked the universalism of Mormonism a reality. Although I recognize the historical significance of the lifting of the ban, I do not interpret it as being the end of racism in the church. Rather, I see it as a triumph of an ideology of universalism that disavows racial difference. This return to universalism also coincided with a shift in racial discourse in the United States. As Michael Omi and Howard Winant describe, "In the aftermath of the 1960s, any effective challenge to the egalitarian ideas framed by minority movements could no longer rely on the racism of the past." Conservatives responded by developing a new approach to equality, a color-blind approach. The color-blind approach was a discourse of equality that was premised upon the complete removal of racial considerations "in the selection of leaders, in hiring decision, and the distribution of goods and services in general."[56] Whereas on the surface a color-blind approach to equality appears to be a solution to the race problem, in fact the disavowal of the continued significance of race only serves to perpetuate the institutionalized racial hierarchy of U.S. society. Further, it had the unexpected consequence of producing claims of "reverse discrimination" by white men who argued that they were disadvantaged by affirmative action policies.

Bringhurst, writing twenty-five years after the ban on black men holding the priesthood had been lifted, acknowledges the significance of the reversal of this policy. He notes that since 1978 the church has "pro-actively sought to reach out more effectively to blacks both within the United States and abroad." However, he also identifies two changes that the church needs to make if it is to truly come to terms with its racism. First, it must acknowledge and come to terms with "the racist folklore previously used to justify black priesthood denial and the inferior place of blacks within Mormonism."[57] Second, if the church is to overcome its past and look to a future that is less racist, the composition of the General Authorities, the highest leadership of the church, must reflect the demographic diversity of the membership, including calling men of African descent to serve in these venerated roles.

Conclusion

The invention of the Polynesian-Israelite connection not only served as a rationale for the shift in nineteenth-century Mormon missionary work from haole to Hawaiian but also allowed the missionaries who remained in Hawai'i to embrace the universalistic principles of their faith. In so doing, they were able to effectively negotiate one of the most troublesome aspects of modern Mormonism: the contradiction between universalism and racism. Although the story of Hagoth is only four verses of the entire *Book of Mormon*, the effect has been profound. Polynesian members of the church believe that the missionary work of the white missionaries in the nineteenth century was preordained. Their testimony of the truthfulness of the gospel and their exalted position in the church as descendents of the House of Israel is made possible by this story. The racial hierarchies that support this narrative are masked by the belief that once a person is baptized they become brothers and sisters who are equal in the eyes of God.

The prophecy by Cannon marks a moment when the church was able to imagine a new social community that it would be able to both save and exploit as it proselytized among Native Hawaiians and as new missions were established throughout Polynesia. These missions, according to the church, were seen as altruistic; without the saving grace of the gospel Polynesians would not be able to achieve salvation and experience the fullness of their destiny as a chosen people. A critical aspect of the covenant made between God and His chosen people was for land where they could build Zion on earth. The gathering principle, as it played out in Hawai'i, afforded some Native Hawaiian Latter-day Saints a place where they could return to the 'āina by establishing self-sufficient religious communities. And yet, these settlements were considered a literal colony where labor and natural resources were extracted to help fill the coffers of the church in Salt Lake City, Utah. In the next chapter, I describe how gathering happened in Hawai'i and begin to expose some of the political implications of this religious principle.

2

Lā'ie, a Promised Land, and Pu'uhonua: Spatial Struggles for Land and Identity

In 1865 the Mormon church purchased six thousand acres of the Lā'ie ahupua'a (a subsection of an island district that stretches pie-shaped from the mountain to the sea) to provide Hawaiian Latter-day Saints with a gathering place in Hawai'i where they could live among coreligionists. It also became a site where many Native Hawaiians could revive their cultural relationship to the land and the sea. Chapter 1 described the process by which Hawaiianness came to be articulated with Mormonism through an invention of Hawaiians as a chosen people. The designation *chosen* marked Hawaiians as having, in the words of Tikva Frymer-Kensky, "an irrevocable relationship with God. It is this permanence that lies at the heart of Israel's covenant with God—it is indissoluble, will never end, and therefore always demands Israel's survival."[1] With the articulation of Hawaiians as descended from the House of Israel, it became the obligation of LDS missionaries to restore the gospel to Hawaiians and to ensure their survival. Land, in addition to being central to God's covenant with Israel, became a critical aspect of the success of the Mormon church in Hawai'i. As Grant Farred writes, "Land constitutes, after the subject's body, the most critical site of the biopolitical because it determines the conditions of life for both the imperialist and the colonized."[2] I argue that Lā'ie served the institutional needs of the church while also meeting the cultural needs and desires of Hawaiian Latter-day Saints. In this place a Hawaiian Mormon identity was reinscribed even as it was rearticulated during times of conflict and struggle. For Native Hawaiians, it was a place of refuge in the aftermath of the political storm we now call the Māhele—a set of procedures that privatized land.

In this chapter I trace the spatial struggles over land and identity in Hawaiʻi beginning in the mid-nineteenth century when ʻāina (land, that which feeds) was transformed into a commodity that could be bought and sold. Although the Māhele was intended to be a strategy to secure Native rights to land, it became a process by which they could be alienated from it. As Jane Jacobs notes, "Space is a part of ʻan ever-shifting social geometry of power and signification' in which the material and the ideological are co-constitutive. . . . These spatial struggles are not simply about control of territory articulated through the clear binaries of colonialist constructs. They are formed out of the cohabitation of variously empowered people and the meanings they ascribed to localities and places."[3] Here Jacob states that spatial struggles were neither simply about control of territory or land or clearly delineated between a coherent us versus them. In Lāʻie, the spatial struggles I examine were not simply about whether the land was controlled by LDS missionaries or by Native Hawaiian Latter-day Saints. Rather, these struggles were constituted by larger political and economic struggles in Hawaiʻi, where land was just one site of contestation and conflict. In Lāʻie, spatial struggles were produced on the ground through the everyday interactions of differentially empowered people living side by side and the meanings and desires they brought to this place.

The Māhele and its aftermath is the backdrop to this story. The privatization of land enabled the church to purchase Lāʻie as a place for Native Hawaiians to gather while also providing the Saints and the mission with a modicum of economic security. As the economic interests of church leaders came to dominate at the turn of the twentieth century, the interests and desire of Hawaiian Saints became subordinated. I begin this chapter with a brief overview of the Māhele that provides the broader context for the struggles over land taking place in Lāʻie. I then focus on the gathering principle, an edict that encouraged Saints to migrate to religious communities free from the sinful world around them. Lāʻie was not the first gathering of Saints in Hawaiʻi. In the 1850s Hawaiian Latter-day Saints gathered on the island of Lānaʻi at a place named Iosepa after church founder Joseph Smith Jr. Despite clear structural differences between the two gathering places, Iosepa has receded into history as a failed experiment tainted by corruption and fraud. Lāʻie, in contrast, has become a promised land in the Pacific. Accounts of visions, prophecy, and miracles are narrative devices used to imagine Lāʻie as a sacred site where the hand of God was at work.

The civilizing discourses of Christian missionary work tinged the gathering principle with colonial overtones. Whereas Native Hawaiian Latter-day

Saints saw gathering as a way to live the gospel principles, it also allowed them an opportunity to reconnect with ʻāina—land as the source of physical and spiritual nourishment. In stark contrast, LDS missionaries gathered at Lāʻie because they were called to do so by the president of the church. Their purpose for gathering was complicated by the dual job of using the plantation to financially support the proselytizing aspects of the mission while also serving as models of industry and wholesome living for Hawaiians. They carried the added burden of having to save these chosen people from vanishing. Lāʻie was more than just a place where Hawaiian saints could live free from the sinful world around them. This chapter examines how the different motivations for gathering played out, along with the impact on the community when those motivations began to shift.

During the period between 1900 and 1931, a change took place in which the gathering principle was replaced by an explicit business model for running both the plantation and the town in order to ensure the economic viability of the church in Hawaiʻi. This shift corresponded to an ideological transformation within the church from a cooperative socioeconomic system to one that was explicitly capitalistic. This economic turn was manifested in two events: first, the relocation of Native Hawaiians from the foothills to the village in order to increase the acreage for sugar production; and second, the separation of the plantation from the mission when the headquarters were relocated to Honolulu. Old timers describe this period as the era of "Old Lāʻie." They describe it as a time when families continued to live from the land and the sea but found it increasingly more difficult to do so. How did Native Hawaiian and Polynesian families struggle to maintain their connection to the ʻāina? How did they adapt to the loss, both physical and cultural, they experienced as their village was transformed into a modern town?

THE MĀHELE AND ITS AFTERMATH

In Hawaiian cosmology, ʻāina was believed to be the older sibling of kanaka (people), born from the cosmological mating of Papahānaumoku (she who births islands) with Wākea (the maker of the sky).[4] As Carlos Andrade explains, "the familial relationships established by the Papa and Wākea story place human beings as the younger siblings of the kalo (taro plant) and the ʻāina (islands)."[5] The familial relationship established by this origin story provided the basis upon which the indigenous land tenure system operated.

Haunani-Kay Trask calls this the kua'ana (elder sibling/younger sibling) relationship, where the responsibility of the elder sibling was to provide nourishment for the younger, and the younger sibling was, in turn, to care for the elder.[6] The values of kuleana (responsibility) and mālama (to care for, preserve, protect, maintain) were the guiding principles that determined each person's role within an ahupua'a system.

The ahupua'a was a subdivision within a moku (district) of a mokupuni (island) that typically extended, roughly pie shaped, from the mountains to the sea. "An ideal ahupua'a," Andrade describes, "extended from the cool, moist uplands, down across the alluvial and coastal plains, out into ocean waters, encompassing fringing reefs and sand-bordered bays.... Ahupua'a life was distinguished by shared use of land and resources, regulated jointly by konohiki (head administrators) and maka'āinana (the people living on the land). The resulting system included kapu, unwritten rules governing the behavior of people." The primary role of the konohiki was to "create order, encourage peace, and support prosperity," and kapu were only one means of achieving these goals. Additionally, these kapu, Andrade writes, "passed an ethic of conservation from generation to generation."[7] Within this system land was not owned. Rather, the reciprocal relationship among ali'i, konohiki, and maka'āinana reflected mutual, if differential, kuleana for maintaining the productivity of the 'āina, and in turn ensured the health of the Kanaka. In this regard, 'āina and the resources that came from this cosmological elder sibling were communally used.

The ahupua'a land tenure system was thriving at the time of the arrival of Europeans to Hawai'i (Captain Cook arrived there in 1778). In less than a century, however, political and economic pressures would, as Andrade notes, "unravel and erode traditional familial relationships [that kanaka] enjoyed with the land, its creatures, and each other."[8] Kauikeaouli (Kamehameha III) attempted to use Western law to "protect and preserve . . . the life ways that had served the Hawaiian people well for many hundreds of years."[9] The Māhele (literally, to portion or divide) was a three-stage process that began in 1845 with the establishment of the Board of Commissioners to Quiet Land Titles (hereafter called the Land Commission). This was followed by the Māhele of 1848, which allowed the Mō'ī (the highest-ranking ali'i), ali'i, and konohiki to relinquish their rights and claims to various parcels of land. The final stage, the Kuleana Act of 1850, set up a process by which maka'āinana could secure fee simple claims to familial parcels and ali'i could secure clear title of their land. These sets of procedures were intended to use the framework of private property to secure the tie that bound kanaka to the 'āina. However, in the end, it became a process by which the familial relationship between kanaka and 'āina was strained and, for some, irrevocably broken.

The groundwork of the Māhele was laid by the legislature in the 1830s with the passing of the Organic Act, which allowed foreigners who swore allegiance to the Kingdom of Hawai'i the right to own land.[10] Prior to the establishment of the Land Commission and the passage of the Māhele and Kuleana Acts, land could not be alienated without the consent of the mō'ī. The definition of ownership came under dispute when a land "owner" tried to sell his property. The Land Commission was established in 1845 to investigate and settle disputes with regard to land awards that were made prior to 1846, and to devise a system whereby individuals could have clear, fee simple title over land.[11] In 1848, the charter of the commission was expanded to establish formal land claims with the intention of protecting both the government and the maka'āinana from permanent dispossession. Scholars disagree, however, about exactly how the land was to be apportioned. Lilikalā Kame'eleihiwa takes the position that the plan was to divide the land into three equal parts vertically, with one share to the government, one to the ali'i, and a third to the maka'āinana. But the reality was quite different, she writes: "The Māhele divided the 'Āina in six ways, between the Mō'ī, ali'i, konohiki, maka'āinana, government, and foreigners, in unequal amounts."[12]

Other scholars suggest that the division was horizontal; after the unification of the pae 'āina by Kamehameha I, the interest in the land by the Mō'ī, ali'i, and maka'āinana was communal and layered one upon the other.[13] According to this interpretation, the Māhele of 1848 divided or separated the interests of the Mō'ī and the ali'i. The Kuleana Act did two things: first, it divided out the maka'āinana's one-third interests in the land from the other two-thirds interests that had already been separated; and second, it established two processes by which maka'āinana could secure fee simple title to land. Thus, the Māhele cut both ways; it severed the horizontal communal interests in the land and then used the surveyor's tools to vertically parcel out land in disproportionate ways.

The Māhele is typically described as a colonial imposition intended to dismember the lāhui (nation). Kame'eleihiwa and others cite the fact that less than 1 percent of eligible maka'āinana were granted Kuleana awards as evidence of the devastation that the process effected.[14] New research suggests that Kauikeaouli, the sovereign of the kingdom, was deeply concerned about the long-term welfare of the makaʻāinana in recognizing that the future of the people and nation was contingent upon land.[15] He saw the process of privatizing land as a way to secure Native claims irrespective of the political status of the government.[16] Donovan Preza maintains that the Kuleana Act was intended to secure the familial rights of individuals to the land where they resided and to the loʻi kalo they tended while also providing other means by which makaʻāinana could buy land. Provision 4 of the act reads as follows: "A certain portion of government lands in each island will be set apart, and placed in the hands of special agents, to be disposed of in lots from one to fifty acres, in fee-simple, to such natives as may not be otherwise furnished with sufficient land, at a minimum price of fifty cents per acre."[17] Preza posits that Native Hawaiians took advantage of this clause in the Kuleana Act and bought 167,290.45 acres (26 percent) of the total acres sold by 1893.[18] This new figure offers an alternative interpretation of the Māhele and suggests that Kanaka took advantage of both avenues of acquiring land, thereby ending up with a larger proportion than previously noted.[19]

In Lāʻie, the privatization of land through the Kuleana Act provided the necessary precondition by which the LDS church could purchase and then control almost the entire ahupuaʻa. Jeffery Stover's research identifies that 145 Kuleana claims were made to the Land Commission by makaʻāinana but only 72 Kanaka were granted Kuleana awards. The two largest awards were granted to Lunalilo (6,000 acres), an aliʻi who was to lose control of his land by 1858 in order to settle his debts, and Kakau, a konohiki.[20] Lunalilo's land was purchased by Henry S. Howland who, Stover writes, allowed Natives who did not receive Kuleana awards to remain on the land. The land was then sold to Thomas Dougherty in 1863 and purchased by representatives of the LDS church in 1865. As new research suggests, the process of Māhele did not immediately translate into dispossession. However, it is also the case that in an ahupuaʻa such as Lāʻie where there were no government lands to purchase, only a very small number of Kanaka were able to secure title to their lands. Indeed, the Māhele did not immediately dispossess Kānaka from the land; rather, it was a gradual process that I will show was never fully achieved. Economic pressures exerted by the increase in sugar production and by political shifts due to revised land laws and the overthrow in 1893 of the government of the Kingdom of Hawaiʻi contributed to the unraveling and erosion of the familial bonds that tied Kanaka to ʻāina—a bond that contemporary Kānaka are working to reestablish.

THE GATHERING PRINCIPLE

A key feature of the early church that resonated throughout its history was the call to gather. The gathering of Saints into cooperative, self-sustaining communities has been traced by Max Stanton back to the founding of the church, when "Mormons were urged to leave their homes and join with co-religionists in a central place commonly referred to be a 'Gathering Place.' The early history of the Church is characterized by this 'Gathering of Zion,' as Mormons call it."[21] The gathering principle linked two dominant discourses of the time: first, the religious millennial discourse that the end of days was near, which made the act of gathering an urgent preparation for this eventuality; and second, the American nationalist discourse of manifest destiny. According to the Mormon immigration historian William Mulder, the gathering principle to Zion, and not polygamy, was the first and fundamental covenant made between the faithful and the Lord. For the newly converted, the holy waters of baptism and the laying on of hands at confirmation held the promise of gathering in Zion. It produced, Mulder writes, "a strange and irresistible longing which ravished them and filled them with a nostalgia for Zion, their common home."[22] In 1830, Zion was still only an imagined community, but as Mulder points out, Smith believed it would be built in the West on the edge of civilization in Indian country. It was in the "empty" lands of the frontier where the promise of an ideal life in the service of the Lord could be actualized.

Kirkland, Ohio, and Nauvoo, Illinois, were two early attempts at building Zion. But the hostility and violence exacted on the Saints by their "gentile" neighbors inspired the Mormons to migrate further west, beyond the reach of the United States, where they could build the Kingdom of God without persecution. "Building the Kingdom," Mulder explains, "meant providing an environment that would regenerate the adult and rear the young so that they would never know themselves otherwise than as Saints."[23] Brigham Young, second president and prophet of the church, lead the Saints across the plains and into the Rocky Mountains, where upon seeing Salt Lake Valley on the horizon he declared, "This is the Place." For the Mormons, the Great Basin was ideal for their purposes of building Zion: in 1847, it was beyond the legal reach of the United States, and after the Mexican-American War its distance from the centers of power made federal interventions sporadic.

The LDS missionaries brought the fervor of gathering with them to Hawaiʻi. Matthew Noall served his first mission to Hawaiʻi from 1885 to 1888. In his autobiography, he expresses how "the spirit of *gathering* gripped some of the Hawaiian saints [who] were determined to emigrate to Utah, where they could be in the midst of the 'New Zion.'"[24] Given the emigration laws that prevented Native Hawaiians from leaving the islands, the church authorities determined that a gathering place was needed in Hawai'i. A site for the gathering also seemed warranted as missionaries continued to garner relative success in their work and the number of Hawaiian converts continued to rise. By 1853 when the number of Hawaiian Latter-day Saints reached a high of 3,008, efforts began to establish a gathering place in Hawai'i.[25] A gathering place would serve as a site of refuge from persecution where Saints could live in peace. As I describe in the ensuing section, it would also be a way for missionaries to model proper Mormon work ethics and righteous living. Two gathering places were developed in the period 1854–1865: the first in the Pālāwai Valley on the island of Lāna'i, and the second at Lā'ie on the northeast shore of O'ahu. Although the gathering principle was mobilized in the formation of both sites, the narrative devices used by historians in their retrospective accounts of these two places construct the former as a site not destined for greatness, while the latter would become a Promised Land in the Pacific.

Iosepa, Lāna'i

The spirit of gathering was upon the Hawaiian Latter-day Saints and the missionaries. However, the gathering principle was taken up within different discourses operating in Hawai'i. As described above, the transition to the privatization of land meant that the church would have to work within the political economy of private property to acquire land. During this same historical moment in the American West, Mormon settlers were acquiring land according to the frontier ideology of empty lands. Prior to the 1860s church leaders had negotiated directly with tribal leaders to acquire land for settlement. Despite these attempts at diplomacy, however, numerous land struggles and bloody battles occurred between Natives and members of the church, which have been documented by the historian Ned Blackhawk. After the 1860s when Indian relations were turned over to the U.S. government, land acquisition was regulated by treaty and federal Indian Agents.[26]

In Hawai'i, land acquisition resembled the contemporary process of looking for real estate. The missionaries tasked with locating a suitable settlement for a gathering place turned to Ha'alelea, a former konohiki who was both a landowner and an agent for other landowners. As principal konohiki of the land of the ali'i nui (high-ranking chief) Leleiōhoku since 1827, as well as the land of the aliʻi nui Kekauʻōnohi, Haʻalelea was able to show the missionaries a number of different properties on Molokaʻi, Kauaʻi, and Lānaʻi islands.²⁷ For nearly nine months, missionaries worked with Haʻalelea to find land that could be transformed into a settlement. Raymond Beck and R. Lanier Britsch make no indication of whether the land that Haʻalelea helped the missionaries acquire was his Kuleana award, part of Leleiōhoku's land, or Kekauʻōnohi's land.²⁸ Based on Kameʻeleihiwa's extensive genealogical research into the māhele process, however, it is likely that Haʻalelea was probably acting as both a husband and the konohiki of lands retained by Kekauʻōnohi after the Māhele.²⁹ Kekauʻōnohi had 128 parcels of land prior to the Māhele, and she was able to retain 76 parcels after it, including "28 on Hawaiʻi . . . , 32 on Māui . . . , 1 on Lānaʻi, 6 on Molokaʻi, 3 on Oʻahu, and 6 on Kauaʻi."³⁰ It appears that many of the properties were probably those of Kekauʻōnohi and that Haʻalelea was acting in her stead. This could explain why the missionaries were able to consider several properties on Molokaʻi, Kauaʻi, and Lānaʻi. It was within this political climate of restructuring that the missionaries went about finding a site to build their gathering place.

In 1854, a site in the Pālāwai Valley on the island of Lānaʻi was identified and acquired as the first Mormon settlement in Hawaiʻi. The Hawaiian Latter-day Saints who moved to Lānaʻi came primarily from congregations on Maui. According to Beck, "It was the first settlement in Hawaii established for the express purpose of gathering church members together to enable them to better understand and live the teachings of religion."³¹ But the gathering place for Hawaiian members of the church was intended as more than a safe haven from persecution; indeed, the settlement would also serve the express purpose of domesticating the natives in the ways of Western civil society.

Britsch describes as pioneers the first Hawaiian Mormons to settle on Lānaʻi. Just as their American counterparts traveled by handcart across the Rocky Mountains to eventually settle in the Salt Lake Valley, these Hawaiian pioneers would toil in order to transform the "barren" landscape of the Pālāwai Valley into a thriving settlement similar to those established in Utah. Britsch draws a clear analogy between Hawaiians settling Pālāwai and the settlement of the West by Mormons: "Settling this community was not very different from doing the same thing in Utah or Idaho. In Utah each village and town started from barren wilderness . . . land had to be cleared, water obtained, homes built, and streets laid out."³² Perhaps from the perspective of the Mormon missionaries it was not much different from the work they had done to build their own communities on the continent. Britsch's use of the term pioneer and his analogizing of Pālāwai with settlement in Utah reveals a settler mentality similar to that described by Grant Farred as belonging to those "intent on rooting themselves, against the temporal force of history, as it were, into the land." Farred explains that the objective of the settlers goes beyond rooting themselves in the land but instead must "ensure that there is no difference between the settler and the land, so that expropriation becomes—through time—renarrativized as historic affiliation with the land."[33] By drawing upon a pioneer and settler narrative, Britsch's framing attempts to create a historical affiliation between the LDS church and Hawaiʻi. Just as pioneer narratives erase the bloody battles that made the expropriation of land possible on the continent, the analogy elides the effects that shifts in land tenure and rights had on Native Hawaiians.

The Lānaʻi settlement lasted only ten years. During that time it experienced many challenges, including poor conditions for farming and low morale among the membership. In 1858 on the eve of a war between the LDS church and the U.S. government over polygamy, and only a few short years into the experiment, all of the missionaries were instructed to settle their affairs and return to Utah. In the midst of the disarray caused by this exodus, Walter Murray Gibson arrived in Hawaiʻi and proclaimed himself the new leader of the colony. Between 1861 when he arrived in Hawaiʻi and 1864 when he was excommunicated and the settlement was closed, Gibson appointed himself president of the church in Hawaiʻi, sold church positions to the Hawaiian Latter-day Saints, controlled all aspects of the Lānaʻi settlement, and extorted money from the Saints in order to buy the Pālāwai property. Those who challenged Gibson left Iosepa and sent letters to Salt Lake City requesting assistance. The first presidency of the church, alarmed by the reports, sent six missionaries to Hawaiʻi to attend to the problem. Despite Gibson's actions, however, about a dozen Hawaiian Latter-day Saints remained on Lānaʻi and continued to work for him.

Lāʻie: The City of Zion

In order to justify the expense of establishing yet another settlement, the decision to pursue a gathering place at Lāʻie drew heavily on Cannon's vision that Hawaiians were a chosen people. According to Britsch, the leadership of the church in Salt Lake City was ambivalent about the status of the Hawaiʻi mission, especially with the failure of the Lānaʻi settlement. On one hand, the severe decline in the Native population made church leaders apprehensive about continuing their financial support of the mission. On the other hand, this crisis also created a desire to want to save as many Native Hawaiians as possible, and the establishment of a new gathering place would go a long way in securing the salvation of these descendents of Israel. Ultimately, Brigham Young decided to continue to support the growth of the mission in Hawai'i because, as Britsch writes, "he felt that he and the missionaries were *obligated* to try to save a remnant of those people" (emphasis added).[34] With the support of the presidency of the church, plans were made to find a new location for the gathering of Zion.

Two missionaries, Francis A. Hammond and George Nebeker, were charged with the task of finding a new site for a Mormon settlement. Unlike the Lāna'i settlement where the Native Hawaiians would work to pay the rent on the land, the church planned to buy the property and establish a permanent gathering place. The church's own economic and political problems back in Utah came in the form of the Morrill "Anti-Bigamy Law" of 1862, which forbade plural marriage as well as restricted churches in the territories of the United States from owning land worth more than fifty thousand dollars. Although the land the church wanted to buy was not located in the territory of the United States (Hawai'i was recognized by the international community as a sovereign nation), the presidency decided to play it safe and loaned the necessary funds to Nebeker and Hammond, who would then make the purchase in their names. The idea was that in time the settlement would become self-sufficient and would pay back the loan.

Nebeker and Hammond began their search for an appropriate settlement site on the island of Kaua'i. Satisfied that they would be able to purchase any land they deemed suitable, Nebeker left Hammond to make the final decision and returned to Utah to prepare both of their families for the move to Hawai'i. The specific details of how Hammond came to decide on Lā'ie are sketchy; however, Britsch's description is illustrative of the ways in which the invention of religion works in his text. The way the story unfolds supports an ideology of the inevitability of progress. According to Britsch, Hammond talked to Thomas T. Dougherty, the owner of the six thousand acres of land that comprised the Lā'ie ranch, and after five days of touring the site he began negotiations to purchase the entire area. The negotiations were brief, and in the end Hammond purchased the plantation for $14,000, including "the stock, horses, and improvements thereon."[35] He took possession of the land immediately, thereby making Lā'ie the headquarters for missionary work in the Pacific and a gathering place for recent converts.

The historian Joseph F. Spurrier emphasizes visions as prophecy to explain why Hammond came to select Lāʻie. As he describes it, "After an anxious night and prayer, he [Hammond] left the ranch house on the property, walked a little distance, and there reported that Presidents Young and Heber C. Kimball appeared to him in vision and indicated that this was the 'chosen spot.'"[36] Once again, chance combines with visions to solidify and justify the missionaries' decisions and actions in Hawaiʻi. It is significant that Hammond's vision includes Brigham Young telling him that this was the place, because he spoke these same words about the Salt Lake Valley. By highlighting the shared language in Hammond's vision, members of the church who read this account would be able to associate Lāʻie with Salt Lake City, thus linking the new gathering place with Zion. Spurrier's book is intended as an informational guide for members of the church. Entitled "Great Are the Promises unto the Isles of the Sea," the first half describes, in brief, the establishment of the Hawaiʻi mission and the growth of the church. The second half includes select chapters from the Hawaiian translation of *The Book of Mormon*. The intended audience of Spurrier's text is the Native Hawaiian members of the church, and thus the emphasis is on revelation, miracles, and visions.

Britsch identifies three benefits of Lāʻie as a site for a permanent gathering place. First, the Lāʻie plantation comprised an entire ahupuaʻa with fertile land, a water source, and productive crops, including five acres of cotton that Hammond hoped would provide a sellable yield. Second, although Lāʻie was located near Honolulu it was far enough away to allow the Mormon settlement to grow at its own rate. Third, there was already a small congregation of Saints living in Lāʻie, and this group could form the nucleus of the community.

Despite the practical reasons for choosing this site, Britsch and other historians of the church in Hawaiʻi also draw upon the Hawaiian belief that Lāʻie was once a puʻuhonua (place of refuge) in order to justify the purchase of the land. For example, David W. Cummings, commissioned by the church to write a souvenir history of the church in Hawaiʻi for the centennial anniversary of the establishment of Lāʻie, draws upon this idea in his account. Titled *Centennial History of Laie, 1865–1965*, Cummings seamlessly combines the gathering of Saints with Lāʻie as a puʻuhonua. As he writes:

> The earliest information about Laie is that it was a small, primitive village—with one striking distinction: It was a "City of Refuge," a sanctuary for fugitives.

A person in flight, no matter from whom, even the King, or for what reason, was safe if he could reach the sanctuary of Laie.[37]

The combined effect is the ability to narratively link the growth of the church with preexisting Hawaiian beliefs in order to create a timeless connection between Mormonism and Hawaiianness.

The establishment of the Lāʻie settlement marked a critical moment of the growth of the church in Hawaiʻi. The acquisition of the Lāʻie ranch had a stabilizing effect on the mission, and missionary work in the islands was able to expand. In comparing the way that the histories of the two Hawaiian Mormon settlements of Iosepa and Lāʻie are told, it is interesting to note that the stories about the Iosepa colony do not include visions or prophecy. As such, it is as though this settlement was not sanctioned by God in the same way as Lāʻie and was, therefore, destined for failure. In Spurrier's account the story of the Lānaʻi colony only takes up a few paragraphs. He attributes some of the difficulties the Hawaiian church leaders faced after the Utah missionaries returned to the continent largely as a consequence of the church members being merely "less than a generation from their pagan past and few, if any, had made the transition from their early task-oriented interaction with the land and sea for livelihood, to the work-a-day, money economy of the new culture."[38] As I demonstrate below, Hawaiian members of the Lāʻie community continued to rely heavily on the land and sea for their livelihood, a tradition mourned by old timers in the community. In the remainder of Spurrier's account of the Lānaʻi colony no mention of visions or prophecy was attributed to it or to this time in the history. In fact, the decision to close the settlement and have its members return to their homes was reinforced in Spurrier's final story of this place—a tale of a miracle. As he writes, "It was after this conference on Lānaʻi that Elder Lorenzo Snow was drowned in the surf, in a landing accident, off the beach at Lahaina. After an hour's search, his body was recovered and under the hands of the elders and by the power of the priesthood, he was restored to life."[39]

The story of Snow's resurrection and its placement at the end of the section on the Lānaʻi colony is a narrative device intended to give credence to the decision to close the Lānaʻi settlement; that is, although the Lānaʻi colony failed, a new gathering place would allow the Hawaiʻi mission to rise from the dead. Within this narrative framework, Lāʻie's reputation as a puʻuhonua is merely one of many testaments to creating the imagined geography that the site was a Promised Land destined for great and miraculous events.

GATHERING, COLONIALISM, AND THE
DOMESTICATION OF THE NATIVE

The Lā'ie settlement would be unlike any other Mormon gathering place, because in addition to becoming a "place of refuge" for saints seeking peace among their fellow believers, it would be a training ground for teaching Hawaiians to live proper Mormon lifestyles. In a letter written by Brigham Young to King Kamehameha V explaining the church's intentions in building the Lā'ie community, Young had this to say:

> According to the precepts of our religion, the spiritual and temporal are so intimately blended that we view no salvation or system of salvation as being complete, which does not provide means for the welfare and preservation of the body as well as the salvation of the Spirit . . . Mr. Hammond, and my other friends . . . will therefore endeavor to teach your Majesty's subjects . . . practical salvation.[40]

Despite President Young's attempt to gain permission from the king to bring both spiritual and temporal salvation to the Hawaiian people, the church was only allowed to improve the physical lives of Hawaiians. The church still functioned under a veil of suspicion by other Christian religions as well as by the Hawaiian government. The edicts by the king did not, however, thwart the goals of missionaries to carry out their mission to save both the body and the soul.

Although the Mormon missionaries were directed by the king to limit their influence to the physical lives of their members—for example, as a precaution against the threat of polygamy entering the islands, they could not perform marriages—missionaries believed that attention to the temporal would reap spiritual rewards. President Young's plan for the Lā'ie plantation was to send four families from Utah who would model proper Mormon lives for the Hawaiians. He expected the families to have "sufficient funds with them to be able to live at a standard well above that of the Hawaiians." The Lā'ie settlement would not merely be a "city of refuge" for Saints but a "school in proper behavior, in hard work, in virtue, and in morality," where "the haoles were to be the teachers, the Hawaiians the students."[41]

The organizational structure of the mission resembled the structure of other gathering places, where church leaders were simultaneously the spiritual, political, and economic leaders in their community. In Hawai'i, however, this structure carried the political overtones of imperialism rather than the utopian society envisioned by the leadership in Salt Lake City. From the very beginning, the mission president was both the spiritual leader and the business leader of the settlement. It was his responsibility to coordinate the everyday workings of the ranch while also tending to the salvation of the Hawaiian members. From winter to fall 1865, Hammond was in charge of the settlement, followed by Nebeker (1865–73). Under his leadership, the settlement went about the process of domesticating the Hawaiians and the landscape. Unlike Iosepa, Lā'ie already was laid out as a ranch with a few houses, cattle, and gardens. In order to accommodate the recently arrived families from Utah, each family would be allotted land that would include enough space for a house, a small garden, and a few farm animals. Wood-framed houses were first built for the Utah families, and temporary shacks were built initially for the Hawaiian families. The plan was to teach Hawaiians the proper ways of animal husbandry through private property ownership—but with one catch. Neither Hawaiian nor Utah families would own the land upon which they lived; indeed, even today the church owns the land while individual families own homes. Also that first year a school was started, one for the children of the Utah missionaries and one for the Hawaiian children. Separate church services were also held, justified because of language.

According to Britsch, life in Lā'ie was difficult for everyone. The missionary families struggled to find a cash crop that would allow them to support their families as well as pay back the debt they incurred to relocate to Hawai'i. Under the direction of Nebeker, the Hawai'i mission encountered other adversity as well. Conflict arose between him and other missionary families who felt Nebeker treated the Lā'ie ranch as his own personal economic venture and not a church enterprise. The tensions between Nebeker and other Utah missionaries continued until 1867 when President Young intervened and loaned the Utah families the money needed to get out of Nebeker's debt. Despite the safety net that Young provided, the ranch struggled economically until 1868 when they saw their first profit from a large crop of sugar.

That year proved to be a critical turning point in the success of the ranch. For the church leaders in Utah their financial risk was finally seeing some success, and for both Hawaiian and Utah Saints living in Lā'ie the 1868 sugar crop gave them hope that their utopian community would thrive. Both Britsch and Spurrier credit the Hawaiian members Jonatana Nāpela and

George Raymond for the decision to try sugar as their primary cash crop. Nāpela directed the planting, harvesting, and processing of the sugar. Despite the high yield and solid profits from the 1868 crop, not every year was as successful. Throughout its history, the Lā'ie plantation served as a colonial outpost for Salt Lake City. The sugar and molasses produced in Lā'ie was shipped to Utah where it was put on the market and sold. The profits were subsequently distributed back into the plantation from church headquarters in Salt Lake City. This system continued until the 1890s when the Kahuku plantation took over the sugar mill production. However, sugar continued to be the main cash crop in Lā'ie until 1931 when management of all sugar land was turned over to the Kahuku plantation.

Over the next twenty-three years the plantation would continue to grow slowly. Despite the uneven success of the plantation, the church was able to invest in improving its image in Hawai'i. In 1882 a new stone chapel was built in Lā'ie, along with over twenty-five other chapels throughout Hawai'i. The Lā'ie mission school was also built, and new church auxiliaries were set up and established. The missionary families living in Lā'ie reportedly made little progress in acting as models of wholesome living, as "the moral

'Ī Hemolele, a chapel built in Lā'ie, is shown here surrounded by sugar cane fields in the foreground and the Ko'olau Mountains in the background. Photograph courtesy of Brigham Young University–Hawai'i Archives.

looseness of the converts and members" continued to haunt the new settlement.[42] Britsch does report, however, the Hawaiian members were living physically cleaner lives, which contributed to higher birth rates in Lāʻie than in other Hawaiian communities. Overall, progress moved slowly during these early years, but it appeared that the destiny of these chosen people was beginning to look better than earlier in the century.

From Ahupuaʻa to Plantation

The Native Hawaiians who gathered at Lāʻie were seeking more than just a place to practice their religious beliefs away from the prying eyes of non-Mormons. On the continent, such persecution drove their coreligionists to erect theological and ideological walls to separate them from the sinful, dangerous world that surrounded them. For the Hawaiian church members, Lāʻie offered them an opportunity to return to the ʻāina. As I read the oral histories of Native Hawaiian and Sāmoan members of the church, I came to see how they managed to negotiate the complex relationship between the motivations and interests of the church and of their own. In telling their stories they describe Lāʻie in complicated ways. Whereas many old timers made a clear distinction between an "old Lāʻie" and a "new Lāʻie," their descriptions reflect a matrix of relationships that operated in the town between the church, the Polynesian community members, and, at the margins, the Asian laborers. Here I underscore the ingenuity of Native Hawaiians who resisted the "presumed" markers of colonization such as religious conversion and dispossession of land.[43]

During the first twenty years of the Lāʻie experiment, Native Hawaiians were able to maintain a lifestyle that balanced the need for cash while also being able to rely on the resources available in an ahupuaʻa. When the church purchased the ahupuaʻa, approximately 125 Native Hawaiian families were already living there, 72 of whom held Kuleana awards. Stover reports that by 1872, "44 kanaka saints had gathered."[44] They were motivated to settle in Lāʻie because of the opportunity it afforded them to maintain customary food practices within an ahupuaʻa system at a time when access to land became increasingly difficult.

The Latter-day Saints who gathered at Lāʻie were given a house lot and a loʻi (water garden) where kalo (taro) could be cultivated. These lots were located in the foothills near the Native Hawaiians who had Kuleana awards. These Saints were able to draw upon the natural, fresh water, and coastal resources the ahupuaʻa offered. According to Cynthia Compton, they gathered "timber, ferns, [and] medicinal plants" from the mountains and grew "'awa, sweet potatoes, fruits and dry kalo . . . in the higher elevations. [They also grew] wet kalo, fruit and other crops . . . in terraced hills and flat lands."[45] From the bay and the ocean came an abundance of fish, limu (seaweed), heʻe (octopus), and a variety of other delectable morsels. Mission President Harvey Cluff (1879–82) explained in an article in the *Deseret News,* an LDS newspaper in Salt Lake City, how Native Hawaiians lived on the land and drew resources from the ahupuaʻa tax free:

> A benefit possessed by native members of the Church, who settle here, is in receiving sufficient land to produce kalo and vegetables, free of taxation and, as the business of the plantation increases, the young and able work hands find ready employment, while the females are employed to divest the cane of its foliage, thereby earning means to make themselves comfortable. They also have free access to the fisheries, game, and timber.[46]

This return to the ʻāina was no small endeavor. Given the historical context of the time, Lāʻie was literally a place of refuge for Native Hawaiians who were finding it more and more difficult to remain on the ʻāina.[47]

These Saints were not alone in their desire to maintain a connection to ʻāina. Robert Stauffer's examination of the hui movement (a co-operative established to buy ahupuaʻa) of the late nineteenth century demonstrates a desire to return to the land. Hui were formed across the pae ʻāina when groups of Native Hawaiians pooled resources and capital to purchase ahupuaʻa. Stauffer found that Native Hawaiians throughout the islands were motivated to retain and perpetuate their customary practices of drawing upon the resources of an ahupuaʻa for their survival and for the foundation of their identity as Kanaka Maoli (the true people).[48]

In addition to being able to rely on the ahupuaʻa for sustenance, Native Hawaiians were able to regenerate the practice of kalo production. As water gardens, loʻi kalo require a fresh-water source, typically a stream from which water can be channeled and circulated through one patch and on to another using a complex network of ʻauwai (irrigation canals). The abundance of loʻi and the significance of kalo production for the Saints reflects Native Hawaiian desires to perpetuate ʻāina and can be seen in the physical layout of the village. Lāʻie was divided between the mission compound located on the lowlands nearest the ocean and the kula area or uplands where Native

Hawaiians built their homes and lo'i kalo. The journal of the missionary Benjamin Cluff describes the spatial layout of Lā'ie shortly after the establishment of the mission: "The little village occupied by the twelve missionary families, with the large plantation house in the centre, is about three fourths of a mile from the sea, and on a low hill which rises higher further back, then ends in a broken mass of immense rocks and cliffs. Native houses dotted the plantation, but were most abundant above the plantation house, among the 'calo' patches."[49] The location of the "native houses" was significant because they were placed near water sources where lo'i could be maintained. Stauffer's analysis of the Māhele concludes that although Native Hawaiians did not get the largest proportion of land, they were awarded the most valuable land. In Lā'ie this appears to hold true as the maps from the Māhele indicate that most of the Kuleana land parcels are located along the stream where fresh water kept the lo'i productive.

The ability of Native Latter-day Saints to maintain kalo cultivation is significant. Throughout the islands kalo production was being systematically pushed out for the expansion of sugar production.[50] As a gathering place originally established for Native Hawaiians, the economic imperatives of

In the late 1890s Lā'ie looked like a farming village with white clapboard houses surrounded by farmland. Photograph courtesy of Brigham Young University–Hawai'i Archives.

the sugar plantation were a close second to the needs of the Saints and the mission. The initial policy was to hire Native Hawaiians living in Lāʻie and provide them with the cash they needed to pay their taxes and meet other financial obligations of a cash economy. Missionaries from Utah, when not proselytizing, were used as a reserve labor source for the plantation. The revenue from the plantation was used to support those missionaries proselytizing in other parts of Hawaiʻi.

Within this structure, Compton argues, Native Hawaiians had a lot of bargaining power. They drew upon their status as laborers and their venerated genealogy in order to meet their needs and interests. The result was a five-day work week where Saturday was reserved for caring for kalo, harvesting, and producing poi, the main food staple for Hawaiians. No work was done on Sundays. The rhythm of work on the plantation was not just governed by kalo but also by the rhythm of the sea. During the seasons when fish were running in Lāʻie Bay the community would gather at the ocean. On those days work in the fields and at the mill had to wait.[51]

Kalo production was both fundamental to Native Hawaiians and seen by church leadership as critical to the overall success of the mission. In a letter written to John Taylor, president of the LDS church, mission president Edward Partridge (1882–85) highlighted the significance of kalo for the success of gathering Saints to Lāʻie:

> Matters at Laie are progressing about as well as could be expected we have not the necessary inducements at present for saints to gather in very great numbers to this place, not being able to provide them with the kalo for patches that each family requires for their sustenance.
>
> It is my opinion that when we get out of our embarrassments [debts of ten to twelve thousand dollars] sufficiently that we can sink some wells and have water to make lois for the natives to raise their kalo many will be induced to gather here who do not feel to do so now. I do not feel to urge many to come at present, circumstances as we are with regard to these matters.[52]

The mission presidents were aware of how important kalo was to the success of their work. Partridge recognized that Native Hawaiian church members migrated to Lāʻie for pragmatic as well as religious reasons. He was keenly aware that the success of the mission was linked to the production of kalo. But this letter also reveals a second concern, the debt of the mission. For Partridge, the production of kalo was also linked to the production of sugar;

they needed more laborers to work in the fields, and offering Hawaiians lo'i for kalo was a very big carrot. However, increased sugar production also required an increase in acreage for cultivation. Should land be used for kalo or sugar cultivation?

The economic needs of the plantation were at times at odds with the religious imperatives of the mission and the cultural interests of Native Hawaiians. Partridge's solution to the paradox was to levy a tax on kalo and he'e. As mission president, Partridge was responsible for the religious and spiritual well-being of the Saints as well as the secular needs of the mission including the viability of the plantation. When he levied taxes on kalo and he'e, he did so by appropriating the Hawaiian title of konohiki. Within a Hawaiian social structure, a konohiki was appointed by the ali'i to, as Andrade points out, "ensure that the activities of the maka'āinana ran smoothly."[53] The familial relationship to land described above established the parameters of the kuleana (responsiblities) of the konohiki and set the standards for how they should interact with maka'āinana. Under the indigenous system, konohiki were responsible for instituting kapu (unwritten rules for managing resources) only when necessary for protecting and preserving the natural resources of an ahupua'a. Land and water use and management were required not to increase profits, as they were under the private property tenure system, but to ensure a heathly ecosystem for future generations. As managers of the land, the LDS leadership adopted the konohiki title. However, within the post-Māhele geopolitical context, as konohiki who were not genealogically accountable to 'āina or maka'āinana, their resource management decisions were informed by the economic necessitities of maintaining the mission. By appropriating the title of konohiki, Partridge drew selectively upon indigenous discourses to ensure his preferred outcome.

As the needs of the plantation and mission increased, the relationship between missionaries and Native Hawaiians became more strained and tension mounted over the meaning and use of the land. Missionaries began to relate to the land in increasingly capitalistic ways. On more than one occasion Native Hawaiians and missionaries clashed over how the land should best be used. Although the Māhele might have initiated a process by which Kānaka could be and were alienated from land, it did not sever the familial relationships described above. Rather, Kanaka continued to relate to the 'āina in pre-Māhele ways.

Under the ahupua'a system maka'āinana were not bound to the land or the ali'i but were free to transfer their labor and allegiance to another ahupua'a and aliʻi if the current ones did not meet their responsibilities. Lance Chase documents one such tension between Hawaiian church members and the paternalistic actions of mission president Fredrick A. Mitchell. The crisis emerged when Mitchell replaced George Nebeker as mission president in 1873. At the time, it was common knowledge and practice that Hawaiians in Lāʻie cultivated and sold ʻawa (kava) as a secondary cash crop. As Chase writes, "They believed that the tuber, ground up and mixed with water, could effectively treat ailments as varied as leprosy, tuberculosis, and toothaches. Taken in large quantities, ʻawa has a narcotic effect, and it was used to make a traditional drink for social and ceremonial occasions."[54] When Mitchell became mission president one of his first orders was to dig up and burn the entire ʻawa crop. He believed that drinking ʻawa was similar to imbibing in alcohol and caffeine, lifestyle choices that were in opposition to the Word of Wisdom.[55] Chase notes that Harvey Cluff, the assistant to the mission president, believed that Mitchell's demands were unreasonable because the village relied heavily on the income that was generated from the crop. He was not surprised by the community's rebellious response to the demands. The actions that the Hawaiians took in response to Mitchell's insistence that his announcement be followed without question is an example of how Hawaiians asserted their agency in the face of paternalistic actions. Those local members of the church who decided not to comply with Mitchell's unreasonable demands organized an Ahupuaʻa Hui that would pull together the capital needed to purchase land in the ahupuaʻa of Kahana Valley. They took up donations from community members in Lāʻie, to Mitchell's dismay, as well as solicited funds from members in the outer islands. Undaunted by Mitchell's attempts to thwart their plans, and unmoved by their disfellowship from the church, a group of Hawaiian Mormons succeeded in purchasing land in Kahana where they continued to grow ʻawa for sale and for personal consumption. This story demonstrates that Hawaiian Latter-day Saints were both faithful to their beliefs and committed to their own sense of cultural perpetuation even when it flew in the face of Mormon doctrine or the edicts of church leaders.

As the economic needs of the plantation increased, the interests of the Native church members were marginalized, and as such the two narratives of gathering came into direct conflict. These conflicts are highlighted by a legal case in 1881 regarding loʻi used for kalo cultivation on church land that was brought by two Native Hawaiian sisters against the mission president Harvey H. Cluff (1879–82) and the Chinese farmer to whom the land was leased. The leasing of land to Chinese farmers was a strategy that Cluff believed would solve two of his problems: the need for cash and the need for water. The periodic droughts that plagued Lāʻie put a strain on the success of sugar cultivation. Another source of water needed to be found, and Cluff saw the Chinese farmers as providing that solution. In exchange for leases to rent loʻi, Chinese farmers would drill a well and provide water for their rice paddies, the Natives' kalo, and the church's sugar plantation. What they did not expect was fierce opposition on the part of Native church members.

The sisters and their supporters drew upon their indigenous notions of ʻāina as well as their venerated status within the church to support their position that the land was originally purchased by the church as a gathering place for Native Latter-day Saints. Although the church legally held title to the majority of land, Native church members who did not have Land Commission Awards believed that the church purchased the ahupuaʻa for their use. When the two women demanded that the church recognize their right to the loʻi within the boundaries of the leased land, they did so based on an indigenous understanding of land that was not constrained by legal definitions of private property ownership. Although Stover calls this case "simple," I argue that it is anything but simple. Indigenous notions of land are both physical as well as spiritual. Compton documents that the sisters organized an occupation of the loʻi and physically barred access by the Chinese tenants to the land. The women also relied on Western and indigenous strategies to challenge Cluff's decision to replace kalo with rice cultivation. They hired a lawyer and sued the Chinese growers and Cluff for the return of their loʻi. Additionally, they hired "an old Kahunapule or high priest who had long practiced the art of 'praying to death' and because of superstition had, no doubt, succeeded in many cases." As Cluff goes on to note in his autobiography, "This 'praying to death' was now to be used on me."[56] Despite their efforts, the court did not support their argument but instead ruled that the land belonged to the church and not to them.

As Jeffrey Stover suggests, this case "demonstrates a long lasting problem faced by both Kanaka Maoli and plantation managers in Lāʻie. This problem stems from the fact that many of the makaʻāinana of Lāʻie, who did not receive Land Commission Awards, continued to live and use the ʻāina despite not owning it."[57] Whereas Cluff was acutely aware of the centrality of kalo for Native church members and their desire to gather, he was also aware that his decision to lease land to non-Hawaiians would be seen as a betrayal. Unfortunately for Native Hawaiians, as the nineteenth century came to a close and new mission presidents brought with them their own vision for Lāʻie, the needs of the mission and plantation would come to take precedence over those of the Saints.

THE MAKING OF OLD LĀʻIE

The 1890s mark a time of dramatic political and economic changes in the church. On September 25, 1890, the president and prophet Wilford Woodruff (1887–98) capitulated to the increasing threats made by the U.S. government and ended the practice of plural marriage by church members. Woodruff's Manifest, as it came to be known, ensured a place for Utah in the United States, and soon thereafter church leaders acting as the political leaders of the territory of Utah were able to lobby for and gain entrance into the union on January 4, 1896. This moment also ushered in a new direction in the economic interests of the church. Until about 1890, the primary economic interest of the institution was communal and cooperative. Under the direction of Lorenzo Snow (1898–1901), who followed Woodruff as president and prophet of the church, the leadership began to redirect its financial interests, as Britsch notes, "towards more typical capitalist American business."[58] The impact of this new direction was felt most strongly in Utah; in Hawaiʻi, this shift was already underway as the plantation began moving more explicitly toward economic financial sustainability rather than cooperative community sustainability, a process I describe in more detail in the following chapter.

Between 1890 and 1919 the principle of gathering gave way to the expansion of sugar production. Matthew Noall (mission president from 1891 to 1895) and Samuel E. Woolley, (mission president from 1895 to 1919), laid the foundation for what would be Lāʻie's transformation from ahupuaʻa to modern town. What both men shared was a commitment to making the plantation profitable and thus ensuring the financial security of the mission. Noall's experience of having served a three-year mission to Hawaiʻi in the 1880s informed the strategies he developed for modernizing Lāʻie and the plantation. Woolley would continue in Noall's footsteps and increase the productivity of the plantation by securing more land and increasing the water supply to "four million gallons of water a day enabling [the plantation] to increase the amount of acreage under cultivation."[59]

When Noall arrived in Lāʻie for his second mission, his first objective was to find a way to turn a profit on the sugar cane ready for harvest. He was able to do this by brokering a deal where the sugar would be milled by the Kahuku plantation and then sold. As the relationship between Kahuku and Lāʻie progressed, a railroad line would replace trucks to more efficiently haul cane for milling. Noall also found other ways to increase efficiency. As manager of the plantation store he standardized the recordkeeping procedures, corrected the mistakes of former general managers, and within a year was able to give Salt Lake City its first accurate account of the economic viability of the plantation. Noall's commitment to standardization and efficiency was not limited to the plantation. Within his first year as mission president he surveyed and redrew the house lots, gardens, and taro patches in the town and established uniform rental fees for the different parcels. He hoped that by making each lot the same and by ensuring equal distribution of land for loʻi, disputes among residents would end. He found that for those residents who had been in Lāʻie the longest this was not an acceptable outcome, but for more recent arrivals the standardization gave them equal footing with older residents.[60]

In addition to the many different ways that Noall attempted to regulate the various components of the settlement, he was most noted for his efforts at modernization. Prior to becoming the mission president, Noall was a general contractor. During his second year, he began designing and building a new mission home that would be named the Lanihuli House. It would stand as the physical center of the town until 1919 when the temple displaced it. Britsch describes the Lanihuli House as a "building modern in all its designs," and "an interesting combination of current continental U.S. stylings with some Hawaiian modifications. It can best be classified as a Hawaiian Victorian. . . . Inside it was spacious, with kitchen, dining room, hallways and six 'dwelling rooms.'"[61] The house would stand as a symbol of Lāʻie's introduction to modernity until 1960 when it was demolished for housing for the Church College of Hawaiʻi. Under the direction of other mission presidents, Lāʻie would see more moves to modernize the plantation and the town. At the turn of the twentieth century, the most significant economic move was made by the mission president Samuel Edwin Woolley. Under his direction, new steam-powered water pumps were installed in artesian wells that allowed the plantation to raise approximately 3.5 million gallons of water a day. The increased supply of water resulted in more acreage of sugar cane and for the plantation to grow overall.

Despite economic stability and the growth of the Lāʻie settlement, it had yet to achieve true Promised Land status. That would come in 1919 when a

equalized land divisions

temple was erected and dedicated in Lāʻie. According to the historian of Mormonism Richard O. Cowan, the idea of building a temple in Hawaiʻi had been discussed on numerous occasions. The first was at the October 1852 conference when the missionary John Stillman Woodbury spoke in tongues, which was translated by Frances A. Hammond. Woodbury's message stated that as the seeds of Joseph, the people of the Hawaiian Islands "would be built up . . . and that a temple would be built in this land." A vision and prophecy of a temple was heard again in 1864 when William W. Cluff, a missionary to Hawaiʻi, had a vision whereby "Brigham Young appeared to him . . . and told him 'This is the place, and upon this land we will build a temple unto our God.'"[62] Joseph F. Smith's visit to Lāʻie June 1915 was equally significant. As Cowan describes this visit:

> Following a meeting at mission headquarters in Lāʻie, Church President Joseph F. Smith invited Elder Reed Smoot and Presiding Bishop Charles W. Nibley to join him for an evening walk in the near by tropical ground. "I never saw a more beautiful night in all my life," Elder Smoot later recalled. While they were strolling President Smith unexpectedly confided, "I feel impressed to dedicate this ground for the erection of a temple of God, for a place where the peoples of the Pacific can come and do their temple work . . . I think now is the time to dedicate the ground."[63]

Later that year at the biannual general conference, Joseph F. Smith (1901–18) made a plea to the membership of the church to build a temple in the Pacific for the faithful followers of the islands. In his speech he referred to their ancestral connection to the House of Israel as well as their openness to hearing and accepting the gospel. He informed the membership that the Saints of the Pacific should not be denied the same privileges of the fullness of the gospel just because they were poor and could not afford the expense of traveling to Salt Lake City in order to do temple work. Cowan's research shows that small groups of Polynesians did in fact make the expensive journey to Salt Lake City in order to do temple work. For example, in 1913 "Stuart Meha and five other Maoris from New Zealand traveled to America to receive their endowments in the Salt Lake City Temple."[64] He notes that the expense of travel from the Pacific Islands to the nearest temple on the U.S. continent created a crisis for many faithful Polynesian saints.

Upon the site where Smith knelt in prayer, the Hawaiʻi temple was built and dedicated in 1919. President Joseph F. Smith had passed away the year

The construction of the Lā'ie temple marked a turning point in the evolution of the Hawai'i mission as it marked Lā'ie as a Promised Land and initiated Sāmoan immigration to Hawai'i. Photograph courtesy of Brigham Young University–Hawai'i Archives.

before, and the temple was dedicated by his successor, President Heber J. Grant (1918–45). In his dedicatory prayer, President Grant acknowledged the divine prophecy that led to the erection of this temple. With the completion of the Hawai'i temple, a new era was to begin in Lā'ie. The temple stood as the physical manifestation of vision and prophecy and established Lā'ie as a Promised Land for a chosen people.

Old Lā'ie: A Hawaiian Mormon Town

Although Vailine Leota Niko was a small child when her family migrated from American Sāmoa in 1922 to arrive in Hawai'i on January 1, 1923, she recalls how her family was warmly welcomed into the Hawaiian community. Niko's family was one of the more than two dozen Sāmoan families called to emigrate to Hawai'i where they would conduct temple work on behalf of their families and the church. After she and her family arrived, they lived in a small house on Iosepa Street next door to a prominent Hawaiian family, the Broads, and on the same street as other notable Hawaiian families such as the Kekauohas, the Kailikeas, the Apuakehaus, the Nainoas, and the Logans.

The act of naming the Kanaka Maoli families who lived on that street serves as a way to ground genealogy in the land and names this place as, first and foremost, Hawaiian. In addition, Niko describes the Filipino camp and a Japanese camp that housed plantation laborers on the edges of the village. Niko's memories of old Lāʻie reflect descriptions of a town peopled by Hawaiians, Sāmoans, and on the fringes, Asian immigrant plantation workers. Her interview in 1972 for the Lāʻie Oral History Program betrays a longing for the openness and feeling of welcome that characterized the olden days:

> Well there is no comparison to what used to be before. Every house was open to anyone. The doors were open. When we first came from Samoa there was not a time when you passed a house and where the head of the family or anyone would come out and say "Hele Mai," you know, in their way say "Hele mai e ai." They would say, "come in and have something to eat," or "come in." They were happy and they welcomed you to their place and they were so hospitable. And that is the feeling.[65]

Although Niko's description is nostalgic it is not unique. Many long-time community members share her sense of old Lāʻie as an open, welcoming place where people were happy. The Lāʻie community oral histories also tell a story of a place struggling to contend with the economic realities that surrounded them. Although what Niko describes is a Polynesian village, this village is firmly situated as a church-owned company town.

After 1919 when the mission headquarters were moved to Honolulu, Lāʻie simply became a business enterprise for the church. As Britsch contends, "this is not to say that the Church suddenly turned its back on Lāʻie and its people, but times were changing."[66] The severing of the mission from the plantation had at least one immediate consequence. When the headquarters moved to Honolulu, the highest-ranking haole church leaders migrated to town, leaving Hawaiian and Sāmoan men as leaders in charge of the spiritual needs of the community. This explains the absence of haole community members in Niko's description of Lāʻie in the 1920s and 1930s.

Despite these changes Lāʻie maintained its affiliation as a Mormon town. This sentiment is best expressed by Amoe Meyer who migrated to Lāʻie in 1927 to teach school at Lāʻie Elementary. Two things struck her as unique about the village. First it was a well-established Mormon community, and second, it was predominantly Hawaiian and Sāmoan. She remembers that the only haole families living in the community were missionaries or the family of the mission president. As a haole herself who grew up in Honolulu, she was not unfamiliar with the LDS church. However, moving to a LDS community was an adjustment. As she admits, "I was kind of scared and you know what? In Lahaina when I left, some of the people over there said, 'Now, you be careful, don't you go there and marry a Mormon!'" She laughs, "But the trouble was, the year hadn't even passed, and I was married to a Mormon."[67]

As I describe above, at various points in the history of the church in Hawai'i, the interests of the church has had unexpected benefits for its Native Hawaiian members. For example, although the church hierarchy was clearly delineated along racial lines with haole occupying the highest leadership positions in the Hawai'i mission, the membership was primarily Hawaiian. Edward L. Clissold notes in an interview that until about 1921 the church in Hawai'i was almost exclusively Hawaiian: "Out in the country districts the people spoke Hawaiian, their services were conducted in Hawaiian and the temple that had just been opened was attended by Hawaiians, for the most part . . . Between 1920 and 1950 we began to bring in the other nationalities" through the migration of Sāmoans and through a concerted effort to convert the local Chinese, Japanese, and Filipinos living in the area.[68] Clissold stresses that at its core, the church continued to be Hawaiian. As a "Hawaiian" church, one of the unexpected outcomes was that the Hawaiian language continued to be spoken at home and in church until the 1960s. A second unexpected benefit was that Hawaiian, and later, Sāmoan men became the spiritual leaders in their community.

Paul F. Nāhoa Lucas argues that after the overthrow of the Hawaiian monarchy in 1893, "the English-mainly campaign transformed into an English-only one, as advocates stepped up their efforts to accelerate the extermination of Hawaiian."[69] Despite the strident campaign to assimilate Kanaka Maoli through the prohibition of Hawaiian, Lucas emphasizes that this campaign was not completely successful. As he explains, "The use of Hawaiian went 'underground' and remained largely in use with families who continued to value the Hawaiian language, in churches, and Hawaiian societies."[70] Thus, although we can trace the persistence of Hawaiian in these "underground" spaces, by the 1960s even these last bastions of the language were beginning to shift to English.

The oral histories with Lā'ie community members tell a similar story of how the Hawaiian language was spoken at church and at home. By the 1960s, however, the shift to English was well under way as Hawaiian-speaking leaders were replaced with younger English-speaking Saints. Although this loss was devastating, it is nevertheless significant that the Hawaiian language was able to thrive for so long in this Mormon community. With the haole members of the church attending the English-speaking congregations in Waikīkī, church services in Lāʻie were conducted in Hawaiian, and later, Sāmoan languages. Moreover, as Lucas suggests, communities that were beyond the surveillance of the public school system and that placed a high value on language and cultural practice continued to speak the language. It is a testament to the Kanaka members of the church in Lāʻie that the Hawaiian language was able to survive there as long as it did.

Old Lāʻie: A Polynesian Village and Company Town

Old timers also describe Lāʻie as a plantation town. When the church bought the ahupuaʻa it introduced and structured the community around market values. The impact of this was felt most strongly after the mission and the plantation were divided in 1919, and then again when Lāʻie plantation was sold to Kahuku plantation in 1931. In response to these economic changes, Lāʻie community members found paid employment at the Kahuku sugar plantation and at the poi factory in Lāʻie, and as workers for the County of Honolulu. They also continued to rely on fishing and the loʻi kalo and family gardens to supplement the low wages in these other industries. During the Depression many found work in WPA jobs, while others were able to secure regular employment at the temple. In these ways Lāʻie did not seem much different from any other Polynesian community.

By contrasting the business interests of the church with the survival strategies of Lāʻie community members, the old conflicts between the community and the church's economic plans resurface. Oral history accounts of early-twentieth-century Lāʻie describe the plantation hierarchy in ways similar to other plantation towns, for example in Viola Kawahigashi's statement that "the missionaries were operating the sugar plantation." Kawahigashi's personal memories and the stories she heard from her grandfather tell a story of resistance. During the late nineteenth century, many Hawaiian members of the community initially worked on the plantation but decided that working all day in the sun for only fifty cents a day was not worth the money when they could work in their gardens and fish in the streams and ocean in order to provide for their families. She admits that her grandfather was able to make this choice because he also had a job as the tax assessor "and marriage license agent."[71]

Kawahigashi recalled that one of her fondest memories of childhood was the significant amount of time she spent with her grandparents. Her grandfather and grandmother "raised corn, pumpkin, bananas, potatoes, tomatoes, [and] onions" in their garden, but went to the mountains behind Lāʻie town "to get pandanus or lauhala; it was an all day adventure." The "all-day adventure" included harvesting the thorny lauhala, and walking along the streams and fishing for ʻōpae (shrimp) and ʻoʻopu (fish) for lunch. Her grandfather would build a fire, then wrap their fresh catch in ti leaves and roast them on the open fire. She also enjoyed "roving around for guavas and mountain apples and rosy apples that were abundant according to the season."[72]

The adventure trips to the mountains were also a time to work. Her grandmother cleaned and prepared all of the lauhala before loading them into the wagon to be taken home. They made the trip only twice a year, which meant that her grandmother needed to collect as much lauhala as she could during each trip. She recalls that her grandmother worked with the lauhala early in the morning, before the day got too hot and dried out the leaves, and then again in the evening after the sun had set. She remembers fondly that her grandmother would weave "large mats for the floor. She wove baskets, fans, and hats for our use in our home and for ourselves." She even remembered how her grandmother would give lauhala mats to their friends and relatives who would visit from Honolulu, "because the city folks didn't do very much weaving . . . And also for the missionaries when they were leaving for their homes after their missions here in Hawaiʻi."[73] Kawahigashi's memories of spending time with her grandparents in the mountains behind Lāʻie and learning to weave lauhala mats is one example of the cultural persistence that took place in this Polynesian village.

Kawahigashi's oral history offers rich detail of the ways in which Lāʻie was both a company town and a Polynesian village. One of the characteristics of a plantation company town was that many of the commercial establishments were associated with the plantation. There was a plantation store that sold sundries and offered credit to plantation workers, which was taken out of their paychecks. Next door to the store was the plantation office where workers could pick up their paychecks. There was a barbershop, a blacksmith shop, and an icehouse that was operated by the Lāʻie plantation store. The only other store in Lāʻie was the Nakayama store, which was on the edge of town. As a child Kawahigashi worked in the fields during the summer and remembers picking up her paycheck, once a month, at the plantation office.

Although the plantation provided employment for many community members, they did not earn enough there to support their families. Similar to the story told by Kawahigashi, the oral histories document how local families were able to survive in a cash poor economy by relying on traditional forms of utilizing resources from the land and sea as well as from gardens, various types of livestock, and communal agriculture. For example, Thomas Au explains how his family supplemented his father's meager income: "My father used to raise a lot of chicken, ducks—he makes salt eggs [from duck eggs] and sell some, and some for the family. And my mother used to go down the river catch small shrimp from the river, small little fishes. And when the sea is calm, she would go down, get squid for us, limu and all those things. Yes, that's how we lived." When Au married and started his own family he drew upon his parents' example in order to support his family. While he worked at the plantation, "the pay was cheap, so I had to do something. So I started raising animals, and that's how we had our meat and pork. Anytime we needed—the freezer get low—then we send them to the slaughter house, send the cow to the slaughter house."[74]

Even when children did not work on the plantation, they still contributed to feeding the family. As a child, Au remembers collecting small shrimp in a nearby river: "Well, the only thing I knew—down the river here on the highway—right close to Matsuda's service station, is a river over there going [to] the ocean. And that river there, in those days, didn't have so much grass as now. And over there, little children can go swim, and catch little shrimp in there—they call it ʻoʻopu [ʻōpae]. We tried to catch the little fish, āholehole."[75]

For Au, the loʻi kalo that were spread throughout Lāʻie were a critical part of their survival strategy and were seen as an expression of Hawaiian values. As he explains, "Taro patches, yes. Where is the [Polynesian] Cultural Center now, we had all taro patches, mostly. All taro patches over there; I remember all taro patches. And right by the married student homes from there toward coming here to Goo's store—on your left side, on the beach side, they had taro patches over there, too. Hawaiians grow them over there too."[76] Even in old Lāʻie, the principle of kuaʻana continued to be practiced as each family had their own loʻi kalo and everyone supported each other in times of need. Au remembers it this way, "Oh, everybody make their own poi, you see. And those days, if your taro patch not ready to harvest—the taro for make poi— you come see me, and then you can have some bag, whatever you want. Then when your taro are ready to harvest, then you give me back your taro. That's how we worked before. And that's how we worked together, lived together.

So, not like today."[77] As described above, today the Polynesian Cultural Center, Brigham Young University–Hawaiʻi student housing, and other development projects have replaced the loʻi. As Au suggests, when development is privileged over mālama ʻāina (caring for the land) the price we must pay is our connection to the ʻāina.

For Niko, the ability to feed one's family by relying on the land and the ocean was what gave Lāʻie its special feeling. Her memories of old Lāʻie echo those of Au; she remembers a time when there was little competition and individualism among families who relied on each other for their mutual well-being. There is a way in which we can read these examples as the persistence of a Hawaiian and Polynesian sense of land as ʻāina. The descriptions of Lāʻie as open, welcoming, cooperative, and reliant on the land and ocean for food were the characteristics that also define this company town as a Polynesian village.

However, what seems to be missing from these narratives is any kind of explicit critique. In sharing her grandfather's decision to quit working for the plantation, Kawahigashi's narrative points to the presence of discontent between the membership and the plantation. However, absent in the rest of her oral history is any kind of criticism of church business practices. This kind of silence around the business decisions and practices of church leaders was not limited to the plantation days. The absent presence of critique reflects an ideology of faithfulness where faithful membership in the church is premised on faithfulness to church business and managerial practices. To be sure, ideologies of faithfulness were not about one's active membership in the church; rather, it was a way to solicit community consent to church projects even when those projects went against prior beliefs, understandings, and values. Arguably, Kānaka Maoli and Sāmoans living in Lāʻie during the plantation era (1868–1931) experienced the gap between the land as private property and indigenous conceptions of the land as ʻāina as relatively narrow compared to today. As the town continued to grow, however, it experienced growing pains associated with an increase in development, migration, and commercialization, themes I will return to in chapter 3.[78]

Conclusion: Remembering the ʻĀina

The gathering principle provided the motivation to search out and establish a Promised Land where Mormon families from Utah could teach Mormon families from Hawaiʻi the proper ways to live as Saints. In addition, Cannon's prophecy provided the rationale for the church to pursue such an extreme venture at a tumultuous time in its own history in Utah. The combined effect was the establishment of Lāʻie as a Promised Land in the Pacific that would become a place of refuge for Polynesians, a chosen people descendent from the House of Israel.

I have argued that attention to the more subtle forms of colonization is important because it is through the process of domesticating the natives that the church is able to garner consent from those Hawaiians who joined the church. The process of domestication, teaching the Hawaiian Latter-day Saints how to live Mormon lives in a yeoman farming fashion, was indeed paternalistic but not, however, altruistic. In fact, the church's ability to acquire land and establish economic stability through the sugar industry was a direct result of a tumultuous battle over land and power. By writing this connection out of the histories of the church in Hawaiʻi, LDS historians have created a picture that allows the church to remain untainted by this colonial legacy.

Kānaka Maoli in Lāʻie and across the pae ʻāina are continually forced to choose between two competing meanings of land: that of land as ʻāina, our older sibling and the source of nourishment for our bodies and spirits, and that of land as commodity. While story and language enable indigenous relationships with place despite colonization and selective assimilation, an ideology of faithfulness works in Lāʻie in a manner that at times silenced or redirected indigenous criticism of church practices. However, this same ideology allowed Kānaka Maoli and Sāmoan members of the church to maintain a sacred relationship to the ʻāina that was at once indigenous and Christian. The story that Tom Fanene shared during his oral history interview about how the site of the Church College of Hawaiʻi was divinely chosen is particularly instructive. As the story goes, one morning at about 9:30 a.m., Fanene, his brother Ailama, and Clinton Kanahele were about to begin working in his brother's watermelon patch when two angels appeared above the temple. They watched as one angel pointed his finger at the site that would become the gateway into the college and the other pointed toward the village. Then they watched as the angels ascended up the hillside and disappeared. At the time they were amazed and confused about the meaning of their vision, but when the plans were revealed for the college they knew that the angels had shown them the site where the buildings would stand. This vision only strengthened Fanene's belief that the Lord had a purpose for Lāʻie and that the temple, the college, and the cultural center were built using the Lord's money. For him, this story was a reminder to himself and a message to others that each community member has a responsibility to give their time and energy toward building up Lāʻie and preserving its sanctity.[79]

As I have demonstrated, Kānaka Maoli in Lāʻie have struggled with and against various economic development plans initiated by the church in order to maintain a familial relationship to the ʻāina and each other. What is distinct during this time period is that Kānaka used an ideology of faithfulness to challenge the economic decisions of mission presidents. As these stories demonstrate, they were not always successful. Their attempt to negotiate the tension between the economic needs of the church and their own desires relied upon their status as a chosen people that at times could be leveraged toward their own benefit. By the 1950s development projects such as renovations to the Lāʻie temple, the construction of the Church College of Hawaiʻi as well as student and faculty housing, and the completion of the Polynesian Cultural Center brought into relief the gap between the institutional interests of the church and those of the community. In the next chapter, I document the dangers that emerged as the church moved forward with these development projects. I also focus on the ways in which the community responded to these changes; indeed, some were able to parlay new opportunities into advances for themselves and their families.

3

Called to Serve: Labor Missionary Work and Modernity

As I described in the previous chapter, the process of transforming Lā'ie into a modern town was not without conflict and contradiction. The diminishing significance of the gathering principle corresponded to political and economic shifts taking place in the Mormon church as a whole. Between the 1890s and the 1930s, several policy changes initiated by mission presidents signaled a conscious move toward modernity and rationality. In this chapter I focus on the Labor Missionary Program, which provided the labor for the construction of the Church College of Hawai'i in 1956 and the Polynesian Cultural Center in 1963. These institutions are vectors that point to but do not clearly delineate the lines between modernization and tradition. Instead, they are sites of transcultural syncretism that come into tension with prior, fundamental tensions between the customs and practices of Kanaka Latter-day Saints and the modernization embraced by church leaders. As with other projects initiated by high-ranking church leaders, these institutions were intended to improve the quality of life for Saints both in Hawai'i and across the larger Pacific.

The college and the Polynesian Cultural Center were seen as symbols of progress and rationalized as materially and ideologically contributing to the community. Jürgen Habermas's reading of Max Weber suggests that the embrace of modernity and rationality ushers in a "process of disenchantment" and "a disintegration of religious world views that issued in a secular culture."[1] Indeed, in Lā'ie we see increased surveillance of the community by church leaders and the diminished ability of the church members to live from the land and sea. However, the oral histories of labor missionaries reveal a reintegration of their religious worldviews that reverberates in their narratives of why they accept their callings.

The rationalization of religion offers an interesting perspective of modernity. On the one hand, Weber saw the process of the "rationalization of religious life" as parallel to the rationalization of economic life; additionally, religious rationalization and institutionalization did not replace tradition and "magic" but made concessions to the traditional beliefs of its membership. Religious rationalization, as I detail below, reinforces the missionary emphasis of the church by making it relevant to a broader range of people. But as the church expanded across Polynesia and into Asia, the increased bureaucracy that came from expansion produced a structure that was increasingly more impersonal and alienating. In order to minimize these impacts, the church again drew upon ideologies of faithfulness to retain a level of particularity even as it became increasingly bureaucratic. As Weber reminds us, religions are in the world, and, consequently, the spiritual rationale for the development projects and the callings that propelled people to travel across the Pacific have material effects. This chapter examines the spiritual and material effects of modernity by concentrating on the Labor Missionary Program.

In this chapter I focus on those moments where progress and modernity were differently negotiated by Native Hawaiian, Polynesian, and haole members of the church. By focusing on the attitudes and perspectives of differentially situated members, I shed light on the changes that took place within the organizational structure of the church. Additionally, I build on the foundation established in previous chapters that identifies the emergence of the Polynesian Latter-day Saint identity. As I argued in chapter 1, Cannon's vision articulated with interpretation of scripture to make the case that Hawaiians and, by extension, Polynesians were a chosen people whom the church was to serve. As the church in Hawai'i increasingly became more institutionalized and bureaucratized, its Hawaiian members experienced a loss of autonomy—indeed, it appeared as though the intention of the church was to reproduce itself rather than to provide a place of refuge for the Kānaka members. But this story is not completely fatalistic. Despite these changes, the shared identity as a chosen people provided a rationale whereby Hawaiian and Polynesian members struggled to assert control over their daily lives while also turning to cultural practices and customs as a mechanism for bringing meaning to their secular and religious activities. In this way Hawaiian and Polynesian Mormons drew upon changes in their material conditions as well as religious doctrine to legitimate their struggles against LDS rationality.

The meanings that Polynesian missionaries bring to their callings as missionaries, as immigrants, and as laborers reveal a candid engagement with modernity and capitalism as they use their membership in the church as a mechanism for the maintenance of a style of life that is both "traditional" and "modern." As Weber theorized, "Men act in obedience to religious or magical beliefs so that they 'may prosper and have a long life on earth' . . . Such actions are moreover relatively rational: though not necessarily based on consideration of means and ends, they are still based on rules of experience."[2] As I demonstrate below, Polynesian labor missionaries accepted a calling for rational reasons that were both religious and pragmatic. I contrast these stories with the oral histories by haole missionaries and church leaders that tend to reinforce imperial discourses of cultural decline and primitivism as they reflect an image of Polynesians as childlike and in need of saving and protecting from the corruption of modernity and capitalism. How do Polynesian Latter-day Saints maneuver within this highly paternalistic structure? By situating the specific case of Lāʻie within a larger historical context of massive development and the shift to a tourist economy in Hawaiʻi beginning in the post–World War II era, I highlight what is at stake in the tension between what Native peoples hope to gain from their active manipulation of modern capitalism and what was lost when development was allowed to progress unchecked.

MORMONISM AND MODERNITY

With a sense of irony and humor, Thomas "Uncle Five Cents" Au reflected in an interview in 1980 on his childhood memories of growing up near the stream in Lāʻie:

> In those days the water was not too deep, it's shallow. The thing is, those days, you're not afraid to go in those streams because there wasn't any broken bottle, or broken cans like today. Today you cannot go in there because since they— beer was allowed to drink, people just throw bottles in there, their cans and everything. And now they have so much grass, and the water is not good now because it's polluted because they throw a lot of dead animals in there. I remember the waste of the chickens, sometimes they dump them up here . . . So you can't go fishing out here. So the best place to go fishing is down the store or the market. (Laughter).[3]

Au's reflections on the contamination of the stream can be seen as a sign of the fate of modernity. In contrast to the early twentieth century when Uncle

Five Cents was a child and played in the stream and caught ʻōpae (shrimp) and little fish called āholehole, at the time of his oral history interview the stream was so polluted that it was no longer safe for swimming or fishing. As the community grew and land was cleared for new construction it became increasingly more difficult for families to draw sustenance from the land and the sea as they had done for generations. Within a context of modern rationality, the stream stands in for and comes to signify the community's loss of autonomy. In modern Lāʻie the stream was no longer a site for food production as it had been in the (recent) past, but instead was replaced by food acquisition at a grocery store, a place where the source of food is depersonalized and abstracted from any original context. In his humorous way, Au is correct—in modern Lāʻie the best place to go fishing is at the grocery store.

For Weber the paradox of capitalist modernity lies in the irresolvable tension between those institutions constructed to make human life more ordered, rational, and predictable so as to bring a greater sense of control to human social life. However, the unintended consequence of rationalization is that these same institutions actually produce less autonomy and less self-control—a fate that is tied to our inability to completely understand and control the structures and institutions we have constructed. As Au clearly articulates, families are now dependent on supermarkets and imported food and not the land and sea. For Weber, once society begins to go down the road of modernization there is no turning back, and although he theorizes the need for struggle against oppressive structures, the fate of modernity is that we can never escape it. Although I find Weber's understanding of modernization and its impact useful for explaining the shifts that took place in Lāʻie, it also raises a red flag for indigenous self-determination. According to this framework, the time before modernity, the time of tradition, is seen as the authentic. As indigenous peoples adopt and adapt to modernity they are seen as less traditional and less indigenous. My approach attempts to depart from this framing by suggesting that modernity and tradition are not binary oppositions such that the further indigenous peoples move away from the time of tradition the less indigenous they become. Rather, I am interested in how indigenous communities engage with modernity, the ideologies they bring to these contexts, the meanings they make, and the way tradition is deployed (sometimes in the service of capitalism and bureaucracy). In order to disrupt the colonial and racial frames that define native peoples as anachronistic, we must first acknowledge the copresence of the settler and native and acknowledge that people may have very different motivations for embracing modernity.[4]

Indeed, Mormonism's engagement with modernity has been a troubled one from the beginning. The church emerged in the 1830s in the United States during the height of what Weber calls the rise of capitalist modernity. As the nation became more disenchanted and increasingly bureaucratized, Joseph Smith declared himself a prophet who had returned Christ's true church and teachings to the world. Smith offered converts and the faithful a return to enchantment and, through the gathering principle, a retreat from the world. As a charismatic leader, he held out the promise of overcoming the vast alienation of capitalist modernity by bringing meaning back to people's lives.

I draw heavily upon the work of Weber, who was a contemporary of Smith and whose body of work attempts to make sense of the economic and political changes taking place in the nineteenth century. Weber's work on the role that religions play in the production of modern capitalism is useful for thinking about how the Mormon church has come to be one of the fastest growing and wealthiest of the global religions.[5] It seems to me that the church is interesting because it emerged in the 1830s as an alternative to the alienation of Western civilization. Yet it did not, nor could it, remain as a retreat from the world. Rather, historians suggest that even in its early years the church was already engaging with the modernization occurring around it.[6] This is not to say that the church was outside of modernity but rather that it was modernizing alongside, if belatedly, the rest of society in the United States. The modernization of the church is unique because on the one hand it mimics the process of bureaucratic centralization of state making, yet on the other hand it needs to reproduce the authority of the prophet as seer and revelator. To do this, religions incorporate the traditions, myths, and magic of the local congregation, thereby retaining elements of enchantment within its modern form.

For Weber, one of the defining characteristics of modernity is the process of bureaucratization. Bureaucracies are necessary because they are an efficient way to manage a complex organizational structure such as a religious institution or a state. However, maintaining a bureaucratic system requires a steady stream of income. For states, taxation provides the means to maintain an administrative apparatus. For the Mormon church, one's faithfulness is measured in part by a tithe. The law of tithing was first instated in 1838 as, in the words of John Heinerman and Anson Shupe, a "10 percent obligation 'levied on what a man is worth.' That is, on his surplus property, interest from investments, and so forth, and not on gross personal income."[7] During the nineteenth century it was not uncommon for tithing to be paid in kind through goods, livestock, produce, or higher-stakes donations such as land, stocks, or bonds. By the twentieth century, tithing was expected to be paid in cash, and church authorities required all employees of church-owned businesses to be full tithe payers or else lose their jobs.

As the LDS church became more bureaucratic, the hierarchical structure of authority became more stratified as midlevel administrators carried out the wishes of the upper leadership. The hierarchical model allowed business to be done on a regular basis, but it also created a gap between the leadership at the top which was buffered by the managers in the middle and the masses at the bottom. David O. McKay (1951–70), the ninth president and prophet of the church (and recognized as the first modern prophet), found the distance created by the bureaucracy to be a hindrance to his success as a prophet. The biographers Gregory Prince and William Wright describe McKay's dilemma as a byproduct of the natural growth of the church: "As the church grew in size and complexity, greater and greater amounts of [McKay's] time had to be devoted to administrative functions, a dilemma that was not resolved until years after his death, when most administrative functions were handed off to the Quorum of the Twelve [Apostles]."[8]

The bureaucratic centralization of the church took advantage of the existing theological hierarchy where the prophet is the pinnacle who holds the dual role of seer and revelator as well as president of all secular—political and economic—aspects of the church. He is supported by first and second counselors, who in combination with the prophet represent a triad called the First Presidency. The First Presidency is intended to mirror the spiritual trinity of God the Father, Jesus Christ, and the Holy Ghost. This structure was established by Joseph Smith who proclaimed himself both prophet and president, thereby making him the central authority over both spiritual and secular concerns of the church. Brigham Young, Smith's successor, maintained the organizational structure, which continues today.[9] Below the First Presidency is "the Council (or Quorum) of Twelve (Apostles) who meet weekly in the temple at Salt Lake City to set policies on Church affairs." Heinerman and Shupe locate the rationale for this structure within church theology: "Just as there are various other, lower councils in the Celestial Kingdom, so the earthly LDS Church has its First Council (Quorum) of the Seventy, which oversees the actual administration of diverse Church operations. (The Council of the Seventy, the Council of the Twelve, and the First Presidency constitute the General Authorities of the Church)." As McKay's dilemma illustrates, the bureaucratic centralization of the church in the twentieth century widened a gap between the General Authorities at the top of the hierarchy and the laity below. Heinerman and Shupe argue that this structure produced "a theologically justified chain of command and the effective insulation of higher leaders from official dealings with most rank-and-file members (except when the leadership desires it)."[10] As the church became more bureaucratic the laity could no longer expect to have direct contact with the upper echelon; as such, under this strict hierarchical model it was no longer possible to "drop-in" on a General Authority.

The illusion of a personal relationship between the membership and the General Authorities continues to be maintained structurally through General Conferences held biannually where the General Authorities "speak" directly to the global membership. At General Conferences the membership is instructed, informed, and reminded of its faith and duty. At the local level Stake Conferences are also important because they instruct the particular community on their duties. Within the context of a depersonalized, bureaucratic institution, conferences are an important mechanism for maintaining a sense of a connected, personalized relationship between the individual members and their leaders. It is at General Conferences where individual members can still be "face to face" with their prophet. In the late nineteenth century and the early twentieth, Polynesian members of the church spared no expense to attend the General Conference in Salt Lake City. The opportunity to be in the presence of a living prophet and to receive direct guidance from him motivated many to travel thousands of miles and emigrate from Hawai'i, Aotearoa (New Zealand) , Tonga, and Sāmoa to Utah.[11]

MODERNIZATION AND THE LABOR MISSIONARY PROGRAM

The Labor Missionary Program relied on the apparatus of the Stake Conference and the calling in order to ensure the will of the LDS church. In Lā'ie, there were two distinct phases of the Labor Missionary Program. It was used in 1955 to build the permanent structures for the Church College of Hawai'i (completed in 1958) and again in the 1960s to build the Polynesian Cultural Center (completed in 1963). Although the specific histories of these two phases differ in terms of who is called to serve, the literature and the oral histories relating to it share a common rhetoric about the program: the Labor Missionary Program benefited the church by raising the status of the church in the local community, it taught missionaries valuable construction skills, and it built the testimony of many missionaries.[12] This quasi-contractual language of the mutual benefit of the program for church and missionary alike masks the power dynamics associated with migration and Americanization. The Labor Missionary Program offers an example of how the church facilitated migration and how the program reintroduced an earlier religious project of civilizing the natives by modeling "American" values of hard work and domesticity.

Two men are credited for making the construction of the Church College of Hawai'i a reality: Wendell B. Mendenhall, who served as president of the Church Building Committee (1955–65) and on the Pacific Board of Education (1957–65), and Edward L. Clissold, who was the stake president and highest-ranking religious leader on O'ahu. The Labor Missionary Program was an outgrowth of the Church Building Committee, however its origins lie in the Pacific Board of Education founded by President McKay. President McKay created the Pacific Board of Education to help transition the schools

An aerial photograph taken in the 1970s shows the close proximity of the Polynesian Cultural Center (foreground) to the Church College of Hawai'i behind it. The temple is located just beyond the college out of view in this photograph. Photograph courtesy of Brigham Young University–Hawai'i Archives.

operating in Polynesia from mission schools to fully modern, professionally staffed American schools and to use the resources of the Church Building Committee to update existing facilities and build new ones as needed at each of the sites.[13] One unique aspect of this program was that it circumvented the authority of the Council of Twelve, as Mendenhall was to report directly to the prophet.

Prior to the formation of the Church Building Committee, each mission or religious congregation was responsible for providing the labor or contracting the labor to build permanent buildings. As I described in chapter 2, missionaries and Native church members all contributed labor on the plantation as well as when homes, churches, and schools needed to be built. The missionary Matthew Noall oversaw the construction of a chapel in Honolulu, and as mission president he put his contracting skills to work as he designed and helped build Lanihuli, the new mission home, in Lāʻie. But relying on local and proselytizing missionary labor was unpredictable, and it came to a head when trying to complete Liahona High School in Tonga. The high school was part of an expanding education program throughout the Pacific, and when it became clear that labor was needed to complete the program's objective, leaders turned to the volunteer system already in place, the missionary program. As R. Lanier Britsch tells it, "[The Labor Missionary Program] was later used in Sāmoa and New Zealand, and it was in New Zealand that the program was brought to fruition."[14]

According to Owen J. Cook, the executive secretary of the Pacific Board of Education, some General Authorities initially expressed apprehension and confusion with the program. As Cook recalls, "Some of the Brethren [General Authorities] were saying these labor missionaries were called on missions and they objected to that ... because the proselytizing mission was the 'mission' and [they couldn't] become accustomed to the idea that they could have labor missionaries."[15] On one level, the General Authorities found the program to be problematic because it did not conform to their understanding of the mission, which by the 1950s was narrowly associated with proselytizing. As the history of Mormon missionary work in Hawaiʻi demonstrates, calling men to serve the Lord by giving their labor toward the cause of building Zion was common in the nineteenth century. The Labor Missionary Program, one could argue, merely formalized an earlier pragmatic necessity. However, with the modernization that began at the turn of the twentieth century, a line was drawn between what was considered volunteer labor and what was paid labor. Within the ecclesiastical framework of the church, there are no paid clergy. All callings of a religious nature are unpaid and voluntary. Missions are one form of unpaid, volunteer labor. But not all positions in the church organizational structure were unpaid. There were instances, as in the case of teachers hired by the church to work in LDS schools in Polynesia, where members were called to serve in secular positions and given a salary. The Labor Missionary Program fits this description as its laborers were expected to do construction work deemed secular, but individual men were also called to serve the Lord in a volunteer capacity. It is no surprise that the General Authorities expressed confusion about the program. Mendenhall effectively blurred the boundaries between the spiritual and secular, thereby producing a cheap labor force for the church.

But Cook raises a second point of contention that the General Authorities had with the program. If Mendenhall had a request or a problem he was allowed to circumvent the General Authorities and go directly to President McKay who personally handled the issue. In bypassing the bureaucratic hierarchy and having direct access to the president, Mendenhall's work in the Pacific was efficient and productive but it was nonetheless viewed under a cloud of suspicion by the General Authorities. According to Cook, in the ten years that Mendenhall was president of the Church Building Committee, "the Church dedicated about one chapel a day on the average . . . Fifty percent of all of the Church buildings throughout the world were constructed" using labor missionaries.[16]

The Labor Missionary Program mediates a tension between religious duty in the form of being called to serve the Lord as a volunteer laborer and a pragmatic desire to immigrate to the United States.[17] For the Polynesians who participated in the Labor Missionary Program their motivations were split between religious duty and pragmatism; in its ideal form the program was set up as a quasi contract between the laborers and the church. The program would provide young Polynesian Latter-day Saint men with building skills and a means to immigrate to the United States, and for this they needed only to volunteer their labor to the church for two to three years. As one labor missionary recalls, he would not have been able to immigrate had it not been for the program. Arguably, the Labor Missionary Program met the needs of both church and laborer; however, the way historians describe the program presumed that the exchange between the two interested parties was entirely equal. The power hierarchies inherent in this system were masked by the adoption of this quasi-contractual language. By relying on oral histories conducted with former Polynesian labor missionaries and their haole supervisors as well as the historical accounts published in formal church histories, I describe how preexisting power dynamics were reproduced through the building program and the relative impact that this new wave of immigration had on the Lāʻie community.

The call to serve played a critical role in mediating these inequalities. The ideology of the "calling" is part of a larger discourse that relies upon a particular understanding of authority. The sociologist Reinhard Bendix, quoting Robert Beirstedt, draws an important distinction between leadership and authority: "A leader can only request, an authority can require ... Leadership depends upon the personal qualities of the leader in the situation in which he leads. In the case of authority, however, the relationship ceases to be personal and, if the legitimacy of the authority is recognized, the subordinate *must obey* the command even when he is unacquainted with the person who issues it. In a leadership relation the person is merely a symbol [of authority]" (italics added).[18] The prophet represents divine authority "by virtue of his purely personal charisma and by virtue of his mission [he] proclaims a religious doctrine or a Divine command." The authority of the prophet and those who have the authority to speak on his behalf is substantiated and reproduced by the ideology of calling. Bendix locates the reproduction of "claims to authority" within the context "of a 'personal' call."[19] Thus the "calling" is seen as "one's duty" or, in the words of Weber, as "an absolute end in itself—meaning not a means to higher wages but a thing in itself."[20] Just as the idea of a calling is necessary for capitalism, it is also critical to the bureaucracy of the church because it assures that the worker-member will accept the calling and in turn maximize his or her labor regardless of the personal costs.

Being called to serve was rationalized as being about service to the Lord and thus as a sign of chosenness while at the same time masking the role that secular benefits such as money, skill training, education, and migration played in one's decision to accept the calling. Additionally, the personalized nature of the calling supported an illusion of intimacy between General Authorities and the individual member. This mechanism reveals a tension whereby one is called or chosen to serve a particular role within the church hierarchy when the reality is that the appointment itself is pragmatic and fills a gap within the bureaucracy. But within the context of religious rationality, the calling is deeply personal and experienced as an expression of the individual "being one of the elect."[21]

Mendenhall, with the support of President McKay and Stake President Clissold, used the Labor Missionary Program in order to build the permanent

structures of the Church College of Hawai'i. Although the college officially
opened its doors on September 26, 1955, the school was housed in temporary buildings purchased from Wheeler Air Force Base that were disassem-
bled and hauled to Lā'ie by the truckload. During this inaugural year, there
were, according to Britsch, "123 students and 20 faculty and administrators
on hand when the first day of classes began."[22] The first permanent structure
for the college was dedicated in December 1958, three years after the work
began, and President David O. McKay presided over the dedication. This
event is considered to be the physical manifestation of his 1921 prophecy
that a school of higher learning would be built in Lā'ie, and that it would be
the center for higher education in the Pacific.

As Britsch describes it, building a college in three years and under bud-
get was no small accomplishment: "At the height of the work, over fifty
mainland missionaries or supervisors and their wives were working on the
job. An additional seventy-five to eighty local building missionaries from
all parts of the island also participated. Local Saints from Lā'ie also helped
in different phases of the work. The wives of builders contributed much
moral support, and they also cleaned all the windows and laid around

Students gather on the lānai of the David O. McKay Building in the 1960s.
Photograph courtesy of Brigham Young University–Hawai'i Archives.

174,000 square feet of floor tile."[23] This quote is instructive on two levels. First, the hard work and dedication of these laborers is offered as a testament of the divinity of the college because the hand of God directed the building of this inspired edifice to education. Second, the highly stratified organizational structure of the program is illuminated. Richard Cowan identifies one division in the program between supervisors and laborers: "Experienced builders responded to mission calls and acted as supervisors. Young men from the islands, also serving as missionaries, donated their labor, learning valuable skills in the process. The local Saints did their part by feeding and housing these missionaries."[24] Although the language in Cowan's description of the Labor Mission Program reflects this quasi-contractual relationship between missionaries and church, what this division of labor more accurately describes is the racial and gender assumptions imbedded in the program.

First, the supervisors and experienced builders were all white American men. Their job was to oversee the construction projects and to teach "local" young men the skills of the building trade. In return, after their service to the church these local (read Polynesian) young men would leave the program with a skill that would translate into a more permanent occupation. This racial hierarchy resembles nineteenth-century relationships between Mormon missionaries who had the gospel and Native Hawaiians who did not. That is, the former occupy a position of relative power and authority by virtue of possessing the knowledge of the restoration of Christ's church on earth reinforced by the weight of U.S. imperialism, while the latter occupy a relatively subordinate position because they do not possess such specialized knowledge and thus must rely on the benevolence of the former.

Second, the racial dimensions of the program were simultaneously crosscut with gender assumptions as well. Within this highly gender-stratified church it is no surprise that it is men, both haole and "local," who were called as labor missionaries to serve the church while the support staff for these "workers" were wives and "the larger community." Within this framework, wives regardless of race play supplementary roles (nonworkers) to the primary laborers—the missionaries. As I discuss below, the racial and gendered division of labor reproduced hegemonic power relationships that reinforce the authority of white, American men, whose wives trade on this authority as they domesticate the "local" young man in proper American behavior. Furthermore, the language of "moral support" effectively renders the labor of "local" women invisible.

Lāʻie Family Robinson

The racial and gender divisions of labor within the Labor Missionary Program were not unfamiliar to the Lāʻie community; indeed, the program merely reproduced already established institutional hierarchies in the village. As was the case of the organizational hierarchy of the sugar plantation, the leaders of the building program were haole men called from the U.S. continent as supervisors and building experts, while the laborers were Hawaiians, Sāmoans, Japanese, and some haole called from throughout the Islands. The oral history interview conducted with Louise Robinson provides examples of how these racial and gender hierarchies were organized and how they played out at the level of everyday interactions. Robinson fondly remembers the years when her family was called to serve as dorm parents to the labor missionaries; in addition, Mr. Robinson would also have the more formal position as personnel director for the construction of the Church College of Hawaiʻi. They moved to Lāʻie with their youngest daughter as 1955 was coming to a close.[25]

Robinson was very enthusiastic about her family's calling to serve the church in Hawaiʻi. She admits that had it not been for the church, her family would not have had this kind of experience—something for which they secretly longed. Her enthusiasm for her calling bubbles over in her interview as she describes her and her family's role in the Labor Missionary Program. As the mission parents to the labor missionaries who were called from across the Hawaiʻi Islands to migrate to Lāʻie, it was the Robinson's first priority to get the mission home ready for the laborers. According to Robinson, at the height of the program there were approximately 125 missionaries at the home ranging in age from seventy-five years old to fourteen years old. All of the missionaries came from Hawaiʻi but they were "Hawaiian, and some Sāmoans, Japanese, Chinese, Korean, Filipinos, Caucasians, and there were many that were from mixed background."[26]

The mission home was located about five miles outside of Lāʻie in Punaluʻu. The family was responsible for providing room and board for the missionaries, and Robinson took great pride in making sure it was welcoming to the laborers.

There was a large expanse of beautiful lawn, surrounded by forty-five coconut palms, huge ironwood trees, and hau trees and shrubs, bushes and flowers with the Pacific Ocean as our front yard. And nestled among all this was a two-story home, a large lanai, a duplex for vacationers and a caretaker's cottage. Well it was a little spot of heaven, right there . . .

We discovered that it was a nine-room home. The three bedrooms and bathroom upstairs was the Robinson domain. The ground floor was to be shared by us and to be the eating quarters and some recreation for the boys such as reading, and quiet games, and music. And downstairs was comprised of a tiny kitchen, a pantry, one bathroom and a large room in an L-shape for a sitting room. And there was also a large glassed-in room where we placed long tables to serve the meals. Then as the number of boys increased, we had to use the sitting room for an eating area also. The duplex, the lanai, and other small cottages that were moved in on the beachfront were used to house the missionary boys.[27]

Robinson's recollections of the first mission home described a beautiful, tropical beachfront bungalow refashioned for laborers, not tourists. It is clear from her description that she took great satisfaction in ensuring that the accommodations were comfortable for both her family and the labor missionaries. However, the paternalism of this system (the practice of calling haole American families to serve as "parents" to "childlike" missionaries) creeps into her language when she refers to the missionaries as boys whom she must feed and, as she describes below, clothe and teach basic hygiene and etiquette. Although the family metaphor is intended as a way of providing missionaries with an emotional support system while serving the church, the institutionalization of this practice in Hawaiʻi was problematic because of an imperial legacy that had defined the Native as childlike, along with the U.S. federal racial policies that define Native Hawaiians as wards of the state and thus equivalent under the law to children. Once again, the church, attempting to act in an altruistic, well-intended manner, reproduced pre-existing power relations of white American supremacy.

While missionary work was considered volunteer labor, both the Robinsons and the laborers were given a monthly allowance. In addition, the Robinson family had all of their travel expenses, rent, and utilities paid by the church, and they were given a monthly stipend of $200 while they were on their mission. The laborers received room, board, transportation in the truck Owen Robinson purchased, and $10 a month stipend. As Robinson recalls, "several times during the mission each one of them was out-fitted with a nice pair of slacks and an aloha shirt."[28] This same arrangement would be replicated during the second phase of the program.

As I discuss below, for missionaries traveling from Tonga and Sāmoa the role of the church in this transnational migration was critical. But, the use of quasi-contractual language to explain the different interests of the church and of the Polynesian laborer masks structural inequalities and brings to light assumptions about the relative worth of laborers compared to supervisors. One could interpret the pay differential between supervisors and laborers as fair compensation for their relative skill levels—supervisors and building experts had marketable skills that they sacrificed in order to serve the church, and their stipend is merely a token of the church's gratitude for their service. Furthermore, the difference could also be attributed to the fact that, as was the case with the Robinson family, supervisors and building experts brought their families with them to Hawai'i and the stipend was intended to help meet the extra needs of the family. According to this logic, the stipend that local laborers were paid may reflect a belief that they did not have any marketable skills, in part explaining the reason why they had volunteered for the program in the first place. Additionally, as single men they needed less money than families. The stipend differential, although appearing rational, is based upon unsubstantiated assumptions about Polynesian men (both young and old) and their role in their families and community. It perpetuates a stereotype of the native man as out of time in modernity—an individual who must be fed and clothed but whose material needs extend little beyond these basic necessities.

In addition to being taught building trades, the labor missionaries would also be schooled in the basics of civilized living. Louise and Owen Robinson had from November (when they arrived in Hawai'i) until late January when the first labor missionaries arrived to prepare the mission home. They "purchased beds and mattresses and pillows and towels at the war surplus outlet. And bought new sheets and pillow cases and blankets." When the missionaries arrived, Robinson showed each of them how to make a bed. To her surprise, after she had completed the bed, one young man asked her, "And where do I get in it?" "Well, bless his heart," she continues, "he was used to sleeping on a mat on the floor."[29] In addition to the art of bed making, Mrs. Robinson set a "traditional" table for mealtime:

> Every meal we placed on the table for every ten boys, bread and butter, salt and pepper, catsup, mustard, soyu, sugar and peanut butter and jam usually, at least ten sets of each of these. Then I also made their place settings of plates, and glasses, and silverware, napkins, and poured the water, and the milk and helped serve.[30]

Although a local woman was hired to help with the everyday maintenance of the house and some of the cooking, each labor missionary was responsible for keeping tidy his own living space and had access to the laundry facilities. In her unique way, Robinson tried to create a family atmosphere for the missionaries. During her interview, she was proud to report that once Bill Moku, one of the first missionaries to join them at the mission home, started calling them "Mom and Pop," the name stuck, and twenty-five years later the missionaries still referred to them as Mom and Pop Robinson. Once again, within the political context of Hawai'i the training of Polynesian men in domesticity mirrors nineteenth-century attempts to domesticate and tame the hypermasculine Native man.[31]

As Mary Louise Pratt explains, in the contact zone both the colonized and the colonizer must adapt to changes. The Polynesian missionaries were not the only ones who had to adjust to living in this American setting; indeed, the Robinson family also had some adjusting to do. Robinson shared a funny story about how her husband had to adapt to Polynesian ways. The story begins when the parents of William Kanahele, one of the first missionaries to arrive from Lā'ie, dropped him off at the mission home. Before they left, they gave him a big bag of poi. After their first day of work, the laborers returned home for dinner and Mr. Robinson asked the Hawaiian missionaries how to prepare the poi for their meal. Louise Robinson remembered how the missionaries looked a little embarrassed and replied, "just put it in a bowl." As she continues:

> Brother Robinson dished a small sherbet dish of poi for each one. It was thick and hard to get off the spoon. Well, we six sat at the dining room table and ate but we noticed that each one of them played around with the poi but did not eat any. Now here we were, mainland haoles and did not really know any Polynesians to ask about the poi.
>
> The next day, just before dinner, Brother Robinson asked the missionaries again and they gave the same answer, "Just put it in a bowl." So he dished it up again and again they didn't touch the thick gray substance. Well, on the third day, he found a Polynesian to ask and it was explained to him about mixing the poi with water. And that night at dinner, we had three happy missionaries and very shortly after that when more missionaries came, many times Brother Robinson would be elbow deep in mixing poi.[32]

As mentioned above, not only were labor missionaries offered an opportunity to serve the church, they also had the opportunity to learn a trade.

Robinson felt that the missionary program was successful for those missionaries who took advantage of the opportunity available to them. As she recalls,

> Those who really tried learned the trade and they also learned good working habits. And there are many of them that are supporting their wives and their children now by the trade they learned, like electrical trade; they learned to be carpenters, and painters, and cement men and many things of that nature. And many of them also advanced a great deal in the Church.[33]

Robinson's recollections support Cook's contention about the larger objective of both the Labor Missionary Program and the church system in the Pacific: "I felt that our job was to educate these young people, to make leaders of them, to help them develop good families and become what LDS Church youth should become in the communities that they came from or to which they went."[34]

The significance of the pragmatic benefits of the program for Polynesian men cannot be disregarded. Within the economic climate of Hawai'i in the mid-1950s, job opportunities for Polynesian men were limited to work at one of the U.S. military bases on the island or in the burgeoning construction industry, or positions in entertainment and tourism. As Noel Kent describes, the 1950s marked a dramatic shift from a plantation economy to a touristic one and signaled a boom in the construction business as American-based businessmen bought up land across Waikīkī and started to build their mighty hotels. In order to make mass tourism possible, an infrastructure "including airports, roads, sewerage facilities, [and] new beaches" needed to be constructed.[35] Both the hotel magnates based in the continental United States and the local Hawai'i government needed laborers to see these development plans through to fruition. The church building program gave Polynesian men skills that they could then transfer into the much larger construction market. Within such an economic climate, it was no small thing for these Polynesian men to be able to provide for their families using the skills they learned as labor missionaries. For example, as a labor missionary from Tonga, Sione Feinga, stated, "Not only did we provide a service to the Church, but that program provided training for us and we made it a career . . . The majority of us do that for a living, something connected with the building industry."[36]

It took three years for the missionaries to complete the Church College of Hawai'i, after which the Robinson family returned to California. Almost one year after their return to Los Angeles, they were once again called to serve as mission parents to a new group of labor missionaries who were coming from Sāmoa and Tonga to build the Polynesian Cultural Center. After they returned to Hawai'i for their second labor mission, they remained in Lā'ie and made it their permanent home.

THE POLYNESIAN CULTURAL CENTER:
TOURISM AND MODERNITY

The second phase of the Labor Missionary Program in Lā'ie began in 1960 with new group of missionaries, the majority of whom came from Tonga and Sāmoa. As noted above, Sione Feinga migrated to Hawai'i as a labor missionary from Tonga, and he talks extensively in his oral history about how it was that he came to settle in Lā'ie. Feinga was a labor missionary in Tonga for three years before he was called to serve in Hawai'i. The church first established a mission in Tonga in 1891 as an extension of the Sāmoa mission, but by 1916 the membership growth was such they were able to establish the Tonga mission.[37] Max Stanton writes, however, that the church did not become popular until the 1950s—notably after Liahona High School was opened and a large number of the non-Mormon students joined the church. This fact adds substance to Cathy Small's contention that Tongan membership in the church in Tonga was primarily pragmatic.[38] Feinga's memory of his experience as a labor missionary first in Tonga and later in Hawai'i reflects this position. However, his story also demonstrates how religious belief gives meaning to the work that he did, thus balancing the pragmatic with the spiritual. His memory of his experience as a labor missionary begins with the night that he and thirteen other Tongan men were asked to meet with Mendenhall and Clissold. As he recalls,

> After the mission in Tonga [serving as a labor missionary on the construction of Liahona High School], I worked for the government in Tonga on construction for about three months. President Mendenhall and Brother Clissold came up to Tonga and called a meeting. We thought, "Oh, not again. We're going to start building the school again or something else in Tonga." But we went to the meeting that night and we found out that there were only thirteen of us that they wanted to talk to . . . We waited for about an hour and then . . . we went into the room . . . and they started to talk about building again. So we thought they were going to build some more buildings in Tonga. Some of us had started

to work for money, and we said, "No, that can't be. We've just started to make money working for the government." As President Mendenhall started talking he mentioned Hawaii. You know, we kind of quieted down a little bit. He said, "You know, I told you before that someday we might call some of you to go and help build buildings in other parts of the world. Tonight I'm here to call you to go to Hawaii and build the Polynesian Cultural Center. Who wants to go to Hawaii?" You know everyone jumped up. We never thought a calling would come to go to Hawaii ... They called thirty-one of us from Tonga. That was in November 1959, and in March 1960 we left Tonga.[39]

Feinga's sense of dread that he might have to give up his paying job for the volunteer labor of a mission is palpable. His attitude, however, changed as soon as Mendenhall mentioned Hawai'i. For Feinga, an opportunity to go to Hawai'i was an opportunity to migrate to the United States.

Feinga and his friends recognized the relative significance of this opportunity for themselves and their families more broadly, and they were quick

Tongan labor missionaries pose for a group picture. The Tongan labor missionaries organized a rugby team after they settled in La'ie. My uncle, Mosese Lomu, is in the center of the front row. Photograph courtesy of the Lomu family.

to accept this second calling as labor missionaries for the church. Based on the historical chronology of Tongan migration laid out by Small, it began in the 1950s as a trickle of single young men migrating to New Zealand in search of "high wages for unskilled overseas work." Migration to the United States also began as a trickle in the early 1960s, primarily through the sponsorship of the LDS church. Small stresses the key role that the church played in this first wave of migration, however she is critical of accounts that locate the motivation for migration by Tongans as a commitment to the church. Instead, she argues, "it is more accurate to say that the Tongan commitment to the church was motivated by the opportunity it provided for overseas migration."[40] Within this framework, church membership is singularly pragmatic and a strategy for families to maximize their chances for migration. Although Feinga and his fellow labor missionaries embody this historical trend (they were the trickle who established the foundation upon which future Tongans were able to immigrate to the United States), Feinga's narrative does not support Small's claim. I contend that the "dread" he felt the night he was called to serve a mission in Hawai'i was an expression of the conflict between a commitment to his faith and to the pragmatic benefits of immigrating to Hawai'i.

Twenty-five labor missionaries from Sāmoa joined the thirty-one Tongan missionaries, and when they arrived in Lā'ie they met the Hawaiian missionaries who had already moved into the mission home. Feinga remembers that the Polynesian labor missionaries lived in old converted army barracks located where the mechanic shop for the cultural center and college stands today. "Each guy had a little bed. It was fun. So we worked everyday, eight to ten hours a day. We got up, had a prayer and then started work."[41]

The army barracks had been refashioned into a new mission home during the first phase of the program when the number of missionaries grew too large for the original mission home in Punalu'u. These same army barracks were repurposed and became the mission home for Feinga and his fellow missionaries. The mission home was partitioned into two separate spaces, one for the Robinson family and the other for the missionaries. According to Louise Robinson the area for the missionaries was also divided into separate areas: "The boys had one large screened-in lanai with a t.v. for their sitting room, and bathrooms and two to four boys for each bedroom."[42] From Feinga's brief description, it also appears that their workday was very similar to their predecessors. They began with breakfast and morning prayers and then Mr. Robinson drove them to the work site where they were divided into work groups, assigned a task for the day, and then sent off to work under the direction of their supervisor.

Upon their arrival in Lāʻie, the labor missionaries learned that their first job would not be to build the Polynesian Cultural Center but to work on some of the other building projects associated with the college and temple. Feinga lists the projects they completed: "The dormitories for the school, some additions to the temple visitor's center, homes for the temple workers and the temple president and sixteen homes for the faculty."[43] Britsch's research provides a more detailed list of the projects these labor missionaries worked on before starting the Polynesian Cultural Center: "Between 1960 and 1963, the big years of the building program, building missionaries constructed seven chapel complexes on Oahu and another several smaller chapels and cultural halls on the outer islands. . . . They built homes for the faculty at CCH [Church College of Hawaiʻi] and constructed a number of mainte-nance and other auxiliary buildings for the college."[44] It is interesting to note that they built modern homes for full-time proselytizing missionaries.

The tension between pragmatism and faith is punctuated by Feinga's admission that many of his fellow labor missionaries from Tonga were "not the most active Church members, so to speak. Most of us came on the pro-gram and were motivated here [in Lāʻie] to be active again." Although he was motivated by the pragmatic opportunity to migrate to the United States, Feinga narrates his story as religious by making clear that though he and his fellow missionaries were not active before they came to Lāʻie, they became active after they arrived. For Feinga, the program served two purposes, "It not only helped people have a trade, but it also helped to build people spiri-tually." For him, building buildings was an allegory for how the program built spirituality and faith. He continues, "So, not only did we build build-ings, but we built better people in that span of time. And I see a lot of them [former labor missionaries] come from here and there and are called to be bishops. They are very strong Church members because of the experience."[45] Feinga's personal experience reflects this process. At the time of the inter-view he had been serving on the stake presidency for six years, and before that he had been a bishop for three years. Throughout his interview, he returns time and time again to how his calling as a labor missionary in Lāʻie changed his life materially and spiritually.

Whereas Feinga's memories were primarily positive and hopeful, not everyone supported the Labor Missionary Program or the way that the Polynesian missionaries were treated. In his interview Charles Barenaba acknowledged that much good came out of the Labor Missionary Program, and that "many of the labor missionaries are still here and are fine people." However, he also admits that "nobody magnifies the negative things, but there were some concerns in those areas, with the Palangi (white American) missionaries living in the better homes and the Polynesian labor missionaries living in the barracks system at Kakela." Some of the things that concerned the community dealt with "disruptive possibilities, social possibilities, the nitty-gritty about the hours of work, stipends, privileges and all that." Over the course of the Labor Missionary Program in Lāʻie, the village grew very rapidly, in terms of both development and population growth. Barenaba describes it like this: "So much took place. A very . . . swift period all through the late 1950s and the '60s, you know, hammers and nails, saws, going boom, boom, boom. The thing that tempered [dissent] . . . was the belief that this was all in the interest of furthering the growth of the kingdom here on earth and that quelled the suspicions."[46]

Barenaba's interview is one of the few that offer a critique of the Labor Missionary Program or note the muted grumbling among community members. I contend that the muffled voices of dissent can be attributed to an ideology of faithfulness. For example, Feinga names his faithfulness to the church explicitly when he describes the various leadership positions he has held since serving as a labor missionary. He implicitly affirms this faithfulness by framing his experiences as positive and thus not exploitative. Although he earned only $10 a month and many community members helped to build the college and the Polynesian Cultural Center for no monetary compensation, he remarks, "I feel that's the main key to the success of the whole thing . . . the fact that everybody didn't have money on their minds." He clarifies that "if it had been a hiring thing, I don't think it would have been very successful. People would be worrying about money and stuff like that."[47] Perhaps the program would not have been as successful had it been framed as a capitalist venture, but nonetheless money was on the mind of the church leaders who were in charge of the project. In order to ensure that their projects came in under budget, church authorities used the calling to capitalize on the belief, faith, and interests of Polynesian Latter-day Saints.

Community members were not the only ones critical of the program. Max Bean was always suspicious of the Labor Missionary Program because he thought Hawaiians and Polynesians had poor work habits. Bean was called to move to Hawaiʻi in order to supervise the construction of an addition to the temple and the building of a new chapel. He returned to Lāʻie in

1969 to build the married student housing complex. Bean's description of his role as supervisor of Hawaiian and Sāmoan laborers reflects a contradictory combination of paternalism, contempt, and enjoyment. During his first stint in Lāʻie from 1947 to 1950 to build the temple addition, he was often frustrated by the work ethics of the Hawaiian laborers. He recalls that if the wind was not blowing, at about two o'clock the workers would end work for the day and go fishing. Bean admits that he went fishing with them, but ultimately he believed that the project suffered because of these "poor" work habits. His opinion did not change in the late 1960s when he returned to supervise the construction of married student housing. By the time he arrived in 1969, the Labor Missionary Program had been discontinued. He believed that the program ended because it was no longer affordable for the church to hire supervisors who were responsible for training "a bunch of children."[48] He alleged that these "children" damaged or stole tools and did not produce the quality of work that Bean expected of them. Based on his dissatisfaction with the program and with the Hawaiian and Sāmoan workers, it is no surprise that when he returned he brought with him his own crew of workers and only hired a select group of students from the Church College of Hawaiʻi to help with the new project. I highlight this interview because Bean recognized the economic interests that the church had in the program. Within an ideology of faithfulness, the interests of the church to have chapels, housing, and the Polynesian Cultural Center built cheaply were obscured by testimonies of faithful service to the church.

Whereas Pratt describes the power relations in the contact zone as a struggle between the colonizers and the colonized, by the time ground was broken on the construction of the Polynesian Cultural Center, power struggles could no longer be described using a simple binary between Hawaiian and Sāmoan old timers and the haole plantation manager and missionaries. When we look at the events and discussions surrounding the construction of the Polynesian Cultural Center, a matrix of power emerges among powerful haole "outsiders" who become a more visible presence in the community, old timers who are described as the truly faithful, and a new generation of college-educated Polynesians who were mistrustful of the changes taking place around them. On the margins were the new Polynesian immigrants recruited by Mendenhall and Clissold as either labor missionaries or as fulltime cultural experts at the Polynesian Cultural Center. This latter group came to symbolize both the potential benefits of the cultural center as well as what was wrong with it. In struggles between haole church leaders and the next generation, reference to the new Polynesian immigrants was made to support each side of the debate of the relative costs and benefits of the Polynesian Cultural Center.

For Barenaba the cultural costs for constructing the Polynesian Cultural Center outweighed the economic benefits it would provide. The construction projects described in the labor missionary section of this chapter clearly illustrate how quickly the physical landscape of the town changed. The sugar cane fields on the Hauʻula side of the temple were cleared for Church College of Hawaiʻi faculty housing and, later, for married student housing. The watermelon patch cultivated by Tom Fanene's brother was cleared and became the entrance to the main building of the college, and the Lāʻie stream was redirected underground so that other college buildings could be constructed on top of it. Finally, the taro patches that sustained the families in Lāʻie located along Kamehameha Highway were leveled to make way for the Polynesian Cultural Center. The town also underwent a renovation in the 1960s as Zion's Securities, then under the direction of Howard Stone, paid to have old, dilapidated homes torn down and new ones built in their place. Also under Stone's direction a new water system was constructed and new electrical lines and street lamps were installed.[49] This was progress! Or so the haole leadership said.

At varying points along this path of progress the community reacted sometimes with their support and other times with suspicion and outright protest. Old timers who took issue with Howard Stone's attempts to bring them "up to a higher standard of living" dismayed Rita Stone. Speaking of her husband, she stated: "That was the thing that Howard wanted to do, to help them to a higher standard of living."[50] Two things helped change the old timers' mind: first, when the Polynesian Cultural Center opened many people became its employees; and second, as a few families built new homes other families became interested in renovating their homes. Stone describes this process as a "re-educating program" intended to help people "realize" that they needed to raise their own standard of living.[51] Although the standard of living became more modernized after the Polynesian Cultural Center opened and improvements were made to the infrastructure of the town, old timers continue to lament the old days when doors could be left unlocked without worry.

The impact of modernization was described by old timers as a loss of what made Lāʻie special. Thomas Au contrasts the old Lāʻie of his youth with the new Lāʻie: "Laie had changed lots. And not only that—Laie, before, the home, we don't have to lock, just leave the door open. It's free, you can go any place, come back, there's nothing touched, not like today. . . . Today you have to lock your doors, lock your windows."[52] Vailene Leota Niko suggests that some of the differences between old Lāʻie and new Lāʻie were because new people moved in and young people went away to school and came back with new ideas. As modernization continued to transform the community, Niko believes they began to lose the "spirit that we had of Laie." One reason for this shift was perhaps because of the changes to the standard of living. In the old days, Niko recalls, "we relied more on the ocean for our livelihood, but later on, you know, as we grew up, I knew we sort of sought for something better for the family."[53] As young people went away to college and came back, it inspired other families to want the things and ideas these young people brought with them. Niko doesn't see education as a bad thing, but it does change one's way of thinking and the things people desire and want. In Lāʻie the various community improvement projects were intended to make life more ordered, rational, and predicable, but the effort also brought about a tremendous sense of loss.

The new generation of college-educated Polynesians who were born in Lāʻie came home with new ideas that clashed with the ways things had been done in the past. Barenaba admits that he was one of the young people who had returned to Lāʻie with new ideas, questioning the way things had been done: "[We] were just coming out of college and struggling to survive in life, lukewarm in their activities in the Church and all of that, feeling their way around, trying to put their lives together."[54] As noted above, Barenaba and others took issue with the treatment of the Polynesian labor missionaries who were housed in old army barracks while they built new, modern homes for proselytizing missionaries from the U.S. continent. They also spoke out against the Polynesian Cultural Center, specifically questioning its material benefits for the community. This questioning raised clear tensions between this younger generation, old timers, and haole church leaders. Barenaba got the feeling that the real benefits of the cultural center would go to people outside the community.

> Entertainment six days a week with about the only sane thinking going on was church on Sunday and then six more days of entertaining. Whether it's a siva or pese or serving supper, lunch, and dinner, frying hamburgers, it's still a catering kind of thing for kupe (for money) from other strangers. And it didn't seem to us that the individuals there, who were performing in the various

aspects of the Polynesian Center, would have any time to preach the gospel to anybody. It was just a matter of cash and carry business.[55]

His statement exposes the capitalist realities of the center while also calling into question the logistics of this tourist facility as a missionary tool for the church. The Polynesian Cultural Center was to serve several purposes. First, it was to provide jobs for students at the college; second, it was to preserve Polynesian culture; and third, it was to be a missionary tool for the church. Barenaba took issue with all three aspects of its mission. Although students were indeed hired for the cultural center, the majority of the employees were from outside the community. As Stanton notes, early on the majority of Polynesian Cultural Center employees were Polynesian cultural experts who were hired as "managers and supervisors fluent in the languages of the various Polynesian groups and used to the social expectations of the workers in the various 'villages' of the Polynesian Cultural Center."[56] Stanton describes the characteristics of this group as "older, usually married, non-students" who, according to his own personal knowledge, comprised the largest portion of the workers at the center in the early 1960s. As was the case in other church-run organizations, upper-level management were haole, either hired from the continent or recruited from within the ranks of the church leadership in the islands.[57]

This division of labor within the Polynesian Cultural Center had been a concern for some members of the community from the moment ground was broken. For example, Tom Fanene remembers how "the Church had a hard time talking to some of the Sāmoan people who helped in the Cultural Center. Some of them were kind of against working for nothing. They wanted to work and get paid for it."[58] Fanene and his wife Ann decided to be role models for the other Sāmoan families, and they volunteered their labor for the construction of the Sāmoan village. After working his regular job, Fanene would go into the sugar cane fields to pick the leaves used as thatching at the Polynesian Cultural Center. His dedication inspired other Sāmoans to get involved as well. The Aumua family, for example, volunteered in the early morning to work on the Sāmoan village. Fanene's need to become a role model for other families signals how community members recognized that there were different standards being applied to work on the cultural center. One group was the Polynesian labor missionaries who were given room, board, and $10 a month stipend. Then there was the group of cultural experts who were paid to relocate their families to Lāʻie, were given housing there, and were paid to work on, and then for, the center. Finally, there was the local Lāʻie community whose members were expected to freely donate their labor to the construction of the center. Mendenhall and Clissold assumed that since the community rallied together to support the Hukilau, an earlier grassroots tourist venture, they would also rally around the cultural center.[59] They failed to realize the dramatic differences between the Polynesian Cultural Center, a commercial venture introduced by "outsiders" to the community, and the Hukilau, a community fund-raiser where all of the profits went directly into local congregational budgets and projects. Despite attempts by the leaders to use an ideology of faithfulness to rationalize the pay disparities, the leadership underestimated community reaction to the stratification among workers.

George Q. Cannon Jr., an original Polynesian Cultural Center board member and stake president of the Pearl Harbor stake, believes that the community was justified in their suspicion of the project. He suggests that the church leaders in Hawaiʻi felt "railroaded" by the plan, and he believed that had Mendenhall and others kept the community more informed in the process then they would have received more support. He too felt concerned about the project, but his attitude changed once he joined the board of directors and was more involved in the process. He believes that without divine intervention the center would not have been finished. It should have failed because of "the distance [from Waikīkī], the amount of money that it would take to develop the Center, and so on." However, it succeeded, he claims, because when people do the Lord's work they will be rewarded.[60]

Despite this general air of concern, there were those members of the community, like Fanene and the Aumua family, who willingly volunteered to help with the work of constructing the center. Agnes Lua, a woman of Chinese-Hawaiian ancestry born in Honolulu in 1922 but raised in Lāʻie, took lunches to the workers each day. She felt that the community had a stake in the Polynesian Cultural Center because they helped to build it.[61] However, not everyone who contributed to the center felt they were rewarded by the experience. For example, Ruby Enos, who was born and raised in Lāʻie, recalls how the leaders of the Polynesian Cultural Center treated the Relief Society sisters. She was very active in church activities, including the Hukilau. She remembers how the Relief Society sisters made crafts for the Hukilau and sold them "out front." All of their profits went directly back into the ward Relief Society fund for their welfare projects. Because of their reputation for making crafts for the Hukilau, President Mendenhall asked her if the Relief Society could make crafts for the Polynesian Cultural Center. Initially, the Relief Society made lei that were sold at the Polynesian Cultural Center for $5. The center took $2.50 and the other $2.50 was given back to the Relief Society. However, the Relief Society sisters did not feel that they were getting paid enough for their work, and when the Polynesian Cultural Center did not pay them more, the sisters stopped making lei. As a result, the Polynesian Cultural Center ended up importing lei from the outer islands.[62]

Whether community members willingly participated in building the center or scoffed at the disparities, an ideology of faithfulness resonates throughout the interviews. As I have noted, Barenaba's interview is fascinating because he gives voice to the dissenting positions of the younger generation who were educated in American values of free agency and the need to speak one's mind. Even he frames his generation's dissenting opinions within a lexicon of faithfulness: "We were the ones who were not as faithful as Amelale, Tautua, Maiava, Uelu, and some of the Hawaiians, Nawahine, Amaka, Amana, Kalili. We were not as faithful as they."[63] Fanene echoes this belief: "Only the ones who really had faith, they were the ones who helped push the work. I tell you, you are right. If anything came up like this now I don't know if our people could support it. They are kind of weak in their thinking." The interviewer clarifies, "The old people had great faith in the words of our leaders." Fanene answers, "Yes, very, very, great faith."[64] Despite Barenaba's insistence that he and his generation had little faith, other statements he made during his interview indicate that he was an active member of the church who followed the tenets of the faith. He believed in attending the temple regularly and followed the doctrines of the church in the strictest sense. Ideologies of faithfulness are not about one's active membership in the church but rather a way to solicit community consent to church projects, even when consent does not support one's own interests. Stanton's research on the Sāmoan members of the community indicates that the silencing of dissent was a recurring problem: "Loyal members of the Church have been frustrated in attempts to air grievances about the community. With the exception of public institutions and a few business establishments (the band and a supermarket), only Church-sponsored units hold significant power in Lāʻie."[65] This ideology of faithfulness goes beyond disagreement over the center and instead operates at multiple levels in Lāʻie.

Not all dissenting voices were silent. For example, William Kanahele's story of the dedication ceremony for the Polynesian Cultural Center reveals how workers challenge decisions made by the church leadership. Kanahele was born and raised in Lāʻie, and in 1955 he was called to be a labor missionary where he was to help build the Church College of Hawaiʻi. In 1960 he was called to serve as a labor missionary again, this time to help build the extensions on the college, to renovate the Hawaiʻi temple, and later, to begin work on the Polynesian Cultural Center. He took pride in the work that he did on behalf of the church, and he was particularly proud of the work he did at the center. The day the center was to be dedicated, however, was not a good day. He and several other young people who had put so much time and energy into building the center stood outside the gate as the dedication ceremony began. He recalls that some of the younger folks looked to him as their former supervisor for an answer to why they were not invited to the dedication; after all, they were the ones who built the place. Kanahele decided to take action. He and the other labor missionaries who wanted to attend the ceremony went to the gate and demanded to be admitted. At first they were told that they could not come inside the center, but Kanahele insisted: "You don't tell us what we cannot [do] . . . We built this. We built this Cultural Center. You cannot tell us to stay outside here and cannot come to the dedication. . . . Who you think you are?" he asked. "And the guy said, 'well, we're not supposed—you have to get [an] invitation to come to the Polynesian Cultural Center.'" Kanahele did not take no for an answer, however, and demanded to be admitted. "No way," he exclaimed, "We're not going to have invitation[s] to come to the Polynesian [Cultural Center]. We'll come in here right now because we built this."[66] His story ends on a positive note: when the president of the center saw the missionaries coming inside, he went over to them and welcomed them to the dedication and apologized for not getting them invitations.

CONCLUSION

The process of modernization presented a paradoxical challenge to the church and its members. Although the college and the Polynesian Cultural Center each brought new opportunities to Lāʻie and the community, the projects also transformed the way of life in complicated and contradictory ways. The Labor Missionary Program was a resource available to some Polynesian men, and those in it had an opportunity to learn a trade that they could leverage in the booming construction industry after they ended their service to the Lord. The college was, and continues to be, a major educational resource in the Pacific. As a small private four-year accredited university, students from across the Pacific and the U.S. continent have access to an American-style educational experience.[67] Additionally, students living in Polynesia who graduated from church schools such as Liahona High School in Tonga were able to stay in the Pacific to attend college within a church environment rather than having to travel to Provo, Utah, to attend Brigham Young University, the flagship institution for the Mormon college system. Once the Polynesian Cultural Center was completed, additional financial resources were made available to Polynesian students making it more afford-able to get an American college degree. In addition to being a resource for students, the college was also seen as a site where these students would be-come future leaders and teachers upon their return home after receiving a college degree.

Despite the material contributions that the institutions provided, mod-ernization did not come without a price. For many community members, progress was a double-edged sword. Although it provided increased eco-nomic and educational opportunity, it also meant that the autonomy that came with being able to feed one's family from the land and sea was replaced by an increased dependency on a cash economy. With lo'i kalo and farmland leveled, families had to go to work at the Polynesian Cultural Center and the college in order to feed their families. For some community members, this was a price they were willing to pay. For these families an ideology of faithfulness motivated them to give their labor freely to church projects. Also in these stories there is a tension between volunteer labor and paid labor. Within the bureaucratic structure of the church, labor done for reli-gious purposes is unpaid while secular jobs such as teachers and adminis-trative positions are paid. As I have demonstrated, the line between religious and secular work has been fundamentally blurred. This ambiguity amplified the preexisting hierarchies within the community between haole leaders and Hawaiian laborers while also reflecting new conflicts as a second wave of Polynesian Latter-Day Saints began to immigrate to Lā'ie in the 1960s and 1970s. As I describe in the next chapter, at the Polynesian Cultural Center the line between work and religion continued to be blurred. Whereas in this chapter I explored how members of the church negotiated a tension between modernity and tradition, in the next chapter I focus on how they balanced the needs of a tourist facility to commodify culture for profit with their per-sonal desire to perpetuate customs and practices.

4

In the Service of the Lord: Religion, Race, and the Polynesian Cultural Center

O N MAY 7, 1964, EMOSI DAMUNI FOLLOWED HIS COUSIN ISIRELI Racule across the Pacific from Fiji to the Polynesian Cultural Center in Lāʻie, Hawaiʻi. Damuni and his wife Sereima resigned from their jobs—his as a teacher at the local school and hers as a nurse—and immigrated with their family. President Edward Clissold, one of the cofounders of the Polynesian Cultural Center, hired Damuni and Racule to be the cultural experts for the Fijian village. While on a brief trip to Fiji before returning to Hawaiʻi from an extended scouting trip in the South Pacific, Clissold was put in touch with Racule who introduced him to some of the local cultural performers. One of the places they went was to Damuni's school. It was a Wednesday, cultural day, when students and teachers "entertained the tourists or anybody that came to visit."[1] Clissold was so impressed by the uniqueness of the performance as well as the beauty of the place that he insisted that Racule and Damuni be the men to make the Fijian village at the cultural center a reality.

Racule arrived in Hawaiʻi on October 7, 1963, and proudly reported that he and the cultural dance troupe he brought with him completed construction of the Fijian village in five days.[2] Although at that time Damuni could not travel with the rest of the group, he eagerly anticipated the opportunities that awaited him in Hawaiʻi. As he stated in an interview nearly twenty years later, "I think I was chosen to come here by our Heavenly Father. . . . I think I was brought here on purpose, first of all to come and work with Isireli to help him build up the Fijian Village and help the students learn the dancing and the cultures of Fiji."[3] When he and his family arrived in Hawaiʻi they were provided with housing in Lāʻie, and once they were settled he and his wife went to work in the Fijian village as demonstrators. At the time, their oldest daughter was about six years old. She attended the local elementary school while her two younger siblings "were raised in the [Fijian] village with the other children."[4] They would eventually have three more children while working in the village at the Polynesian Cultural Center.

Damuni describes his life at the Fijian village as quite comfortable. One of the first tasks he took on was to finish camouflaging the building.[5] In 1976, Damuni was given permission and the funds to completely renovate the structure to more accurately reflect a traditional Fijian village. Once the structures were adequately camouflaged, Damuni and his family were able to establish a more regular routine, which, as closely as possible, resembled "village" life. The workday began at about six o'clock in the morning. Damuni cleared trash and debris from the area while his wife began cooking the meals for the day. In 1964, there was not a centralized kitchen where the food for the lūʻau was cooked. As Damuni recalls, "Every village had to cook their own food and during the evening we had to go and serve it to the tourists in the big Sāmoan fale. We'd have to go and get coconuts and serve it with the food."[6] In addition to cooking the food for the tourists, they would prepare lunch and dinner for the family because they would not leave work until after the night show, which could run as late as ten o'clock at night.

I begin with Damuni's story because his experiences illustrate how cultural preservation and cultural tourism intersect at the Polynesian Cultural Center. As his story shows, tourism and cultural preservation through replicas of village life intersect in a unique way at the cultural center. In this chapter I argue that attempts at the institutional level to preserve Polynesian culture can be seen as a racial project that relies upon stereotypes of the "happy native." I contrast these dominant discourses with the perceptions and commitments of Polynesians themselves, thus shifting the focus away from the consumption side of tourism to the production side. By analyzing tourism from the perspective of workers, an alternative narrative of culture emerges. As an institution owned and operated by the LDS church, the cultural center adds a religious dimension to how workers understand their jobs at this tourist attraction. As I demonstrate below, religion serves multiple functions at the cultural center. The church uses its influence to garner the consent of workers to perform as the "happy native," but equally important is the fact that religion becomes a way for workers to stave off feelings of alienation. By focusing on multiple levels of meaning making that happen at the center, I explore the limits of preservation while simultaneously tracing what it means to perpetuate cultural knowledge. I theorize that ideologies of faithfulness hold together these different and sometimes competing meanings of Polynesian culture.

I argue that an ideology of faithfulness operates on different levels toward competing ends at the Polynesian Cultural Center. At the structural level of the institution, an ideology of faithfulness functions whereby employees who are also members of the church give their consent to church organizations and projects through a form of coercion—that is, their standing and faithfulness in the church is predicated upon their support of church business practices and projects. This ideology of faithfulness interpellates Polynesian student workers as the site where the perpetuation and preservation of culture is ensured. How do Polynesian workers negotiate the limits of this ideology while also using it as a tool to challenge institutional practices? How do they articulate critique while not appearing unfaithful to the church or its leaders? I argue that their ability to maneuver within the touristic structure of the Polynesian Cultural Center is possible because of their status as a chosen people that they use as leverage to insist that the church meet its larger obligation to preserve that connection.

I intentionally use the word faithfulness because former workers describe their loyalty using the language of faith. Damuni is no exception: "The foundations of this place should be love, faithful loyal dedication, and sacrifice."[7] Damuni links love, faith, loyalty, dedication, and sacrifice to work at a tourist attraction. Through ideologies of faithfulness he has blurred the boundaries that typically divide work from religion and tourism from spirituality. What makes his statement problematic, however, is that when a corporation or tourist facility such as this one frames the labor process as service to the Lord, one's personal belief system and spirituality, one's faith, becomes a mechanism for producing compliant workers.

Ideology is a powerful tool of hegemony because it produces a necessary illusion that all is well, thus masking the material conditions of one's domination.[8] At the Polynesian Cultural Center, an ideology of faithfulness draws upon its association with the church to get workers to consent to performing race. Given the relationship between the cultural center and Brigham Young University–Hawai'i (originally the Church College of Hawai'i), this ideology of faithfulness produces a continuous supply of compliant workers with each new cohort of students who attend the college and with each new generation that grows up under the influence of the church and the cultural center. The power of ideology serves to produce subjects who, in the words of

Leonard Williams writing about Althusser's notion of subjectivity, willingly occupy "their assigned places within the existing social order . . . as if to do so were human nature, without giving their actions and beliefs a second thought."[9] Thus not only is performing for tourists seen as natural and normal (i.e., Damuni's family replicating village life for tourists) but the rhetoric that their work is in the service of the Lord adds a religious dimension to why they buy into the system willingly, voluntarily, and faithfully. The socioeconomic conditions that make tourism an industry within which one *must* work in order to attend college or support one's family is necessarily obscured. For example, the popular history of the Polynesian Cultural Center extols it as an authentic replica of what life was like in Polynesia, albeit in an indeterminate mythical past. However, missing is the irony that the lo'i kalo (water gardens of taro) that in the past were cultivated by Lā'ie families were bulldozed in order to build the cultural center, thus cutting off a sustainable source of traditional food.

In part, an ideology of faithfulness attempts to explain why Polynesian workers labor as hard as they do in a manner that expresses their strong ties to the Polynesian Cultural Center. Workers are expected to ignore the exploitive and contradictory aspects of their job, including the emotional and physical labor of greeting hundreds of tourists a day or memorizing scripts and demonstrations that are performed over and over while appearing natural, normal, and spontaneous. Workers are not, however, ignorant of the racialized nature of their performances or the stereotypes that they perpetuate. As Susan James notes, ideology is not solely a mechanism of control because it can also produce the conditions by which workers "perceive themselves as free agents."[10] Althusser is equally instructive on this point because he moves beyond the Marxian notion of ideology as a tool of capital to include the ways in which the masses can use ideology in counterhegemonic ways. In this chapter the experiences of Polynesian Cultural Center workers offer insight into how religious belief and practices can serve multiple purposes, in this instance, by upholding a capitalist workplace while also producing a space for dissent and the recoding of the meaning of labor.

RACE AND THE POLITICS OF TOURISM IN HAWAI'I

In 1993, the political scientist Haunani-Kay Trask published an essay titled "Lovely Hula Hands: Corporate Tourism and the Prostitution of Hawaiian Culture," which stands as one of the strongest indictments against the tourism industry in Hawai'i. In this essay she calls the industry a colonial project intended to maintain the existing racial, gender, and class hierarchies established in the nineteenth century that culminated in the illegal overthrow of the Kingdom of Hawai'i. Since the overthrow, Native Hawaiians have fought continuously for their self-determination. However, this reality and struggle is effaced by the image of Hawai'i as paradise—that is, as America's sandbox in the Pacific. As Trask writes, "Because the selling of Hawai'i depends on the prostitution of Hawaiian culture, Hawaiian and other locals must supply the industry with compliant workers. Thus our Hawaiian people—and not only our Hawaiian culture—become commodities."[11] In part, Trask provides a formula for how tourism relies on the gendered racial bodies of locals in order to keep the machine going: the tourism machine sells race, workers perform race, and tourists buy race. Within this framework, Hawaiian people sell more than their labor for wages; tourism relies on their gendered racial bodies to sell race to tourists.

Similarly, the Polynesian Cultural Center relies on this formula for its success. One need only visit the center's Web site to see a colorful display of happy natives: a Hawaiian maiden greets a white, middle-class, presumably American, family; a Sāmoan man places a coconut leaf hat atop the head of another white tourist; Tahitian performers teach a group of white tourists a few dance moves. As the historian Jane Desmond notes, the stereotypical image of Polynesians as the happy native was a racial project established in the mid-nineteenth century intended to reinforce the scientific racism of the time: "The Polynesians in particular, and especially the Hawaiians, thus are seen to represent an earlier, sometimes idyllic, stage of civilization through which Europeans have already passed. One of their uses for the colonizing powers is to serve as an example, a living experiment in the evolutionary paradigm of civilization."[12] Within this paradigm the Native never escapes his or her primitive—precivilized—state of being; as such, they are forever out of time in modernity. The visual representations of Polynesian cultures depicted on the center's Web site appear to reproduce this racial paradigm: from the costumes the workers wear to the stylized settings of the models photographed in "nature," the Polynesian Cultural Center sells a fossilized image of the "ideal primitive" to white, presumably American, families.[13] As Trask noted about the overall tourism industry in Hawai'i, Polynesian workers at the cultural center appear to willingly use their bodies as performance and commodity to sell the ideal primitive for wages. What motivates workers to willingly sell their labor and their bodies for tourism? When Polynesian workers come to these jobs, what do they want? What do they get out of this work? Why do they work as hard as they do for this tourist facility?

Polynesian workers describe getting more out of their jobs than just a salary or financial support to pay for college; what seems to motivate many of them to work for and feel loyal to the Polynesian Cultural Center are the nonmaterial religious, spiritual, and cultural benefits. What is sought after is a real connection to the worker's culture, but at the center culture is a commodity fossilized, packaged, and performed for tourists who also desire a real representation of Polynesian culture. I argue that Polynesian workers find themselves in a paradox of selling/performing race at the cultural center: many former workers describe their experiences there as a time in their lives when they took pride in their cultural heritage. It was also a time when they were able to learn about their culture as well as the diversity of cultures in Polynesia, yet this learning took place within a highly racialized institutional structure. The culture that is packaged and sold operates within a racial discourse of the always already primitive Polynesian.

In this chapter I explore the paradox of looking for cultural meaning at a tourist facility that sells race. I trace some of the ways in which Polynesian

Today the Polynesian Cultural Center is one of the most popular tourist facilities in Hawai'i. Photograph by author.

workers perceive themselves as "free agents" because they appear to act out of their own self-interests but, more importantly, their motivation is connected to reclaiming an ethnic identity that, for some, has been repudiated by colonization, assimilation, and racism. What they appear to get from being loyal and faithful is access to a limited number of indigenous customs and practices. How can a tourist facility that sells race be a site where Polynesians express feeling renewed interest and pride in their culture, heritage, and ethnic identities?

The Polynesian Cultural Center: A Brief History

Edward L. Clissold and Wendell B. Mendenhall, the cofounders of the Polynesian Cultural Center, believed that tourism in the form of a permanent facility in Lāʻie would solve the economic problem of providing Polynesian students with financial support to attend the Church College of Hawaiʻi.[14] By the 1960s Hawaiʻi's economy had already begun to move from a plantation economy to a touristic one.[15] Furthermore, the Lāʻie community had proven itself capable of drawing tourists from Waikīkī to the north shore for the monthly Hukilau. The Hukilau began in 1947 as a fund-raising event to earn the money needed to build a new chapel. As noted in the previous chapter, the Lāʻie community was primarily Hawaiian and Sāmoan, and as such the Hukilau activities reflected the cultures of these two groups. Whereas the community began preparing for the Hukilau a month in advance, the experience for the tourists began by watching local men demonstrate a hukilau, a form of Hawaiian net fishing, followed by various arts and craft demonstrations, and then culminating in a lūʻau feast and show featuring the dances and music of Hawaiʻi and Sāmoa. The cultural center, loosely based on the Hukilau model, invites its guests to spend the day traveling from village to village learning about the arts, crafts, and traditions of each culture of Polynesia. The day culminates in a lūʻau followed by a night show, which is a professional-quality revue of the dances and music of Polynesia.

The Polynesian Cultural Center has been selling an image of the happy native to tourists for nearly fifty years. The center is one of Hawaiʻi's premier tourist attractions; it draws approximately twenty-five million visitors each year and currently employs approximately seven hundred students who attend Brigham Young University–Hawaiʻi.[16] It was founded in 1963 by the Church of Jesus Christ of Latter-day Saints to provide jobs for Polynesian students attending the Church College of Hawaiʻi. The cultural center is also unique as a tourist facility because culture, spirituality, and education inform how workers understand their role in this system. The mission statement reflects how these values coexist at the center:

> The Polynesian Cultural Center is a unique treasure created to share with the world the cultures, diversity and spirit of the nations of Polynesia. In accomplishing this we will: Preserve and portray the cultures, arts and crafts of Polynesia; Contribute to the educational development and growth of all people at Brigham Young University–Hawaii and the Polynesian Cultural Center; Demonstrate and radiate a spirit of love and service which will contribute to the betterment, uplift and blessing of all who visit this special place.[17]

In addition to achieving the financial needs of the church and the college, the center is seen as a key missionary tool. The founders believed that presenting both an authentic representation of Polynesian culture and a positive image of the church would open the minds of tourists to the message of the gospel. Although some members of the church in Hawai'i were skeptical of the missionary component of the center in the belief that young people would become seduced by tourism and end up in Waikīkī, the church presidency in Utah made it a critical component for their support of such an endeavor.[18] The tram tour of Lā'ie that includes a brief stop at Brigham Young University–Hawai'i and a thirty-minute layover at the visitor's center of the temple has become an important missionary tool for the church as visitors to the temple can fill out a form requesting more information about the church. Upon their return home, proselytizing missionaries provide the visitors with an opportunity to hear more about the gospel. From inception to fruition, the Polynesian Cultural Center was intended to achieve both the economic and religious goals of the church. It is within the space between the religious and the economic that Polynesian workers attempt to negotiate and articulate a religiously embedded Polynesian identity.

The Polynesian Cultural Center: A Cultural Park of Ethnographic Tourism

Andrew Ross describes the Polynesian Cultural Center as a "'cultural park' of ethnographic tourism." In his view "it is invariably the mass tourist who is now invited to play the role of the classical ethnographer, encouraged by guidebooks to venture beyond the kon-tiki stage shows and strike out for the highlands or the interior in search of authentic village life."[19] The ethnographic experiences of its visitors include eating food cooked in the villages, watching dance demonstrations, and sitting in thatched huts adorned with material objects of Polynesian culture. At a cultural tourist attraction, tourists buy more than just material objects such as handmade lei, tiki (wood-carved statues), and replicas of costumes worn by demonstrators and dancers. The participation by tourists in the demonstrations of food preparation, dances, and leisure activities that happen in the "village" as well as their observation of the performances in the night show contribute to the authentication of the cultural center. In Ross's criticism of this configuration, he observes that "tourism promotes the 'restoration, preservation, and fictional recreation of ethnic attributes' creating a museum-like commodity out of ethnic identity."[20]

In addition to the consumption by tourists of material objects such as poi balls made in the Aotearoa (New Zealand) village and the poi pounded in the Hawai'i village, as consumers of this "cultural park of ethnographic tourism" they utilize a collective gaze that reassures them that what they experience is "more real, more immediate, or more complete" than what can be had in Waikīkī or at one of the other lū'au shows such as Paradise Cove or Germaine's Luau.[21] Tourists can rest assured that the display and performance of Polynesian culture at this tourist facility is made more "authentic" by the natives who perform in the villages and in the night show. Cultural tourism transforms native culture and native people into objects packaged, purchased, and visually consumed by tourists.

Dean MacCannell describes the relationship between tourism and the display and performance of native culture as a tension between the "primitive" and the "modern." He argues that although primitives no longer exist in the world today, it is through the performance of culture such as that done at tourist attractions where the "ex-primitive" emerges. Performance is a key aspect of this framework:

> Enacted and staged savagery is already well established as a small but stable part of the world system of social and economic exchanges. Many formerly primitive groups earn their living by charging visitors admission to their sacred shrines, ritual performances, and displays of more or less "ethnologized" everyday life.[22]

In the context of modernity, the performance of the "ex-primitive" can be seen as a hybrid cultural form. The performance combines the cultural traditions of the "primitive" and the economic opportunity, provided by modernity, to earn money "doing what they have always done." He is not convinced by the hybrid cultural form but rather argues that the "primitivistic" performance is a pseudo hybrid that wears the mask of the primitive to hide the simple fact of capital accumulation. For MacCannell there is no way out of the economic system of tourism. Once profit or economic value is attached to cultural codes and practices that once had use value, exploitation and alienation necessarily follows.

My objective for turning attention back onto the Polynesian Cultural Center is to problematize two underlying assumptions of the literature on tourism—both in general and about the cultural center in particular. First, as Ross's analysis of the center demonstrates, most research on tourism focuses either on the industry side of the equation or on tourists. Studies such as these provide a critical perspective of how tourism operates and what tourists get from this system, yet we learn little about the workers. In order to understand how Polynesian workers make sense of their place in the tourism formula described above, I turn to their own words and explanations. The examples I provide in this chapter come from oral histories conducted between 1982 and 1986 with former employees at the cultural center for the Polynesian Cultural Center Oral History Program archived at Brigham Young University–Hawai'i as well as from interviews I conducted while doing research in Hawai'i and Utah between 2001 and 2002.[23] I focus primarily on the first twenty years of the center's operation (1963–1983) because former workers describe this as a time when "the spirit of aloha" was most prominently felt. Indeed, this was a unique time in the history of the center. As Damuni's story above illustrates, it was a time when parents could bring their children to work, which in turn contributed to a "real" village feeling. The doors of the center were open to members of the community who could come and go as they pleased, young people learned the arts and crafts of Polynesia from kūpuna (elders) who had deep cultural knowledge, and workers felt free to ad lib or go off script depending on the situation or their mood. Between 1976 and 1980, workers describe a loss of "aloha" as parents were instructed to leave their children at home, community members were charged admission, uniforms were standardized, and workers were expected to conform to strict regulations and were subjected to increased surveillance by management.

Second, once we turn our attention to the experiences of workers we begin to challenge binary thinking about culture. Although MacCannell's model offers a Marxist analysis of tourism in a postmodern and post-Fordist era of globalization, he reproduces a binary between (sacred) culture that has use value and (profane) culture that has economic value, wherein the ex-primitive is not preserving "culture" but reproducing capital. Within such a framework, the worker/ex-primitive is always already exploited and alienated from "culture." By turning to the words and experiences of workers whose job it is to perform "ethnologized everyday life," I challenge the binary between the sacred space of culture and the profane space of the market.[24] As Richard Poulson expressed in his interview with me, one of the greatest benefits for him of working at the Polynesian Cultural Center was the opportunity to learn the art of Māori wood carving from an expert. He recalls spending hours after work sitting and watching the master carver Epanaia (Barney) Whaanga Christy. If he was patient, Christy would toss him a chisel and put him to work: "I wasn't getting paid but I would stay there and learn as much as I could from him," Poulson recalls. "Those were opportunities. I know I lost opportunities in New Zealand but those opportunities came in Hawai'i. I wanted to learn. I was ready to learn."[25] When the interaction between Poulson and Christy is examined from the point of the view of the political economy of the industry, this exchange is seen as problematic; that is, the learning that takes place in the space of tourism becomes tainted. By shifting the analytical focus from what is gained by the industry or tourists to what the workers seek, we can better see that the boundaries between the sacred and profane are blurred. Within the space created for tourism the (sacred) transmission of culture from one generation to the next is not tainted but actually helps young Polynesians develop a strong cultural identity that they carry with them throughout their lives. Thus the communal value of the generational transmission of knowledge overrides any individual economic value (i.e., being able to buy a car) that could come from employment at the center. What are the contours of this cultural identity and how does it inform the worker's sense of self?

Culture, Education, and Identities

One phrase repeated often in the oral histories and interviews was that working at the Polynesian Cultural Center was more than just a job. I came to learn that there was more going on at the center than could be accessed by visiting the Web site, touring the villages, or watching the night show. Poulson, who is Māori, began working at the center in 1971, one year after immigrating to Hawai'i from Aotearoa. He continued to work there until

1977 when he was laid off, and a year later he migrated to Utah where he still lives. When I asked Poulson about how he came to be in Hawaiʻi, his recollections turn from a description of the chain of events that landed him and his sister in Lāʻie to the unexpected benefits of his decision to leave home. He admitted that his motivation for moving to Hawaiʻi was to surf. However, almost immediately he found that it was the opportunities to learn more about his culture that kept him there for eight years. Moreover, it was the friends with whom he worked at the center that most influenced him to seek out this knowledge:

> I got to Hawaiʻi and all those times that I could have gone to Māori classes and learned dances and stuff but skipped out and took off someplace else and hid, it finally dawned on me that no matter what happens in my life I am always going to be part Māori, there is nothing I can do about it so why not learn what my culture is about. So that was a good learning experience. I started observing, watching and then start[ed] to learn more about my culture. I learned more about Māori culture than I did in 17 years in New Zealand. I learned more in Hawaiʻi.[26]

What Poulson describes is a situation by which working at the Polynesian Cultural Center provided him with a unique educational experience. From this we can infer in a larger sense that employment at the cultural center is articulated with one learning about one's culture.

As Néstor García Canclini observes, the reproduction of cultural capital takes place through "a set of institutional mechanisms that ensure the transfer of inherited culture from one generation to another." In noncapitalist societies the reproduction of culture necessarily takes place in concert with other activities of "an economic and social nature"; under capitalism, however, there are separate institutions for this "cultural development." Although one such institution is the formal educational system, García Canclini stresses that under capitalism we must also "include the mass media, forms of organization of space and time, and all material institutions and structures through which meaning is carried."[27] In Lāʻie, we have to include the Polynesian Cultural Center. As Poulson's story illustrates, the center provided him with the structure by which he was able to access cultural capital in the form of learning Māori dances and wood carving. It would be easy to draw a comparison between the center as a separate institution where cultural meanings are reproduced and sold as contrasted to an idealized description of life in

New Zealand where the transmission of culture is integrated into daily life. But from Poulson's recollections, cultural education at home also took place in separate institutions; the transfer of culture took place at his mother's marae (buildings at the center of a Māori community or tribe) in the form of Māori funerals and weddings, in classes devoted to cultural lessons, and at church. Although it is ironic that Poulson had to leave home to learn about his culture, the Polynesian Cultural Center is one of many sites where cultural capital is differentially appropriated by members of a society.

Poulson's story is useful because he sees the cultural learning that takes place at the Polynesian Cultural Center as comparable to the cultural learning he rejected as a child. This distinction, again, blurs the boundaries that characterize the center as a workplace and "home." What is less clear from Poulson's interview is what constitutes culture. What are the contours of cultural education at the Polynesian Cultural Center? Who teaches culture and what are students as workers supposed to learn? As noted above, the mission of the center is to preserve and portray culture; furthermore, education is seen as an activity that happens at the college through the financial aid provided to student workers. Whereas Poulson and other Polynesian workers understood their jobs at the center as having an educational component (Poulson was there to learn from kūpuna who were his teachers), the center's founders, managers, and other bureaucrats failed to make the same connection. In their figuring, preservation and portrayal were not educational but commercial. Vernice Wineera's research has found a lack of consensus regarding the role the Polynesian Cultural Center should play in educating Polynesian workers about their culture.[28] For Kenneth Baldridge, a Church College of Hawai'i faculty member and historian, there was a clear divide between the center as a source of financial aid for students at the school to gain an education at an American college that presumably would translate into professional and political occupations upon their return to their home countries and to what degree the center was equipped to educate workers about Polynesian culture. In 1972, one solution offered by Mendenhall was for workers to take courses offered at the college, namely introductory anthropology, as well as courses through the Pacific Institute and Museum.[29] As these course offerings suggest, even at the college Polynesian culture is figured as anachronistic—that is, as culture that existed in the past or is preserved in a museum.

In contrast to Mendenhall and others who looked outside the cultural center to the college as the source for cultural education, many Polynesian

workers saw such education as a key component of their job. Ironically, when
Clissold and Mendenhall traveled throughout Polynesia looking for experts
in the arts, crafts, dances, music, and everyday practices of the region, they
believed that having the best cultural experts would increase the authenticity of the center. They did not foresee how these cultural experts would

become teachers to subsequent generations of young Polynesian workers.

Damuni, who worked for the cultural center for over twelve years, was
always clear about the role he would play as teacher and cultural expert at
the center. As his story above suggests, he came to the center with an understanding of his job as educational. To be sure, what he taught students and
tourists was qualitatively different. During his time at the center, he was a
demonstrator in the village, a performer in the night show, assistant village
manager, and village operations manager. At the time of his interview in
1983, he no longer worked at the center but he did continue to volunteer
his time training young students for the Fijian section of the night show.
He continued to work with these young people despite feeling frustrated
that many of them saw their time there as merely a job. His ultimate goal
was to instill in them the kind of appreciation of the Polynesian Cultural
Center that he held—an appreciation that recognizes its spiritual and cultural significance:

> This is a Promised Land where these kids should learn their culture. It's not
> just a place for a tourist attraction. If one of our children comes here and tries
> to learn the culture, he will have great opportunities over here. He can learn the
> cultures of all the villages. Where else can he get the culture of all these islands?
> Some of our students overlook the opportunity and they come here just to
> enjoy themselves. They come here to dance and make money to go to town and
> buy cars. That's not the main purpose of this place.[30]

Embedded in Damuni's declaration of the purpose of the center is a paradox of performance. On the one hand, he believes the center is more than a
tourist attraction because it is a place where cultural education takes place.
On the other hand, he is disappointed when some students see this cultural
education as merely a job; that they are there to earn money presumably to
buy cars. What he does not reference are the structural changes that had taken
place over the twenty-plus years he had been at the center that produced a
qualitatively different work-cultural experience for the next generation. I
argue that it is an ideology of faithfulness that motivated him to continue to

work with the young people. In this instance, he declares his faithfulness to
two forces—the church and the perpetuation of culture. I intentionally use
the word perpetuation rather than preservation (the term used in the center
mission statement) because for Damuni and others the culture they teach
the young people who come there to work is one that is dynamic, creative,
and ever changing. Indeed, embedded in Damuni's vision is a contradiction:
the dances that he teaches student workers will be sold to tourists as part of
the fossilized primitive past depicted at the center.

But Damuni was not only interested in educating workers, he was also
committed to teaching tourists something about Fiji. He describes how he
ran the demonstrations in the Fijian village as follows:

> I would give them the introduction outside and tell them about the village and
> how it was constructed, how the roof is made with the beating of the *lali* and
> from there I would take them in and explain the building and the culture. I
> would tell them how we have to sit down in the house and how you receive
> people coming in. When I demonstrated to them I asked them if they could sit
> down so they could share the experience. I would try to keep the momentum
> going. While they were still interested in what we were doing inside I would go
> outside and dance for them and explain the dance and then escort them to
> another village. I tried hard to make it interesting for the tourists.[31]

His approach to his demonstrations was modeled on his experiences as a
teacher back in Fiji. He wanted to educate the tourists while also making the
demonstration interesting and entertaining.

Unlike Mendenhall and others who potentially underestimated the degree
to which cultural education would take place at the Polynesian Cultural Center, Christy's story punctuates not only how important it was for him to pass
on his knowledge to future generations of workers, but also how his expertise at the center earned him recognition at the college. For Christy, becoming a teacher was an unexpected outcome of his job at the center. When he
immigrated to Hawai'i in April 1973, he was hired for a two-year position as
master carver and assistant chief in the Māori village, but his contract was
extended. In 1982, when the interview was conducted, he was still working
as a carver for the center. Christy recalls how in addition to his work at the
center teaching carving to a small crew of apprentices and overseeing all of
the carving projects at each of the villages, he had also started to teach students at the college through the fine arts program. At the conclusion of his

interview Christy was asked to reflect back on the contributions he made to the center. In his reply he states that he was just one of many older people who gave their talents to the center and to the church: "I want to give of my knowledge to others so that they may carry on this work. I feel that the talent I have is not mine because the opportunity came through the church. I would probably never have learned how to do carving if I was not selected to be one of the carvers that the church has selected. And I'm grateful to be giving of my time here at the Cultural Center to do this work and to help teach others."[32]

These closing words from his interview are instructive regarding the complexity of an ideology of faithfulness. Christy's statement begins by giving thanks to the church for the talent he is able to pass on to the next generation. On the surface we could read his gratitude as an internalization of an ideology of faithfulness where loyalty to church projects is required of its members. As I have described in previous chapters, however, within the Pacific region Christianity plays a paradoxical role in the perpetuation of culture.[33] Here, Christy is not acting under false consciousness, but instead recognizes how the opportunity to work under a master carver back in 1947 and again in 1960 was made possible by the church. Prior to moving to the cultural center Christy had worked continuously as a carver since 1947, and the LDS church in New Zealand sponsored many of those projects. Although the interests of the church were served—and faithfulness to the church and its project was garnered—Christy's interests were also met: "I'm grateful that I taught Angus, my son, to carve. He is a very good carver. I'm teaching Douglas, too. He's my younger son. He has a long way to go."[34] As García Canclini made clear, in a capitalist society the transmission of cultural knowledge from one generation to the next necessarily takes place in separate institutions. For Christy, Damuni, and Poulson, the Polynesian Cultural Center was an institution where cultural capital—learning the dances of Fiji and Māori carving, for example—were passed from a generation of experts to a few fortunate young people.

However, not all of the "teachers" at the cultural center were content to let management decide which students would have a cultural education and which ones would not. The tension between culture as commodity and the center as a site for cultural education to take place was of utmost concern for Patoa Benioni, especially when it came to how Polynesian students were hired as musicians and dancers in the prestigious night show. Born in Rarotonga but raised in Western Sāmoa where he attended the LDS high school,

Benioni immigrated to Hawai'i in 1961. After his arrival he worked for the Institute of Polynesian Studies at the Church College of Hawai'i and helped build the Polynesian Cultural Center in exchange for tuition. When the center opened, church leaders relied on Benioni's cultural expertise in Tahitian dance and drumming. His intervention into the way students were chosen and trained for the night show forced the leadership to recognize that not all students who came from their home islands arrived at the center knowing how to dance and play their ethnic music. Benioni also challenged the leadership of the center to take their mission statement seriously by preserving Polynesian culture through teaching Polynesian students about the dances and music of the region. He argued that as long as the selection process focused on students who came to the center with a prior knowledge of the language and dances of their culture, they would be failing in their duty. In challenging the policy and procedures for determining who is more deserving of cultural knowledge and who is not, Benioni also challenged dominant ideas about Natives doing what they have always done. His critique of the hiring procedures acknowledges that cultural practices must be taught and passed on from one generation to the next in order to remain vibrant and creative, and that all Polynesian students who want to learn should have the opportunity to learn cultural expressions of their own culture and of the region.[35]

Evident in these examples are glimpses of the contested meaning of culture at the Polynesian Cultural Center. For management, culture is comprised of material objects and practices that can be displayed or performed for tourists, and it is something objective that one can learn in a classroom at the college. However, Poulson, Damuni, Christy, and Benioni all offer a bit more complicated and nuanced understanding of culture. For them culture is dynamic, changing, and alive when it is carried forward to future generations. Many workers recognize the limits of what is possible at the center, while others hold great appreciation for what they were able to learn there. The lack of clarity over the educational aspects of the Polynesian Cultural Center, I believe, relates to the underlying assumptions about what constitutes "culture" at the center or what is "cultural" about it. What exactly are the cultural identities being (re)produced at the center?

The work of Arjun Appadurai is instructive for delineating the difference between the noun "culture" and the adjective "cultural." The term culture implies "some kind of object, thing, or substance, whether physical or metaphysical . . . Viewed as a physical substance, culture begins to smack of any variety of biologisms, including race, which we have certainly outgrown as scientific categories."[36] Indeed, the tourism industry in Hawai'i has not "outgrown" racial categories but rather relies on them to turn a profit. On one discursive level, there appears to be a strong correlation between culture and race. At the center, culture is composed of objects—things that collectively produce the feeling of authenticity. Within this framework, Polynesian bodies adorned in "traditional" costumes are equal to the grass shacks in each village and the arts and crafts produced by workers and sold in the store called the International Market Place. The racialization of the Native as primitive—always out of time in modernity—is what tourists buy at this "cultural park for ethnographic tourism."

Appadurai goes on to contrast the noun "culture" with the adjective "cultural," which "moves on into a realm of differences, contrasts, and comparisons that is more helpful." Its usefulness is twofold, first it signals contrast, context, and difference: "When we therefore point to a practice, a distinction, a conception, an object, or an ideology as having a cultural dimension[,] . . . we stress the idea of situated difference, that is, difference in relation to something local, embodied, and significant."[37] Second, the cultural also signals "those differences that either express, or set the groundwork for, the mobilization of group identities."[38] The move he attempts to make is one that privileges difference over similarity. Within the context of tourism in Hawai'i, however, difference is exactly what tourists want to get for their money. Wineera found that "many of the Polynesian Cultural Center's tourists desire to experience something beyond the ordinary in meeting with Polynesian Others at the site and arrive with the expectation of some sort of spiritual renewal in the encounter."[39] The recognition of difference, in this context, produces two competing group identities, the tourist and the Polynesian other. In this example, the cultural slides back into the naturalizing categories of culture to produce a subset of group identities delineated along well-worn racial lines.[40]

Appadurai's analysis does not end with the comparison of "culture" and "cultural." Rather, he offers the term "culturalism" as a means of designating "a feature of movements involving identities consciously in the making. . . . Culturalism . . . is the conscious mobilization of cultural differences in the service of a larger national or transnational politics."[41] This concept is useful because it provides us with a way to get at the different meanings of culture as articulated at the Polynesian Cultural Center. As noted above, the hegemonic meaning of culture reflects racial discourses of the primitive Native that are sold to tourists. However, I suggest that an alternative meaning of culture, one more in line with Appadurai's notion of culturalism, better explains what Poulson means when he proclaims that his cultural identity was strengthened at the center. When we read Poulson's story through the lens of culturalism, the representation of cultural differences among Polynesian groups displayed at the center becomes disarticulated from a racial discourse of difference and rearticulated with a trans-Pacific politics of self-determination. For example, during my interview with Poulson he admitted that as a child one of the reasons why he hid from cultural events was because he wanted to assimilate into the Pākehā (white European) culture of New Zealand, and as a fair-skinned Māori with sun-bleached blond hair, he found it relatively easy to pass. In Hawai'i the assimilation projects that became institutionalized after the overthrow of the kingdom in 1893 instilled negative connotations with being Hawaiian that we are still trying to overcome.[42] Given this legacy of conquest in some Pacific countries it is significant that people expressed feeling proud of their ethnic identities, because for some it was the first time in their lives that they felt this kind of pride.[43] I take seriously their words and experiences because to do otherwise would reproduce the colonial structures that say we are inconsequential primitives—small people from small islands—who have nothing to offer the world but a good time on their vacation.[44]

One of the challenges of making sense of how race operates at the Polynesian Cultural Center has to do with the relationship between the conceptual categories of race and ethnicity. My approach to understanding how workers make sense of their role in selling race at the center is to see race and ethnicity as complementary empirical and analytical categories. Stephen Cornell and Douglas Hartmann's examination of the social science project and meaning of these categories is useful for understanding how race and ethnicity operate simultaneously at the cultural center. First they contend that what race and ethnicity have in common is that they are both socially constructed categories that rely on "the assumption that human origins are uniquely powerful in determining differences between social groups." By focusing on origins, both are seen as "natural" categories. Second, despite these similarities, there are also key differences: "Race focuses on genes as the critical dimension of origins . . . especially through skin color or other visible physiological features . . . Ethnicity, in contrast, . . . focuses on descent and homeland: it is kinship and provenance that are given power in ethnic conceptions."[45] At the center this translates into a structure that sells race—

an origin story that first draws upon racial divisions within Oceania and then rearticulates those divides for religious conversion and expansion—that is, brown-skinned Natives who are paid to perform their fossilized primitive culture.[46] But it is also a structure where Polynesian workers experience a strong connection to their ethnic group, or localized identities based, in the words of Cornell and Hartman, on "self-assertion of collective identity and blood ties, based on descent or homeland."[47] They stress how race and ethnicity are not mutually exclusive categories but rather acknowledge that individuals and groups can move from one category to another.

By using the analytical tools of both race and ethnicity, we are able to see a more complex view of what is bought and sold at the Polynesian Cultural Center. For example, when Poulson first started working at the center he danced in the Māori section of the night show. After meeting his wife Noe he was motivated to learn the dances for the Hawaiian section, and from 1971 to 1975 he performed in both the Māori and Hawaiian sections of the night show. For Poulson, learning the dances of Hawai'i only strengthened his Māori identity as he was able to experience firsthand the genealogical, linguistic, and mythological connections between Hawaiians and Māori. Learning the dances of Hawai'i also brought him closer to his wife. Using the language of ethnicity helps to understand how Poulson and other Polynesian workers experienced learning from different cultures as part of the process of remaking their individual ethnic identities.

Ezekial Kamai also came to embrace Polynesian culture by dancing in the night show.[48] Born in Honolulu, his family moved to Lā'ie when he was about a year old. After going away to college for one year and then on a mission for two years, he returned to Lā'ie where he attended the Church College of Hawai'i and found a job working at the Polynesian Cultural Center. As was the standard practice of the time, Kamai danced in two sections of the night show—the Hawaiian section (his own ethnic group) and the Tahitian section, with a switch later to the Māori section. In the Hawaiian section of the night show he learned how to do the spear knife dance, how to dance kahiko (ancient hula), and how to blow the conch shell. Additionally, by learning the movements and meanings behind the dances of other ethnic groups he says he was able to develop a deeper appreciation of the different cultures represented at the cultural center. He believed that without this opportunity he would not feel the connection he has for all of the cultures of Polynesian. This experience also prepared him for his eventual marriage to a Tahitian woman. He felt that learning the dances and music of Tahiti provided him with a basic cultural understanding of his wife's ethnic background. Kamai's story is by no means unique. Indeed, many former workers share stories of working in various villages or dancing in different sections of the night show as being the basis by which they learned to appreciate Polynesian culture.

In reading these examples through the lens of race, we see how the policy to allow people to perform in at least two sections of the night show relies upon a disavowal of ethnic differences and produces an "abstract native" where the floating signifiers of racial differences can be easily transferred from one brown body to another as quickly as a change of costume.[49] At issue here is the clear conflict between how a people represent themselves and how they are represented by others. Ralph Barney, a haole teacher at the Church College of Hawai'i, was ambivalent about the inherent conflict between wanting to represent Polynesian culture as a dynamic, creative process and the financial needs of a tourist facility. He saw "fiberglass canoes" as good management, "so you don't have to carve new canoes," but he recognized as a problem "putting fuzzy wuzzy wigs on Sāmoans and letting them be Fijians. A lot of that hokey [stuff] that comes from good management is the kind of thing that has the people from the countries themselves shaking their heads and saying, 'Hey, what kind of a place is that?'"[50] As the Polynesian Cultural Center developed a greater business sense it experienced many more tensions between the sacred realm of culture and the profane realm of the market.

It is clear from the oral histories and the interviews I conducted that Polynesians were well aware of the tension between the management's need to sell race and the workers' desire to perform ethnicity. In his interview, Tommy Taurima stresses the importance of teaching young people their culture; however, he also recognizes that it was unrealistic to expect the Polynesian Cultural Center to preserve every aspect of Polynesian culture.[51] The most important thing he thought young people should learn was protocol— appropriate ways of behaving in any given situation. He felt that if they understood proper protocol then young people would be well prepared for anything. As such he stresses quality over quantity; although they cannot teach young people everything, what students do learn they learn well and they can take it with them after they leave the cultural center. Nāpua Stevens Poire, a kumu hula (source of hula knowledge and instructor) agreed that not every aspect of Polynesian culture was or should be preserved at the center.[52] She was proud at how well Hawaiian mele (songs), hula (dance), and moʻokūʻauhau (genealogy) was preserved, however the traditional forms of building huts and canoes were not maintained. Once again, she too emphasizes quality over quantity; what mattered most for her was that her knowledge of the hula would be passed on to future generations. Indeed, the quality of the performances at the Polynesian Cultural Center is undisputed. What is not questioned, however, are the political implications of preserving only the performative aspects of Polynesian culture that have been decontextualized in order to be palatable and nonthreatening to tourists. In preserving mele and hula devoid of their cultural meaning and practice, workers do not learn how to live and survive in their homeland but instead become dependent on tourism rather than the ʻāina to feed their families.

What these few examples illustrate is how management and Polynesian instructors took a pragmatic approach to the representation and preservation of culture at the Polynesian Cultural Center. Despite this similarity, there are also important distinctions, namely the significant role of the center as an institution of cultural education. And as Wineera makes clear, "in the Polynesian Cultural Center's representation of culture, employees respect an unseen line of demarcation which exists, not between outside and inside, but which resides, always, on the inside, separating, safeguarding, that which is sacred (tapu-Māori) from that which is noa (Māori for common, profane)." And as Wineera explains further, "As most Polynesians know, there are many elements of culture which are sacred, private, unsuitable and inappropriate to be shared with tourists either as entertainment *or* education, and to label ethnic entertainment as 'phony' when it excludes these ceremonial or ritual elements is patronizing."[53] Indeed, many explicitly sacred ceremonies or rituals are not a visible aspect of what is ethnologized at the cultural center. However, workers express feeling a spiritual connection to the cultural center that in part contributes to their loyalty and faithfulness to its mission. It is to that relationship between work, religion, and spirituality that I turn next.

Work, Religion, and Spirituality

According to Elliot Cameron, former president of the Church College of Hawaiʻi, "the umbrella of the gospel" is what allows work, religion, and cultural preservation to coexist at the Polynesian Cultural Center.[54] Typically, work and religion are not discussed in the same frame because religion is presumed to be sacred, to be kept in the realm of one's private life, whereas work is not sacred but quite public. As I have illustrated in previous chapters, the gospel can be seen as an umbrella that functions as a barrier protecting members from such things as land dispossession (see chapter 1). I have also demonstrated how the gospel is used to garner the consent of members for church projects even when those projects reflect the interests of the organization, not the people (chapter 3). At the cultural center the umbrella of the gospel is ever present in both positive and negative ways. In the remainder of this chapter I explore how the gospel is mobilized in the self-interest of workers, which I contrast with how the church uses the gospel as a mechanism to ensure, to repeat the words of Damuni, "love, faithful dedication, and sacrifice."

As I noted in chapter 3, within the internal logic of the religious-corporate structure of the LDS church the division between the spiritual (the gospel) and the profane (work) had already been trespassed before the Polynesian Cultural Center was built. It was no surprise then that a religious component would be integral to the development and operations of the center. As stated above, from the beginning the center was to serve as a missionary tool for the church. Concessions were made early on such that no active proselytizing would take place at the facility; however, upon inquiring, as well as through the town tram tour, visitors could learn more about the church. Terry Webb argues that while not explicit, Mormon theology is reflected in every aspect of tourists' experiences at the center. From the organization and layout of the facility to the demonstrations at each village to the dress code for performers, the beliefs of the church surround tourists as they travel through this space. Whereas for tourists the religious codes can be effectively masked by the veneer of cultural tourism, these religious codes are made explicit for the workers. They take the form of group prayer performed by workers at the beginning of the day to the spontaneous sharing of one's testimony of the truthfulness of the gospel. The codes are reinforced in the lessons students receive in religious classes at Church College of Hawai'i as well as in the stories shared among workers about how the center was a realization of divine prophecy. Although the center was intended to be a missionary tool for tourists, it also served to bring nonmember workers into the church as well as strengthen the beliefs of inactive members.[55]

During his interview, Damuni shared his conversion story. He admits that his primary motivation for coming to the Polynesian Cultural Center had to do with perpetuating Fijian culture by teaching future generations. Although he was resistant to the lifestyle constraints placed on workers by church leaders and managers at the center, he eventually followed his wife and children and joined the church. Initially reluctant to hear the formal lessons offered by the missionaries, Damuni's exposure to the teachings of the church came from his family and from work. As he recalls, "I don't know what made me change, but my children attended Primary and Sunday school and they learned the Gospel before me. I learned it in the Village with the people that I worked with."[56] It was not uncommon for workers who were not members of the church to convert after working there. Damuni's story draws a subtle but important distinction between spirituality (that which is sacred and private) and religion (the institutional structure of the church). When he talked about his feelings for the center before joining the church he describes it as a place that was created "not only to entertain tourists coming into our place, but it was also built for special things."[57] He saw it as a place where the sacred work of perpetuating Fijian culture could take place. Although his perspective of the center as a special place did not change after his conversion, the rhetoric he used to expand on what is expected takes on a religious tinge. Recall, for example, how he acknowledges the Heavenly Father for having had the opportunity to work at the center. In this example we can see the ideology of faithfulness at work for the individual and for the institution: we can read Damuni's conversion story as simultaneously an extension of an ideology of the sacredness of cultural transmission as well as indoctrination that produces a worker who should be faithful, loyal, dedicated, and self-sacrificing.

Cy Bridges, an ecclesiastical leader and a Hawaiian cultural expert, came to the Polynesian Cultural Center already speaking Hawaiian and knowing how to dance hula and play music. An ideology of faithfulness allowed him to reconnect with the church. In reference to a public talk he gave at Brigham Young University–Hawai'i just a few years before my interview with him, he had this to say: "I came here as a young inactive kid and I am standing here talking to you as a father, a manager, and a bishop. I said, when I came here I never dreamt that my goodness, that I would, not even close, but . . . here I am."[58] Working at the cultural center from the mid-1960s to the present has provided Bridges with numerous opportunities to pursue his interests in Hawaiian arts and culture. But for him, whether or not he worked at the center he would still be doing these things.

The center has made it financially possible for him to work and pursue his love for Hawaiian culture. In contrast, he acknowledges that without his many years of involvement with the center he would not be both a cultural leader and a religious leader in his community. When he stood before the auditorium of students at Brigham Young University–Hawai'i he not only declared how far he had come as an employee of the center, he also made a declaration of gender. He stood before them as a man, one defined by the middle-class American ideals at the core of Mormon culture. Masculinity, in this case, is defined by fatherhood, a middle-class economic position, and religious volunteerism. In addition to the spiritual opportunities as well as the economic ones provided to Bridges by the center, it was also a way for him to achieve the ideal of Mormon masculinity. I contend that this ideal of Mormon masculinity is, perhaps, tweaked at the center. I believe that it is possible to read this declaration as a statement of Bridges's Native Hawaiian masculinity; his ability to serve the Lord is, possibly, a way for him to nourish his family spiritually, culturally, and materially. Whether achieving an ideal of Mormon masculinity or filling a void of Native Hawaiian masculinity, Bridges's role as a cultural and spiritual leader in his community supplants the ornamental or objectified Native masculinity put on display at the center.[59] Through Bridges's service to the church combined with his service to the community, he becomes more than a cog in the tourism machine.

Many Polynesian workers felt a strong spiritual connection to the Polynesian Cultural Center because of the cultural knowledge that was passed on to them. As Webb, Damuni, and Bridges emphasize, a strong religious undercurrent enabled some workers to expand their status and position in the church and the community. The influence of the church is quite explicit for workers, and an ideology of faithfulness simultaneously explains the love workers have for the center while also obscuring the power dynamics that structure the labor process at the center. One seemingly contradictory aspect of the center is that a religious institution owns and operates it. To be sure, the center is neither the first nor the only strategic engagement that the church has had with tourists. The visitor's centers at each of the LDS temples around the world as well as Historic Temple Square in Salt Lake City all have the tourist in mind in their design.

As I described in previous chapters, it is common practice for ecclesiastical leaders to also be prominent businessmen in the community. This dual role as religious and business leaders contributes to the blurred boundary between work and religion while simultaneously obscuring power hierarchies. The presidents Edward L. Clissold and Wendell B. Mendenhall's dual position as both religious leaders and business leaders is one example of how complicated and blurry the boundaries between the sacred and profane are at the Polynesian Cultural Center. When they began working on the project, Clissold was the president of Zion's Security Corporations (the financial arm of the church) as well as stake president of the church on Oʻahu, thus making him one of the most important ecclesiastical leaders in the islands. Mendenhall began working for the church in 1955 when he was called to serve as chairman of the Church Building Committee. His job was, according to Craig Ferre, to "organize and administer a labor missionary program to help build the [Church College of Hawaiʻi]," and later the Polynesian Cultural Center as well as other building projects throughout Polynesia. In addition, both were board members of the Pacific Board of Education, "a committee established by the church to supervise its schools in the Pacific, including the Church College of Hawaiʻi." [60] Their positions in the church allowed them to travel throughout the Pacific, and in so doing to draw from various church contacts to recruit the cultural experts who would eventually build the Polynesian Cultural Center.

Ralph Barney, the director of promotion at the Polynesian Cultural Center from 1964 to 1969 and a haole member of the faculty at the Church College of Hawaiʻi, describes how management blurred the boundary between what constituted work for the center and what was a calling for the church. He recalls how excited the college faculty and other members of the church living in Hawaiʻi were about the center, and many were eager to get involved. Excitement and energy surrounded the opening months of the center as many faculty, students, and community members looked forward to being a part of the project. Barney was brought into the project once it became clear to the center's board of directors that attention had to be paid to promotion. As public relations director at Church College of Hawaiʻi, he was an obvious candidate. President Clissold, head of the center's board of directors at the time, approached him and asked him to take a job as head of public relations at the center, which Barney accepted. He kept his full-time job at the college but was released from his ecclesiastic responsibilities at church. In his mind, the cultural center job was "half-church job and a half-some other kind of job."[61] From his interview, it is clear that Barney was expected to see his new position as both a second job and a religious calling. Although he accepted the position as well as the dual job description, he recognized the limitations of it, especially when he began to work with different groups of Polynesians. One tension that stood out for him was between the couples who were brought to the center, as Damuni's family was, to work in the villages and the people already living in the Lāʻie community. Community members were asked to volunteer their labor or accept low pay because in the minds of church leaders half of the job was religious and thus seen as a calling or service to the Lord.

Although Barney was willing to accept the conditions of his employment at the Polynesian Cultural Center, he learned that not all Polynesian workers were willing to take what they were given without complaint. As he related in his interview:

> The Polynesians had some relatively strong feelings in those early years about being treated as second-class citizens in the Cultural Center. Essentially their notion was, "why do they bring some of these people in at high salaries and on expense accounts, etc. when we are expected to give mostly service?" There was that sort of philosophy, I understand, that operated there. Even within the Center some of these people were brought up from Tahiti and other places and given some fairly solid kinds of financial help while others who were already established in Lā'ie were expected to donate their services. I'm not sure to what extent they were donating their services. My experience was they probably didn't get all that much help—that the Center went out and was willing to help people who they brought up especially to work in the Center, but they didn't give that much assistance to people who already lived in Lā'ie.[62]

The conflict between the Polynesian families who were paid to work for the center and those who were expected to work for free only fueled the already existing tensions in the community. Although there was resistance by some Lā'ie community members to work without financial compensation, most of the interviewees maintain that the volunteer labor they did was what made this site quintessentially special. Indeed, many former workers define themselves as being in contrast to a younger generation of workers who focus primarily on the money they can make rather than on the nonmaterial benefits they receive from their volunteer or low-paying job. Given the policy changes that formalized and routinized their jobs, however, it is no surprise they felt this way.

Although one of the unique aspects of the Polynesian Cultural Center is that it bridges the gap between work and religion, one of the clear problems with bringing religion to work is that religion—faith and spirituality—becomes a mechanism by which management is able to increase profits through free or low-cost labor. Damuni's quote that the center is founded upon "love, faithful loyal dedication, and sacrifice" is at the crux of the paradox—on the one hand these values are used to get free labor, and on the other hand they give meaning to the experiences the workers have of their jobs there. This tension is particularly evident when Bridges explains what it has meant for him to work at the center all of these years. He credits the volunteer labor by missionaries and the willingness of workers to go above the call of duty as the defining feature of what makes the center such a special place.

> For all of us, we were idiots. Basically . . . we wanted to hang out together. We loved the Center. You know. They went out, for the likes of those others who were older than us . . . would go out on the road and wave to the people to come in. 'Cause, you know people wouldn't stop by and they did it just for the love of the Center. I mean love built this place. You know, labor missionaries. To have people outside of the church to think that people [would] give up all of their time to spend the whole day here working to build this place, they can't figure it out. But um, that's what happened. So love built the Cultural Center.[63]

This story about workers going out to the street to flag down tourists who were making the circle island tour of O'ahu was told by many former workers. Whether they were one of the actual workers who, dressed in costume, went to the roadside to entice tourists into the center, or whether they had

The "royal Hawaiian court" poses in front of the Hawai'i village in the late 1960s. Uncle Cy Bridges is the ali'i, and my father, Ned Aikau, plays the ukulele. Photograph courtesy of Brigham Young University–Hawai'i Archives.

only heard the stories, the tale is told with a sense of pride and ownership. As Bridges states, this act of going beyond the call of duty is seen as an act of love for the center and for the church.

Jay Akoi, a Native Hawaiian who started working at the Polynesian Cultural Center in 1969 and continues to work there as a manager in purchasing, blurs the boundaries of what constitutes work at the center.

> Back then it was actually, for us, it was just heaven. It was fun. It was not work. I shouldn't say, it was work. We didn't treat it as work. Whereas people now are on the time clock, five o'clock they're out. You would find us coming in early; working on songs that had nothing to do with our work . . . this is your part, this is your part. We would learn new things. Learning our songs was just fun. We should be going home to our wives, we did not. We stay and jam. The groups would be going on, the Sāmoan section going on, New Zealand section. We'd still be back there [back stage of the theater] . . . we treated it as not so much as a job as being fun, learning our music.[64]

Once again the tension between the Polynesian Cultural Center as a work place and Akoi's experience of it as so much more is exemplified in the first lines of this quote. He knows he should call his job "work" but there were so many different ways that it was not just a job that he stammers to find the words to express how it can be both.

Sione Feinga's reflections on his experiences as a labor missionary provide useful insight into how labor and faith intersect. His attention to the voluntary labor he provided necessarily obscures the way that the church was able to keep the overhead of the project low by relying on unpaid immigrant labor, a theme I examined in detail in chapter 3. That labor missionaries and community members worked at the Polynesian Cultural Center without pay is held as a testament to their faithfulness to the gospel of the church.

> [Labor missionaries and Lāʻie community people] came and spent their days there without any pay. Families, husbands and wives, and I think that is the key to the success of that program. I feel that's the main key to the success of the whole thing . . . the fact that everybody didn't have money on their minds. It was a call and everybody worked with that goal in mind. Each missionary was called for a certain amount of time and he would be finished someday. So if it had been a hiring thing, I don't think it would have been very successful.

People would be worried about money and stuff like that. But because it was a calling it worked.[65]

As these examples illustrate, an ideology of faithfulness was used to direct attention away from the problems of using cheap or volunteer labor to establish a tourist facility. However, Barney and Bridges both make clear that dissent for the project came primarily from a younger generation of Polynesians, many of whom had grown up in Lāʻie, had gone away to college, and then returned with new ideas that clashed with the way things had been done in the past. For Bridges, Damuni, and others, there is a level of disappointment when young people see working at the center as merely a job. This disappointment was evident during my interview with Bridges when he talked about the different attitude that kids have today. In a somber tone, he explains as follows:

> A lot of times the kids that come here to the show they want to know what they can get out of this. You call them in for something; they want to know how much I going to get. And if there are double shows we just bring them ice cream, . . . either ice cream or something to eat. If you don't have it, they want to know how come we don't have this. Eh, we didn't even have that. They gripe about not having soap dispensers in the restroom. I said you lucky dogs. When I danced in the show, we never even had restrooms. We didn't even have showers. We try to provide everything for you guys. We had no lockers. Give me a break you bunch of spoiled brats.[66]

Despite the best efforts of Bridges, Akoi, and Damuni, the next generation appears not to share their feelings for the center.

To be sure, there were young people who did not believe the Polynesian Cultural Center could fully transcend the religion-work interface. In chapter 3 I explored in detail the conflict Charles Barenaba and others had with the center and how their criticism was framed as a generational issue that marked young people's lack of faith. Barenaba admits he was one of the young people who had returned to Lāʻie with new ideas, questioning the way things had been done in the past: "[The young people] were just coming out of college and struggling to survive in life, lukewarm in their activities in the Church and all of that, feeling their way around, trying to put their lives together."[67]

Despite the labor issues that arise when workers use faith and spirituality to garner consent, the spiritual benefits continue to mask important labor issues. Just as the Lord is given credit for the establishment and success of the center, its future success is also attributed to Him. As Feinga states, "I think the Lord will take care of us as long as we do our part. And even the school and other organizations, if we do our part, I think the Lord will help us prosper and stay alive."[68] "Our part" is for the larger Lāʻie community as well as center workers to pay as much attention to their ecclesiastical responsibilities as they do to their cultural and educational work at the center and the college.

THE PROPHET AT THE POLYNESIAN CULTURAL CENTER

As these examples illustrate, at the Polynesian Cultural Center the lines between work and religion, tourism, and spirituality cannot be clearly delineated. This was amplified for me during a visit to the center. On October 24, 2003, I attended the center's fortieth anniversary with my parents, my youngest sister, and my partner. After we parked our car, we headed to the ticket counter to pick up our tickets for the village tour, the Aliʻi Lūʻau, and the special Alumni Night Show. My dad worked at the Polynesian Cultural Center from 1963 when it was opened until 1973 when our family moved to Utah. He loved working there and had wonderful stories about how it was more than just a job for him and for his friends. Upon first glance, the center looked as it always had, with the young men and women greeters in their matching aloha attire serving as sentinels at the entrance ready to assist the latest batch of tourists. But on this particular Friday, the center was closed to the general public; everyone there was either a former worker or volunteer laborer or friend or family of a former (paid or unpaid) employee of the center.

My family and I spent the day touring the villages where we enjoyed watching former workers perform spontaneously alongside current workers. At approximately 3:30 in the afternoon, my mom, sister, partner, and I left the villages and walked back toward the main entrance plaza to meet my father who, hours later, was still "talking story" with old friends. As we neared the plaza we noticed that people were lining up along the sides of the path. Among them was my cousin, who waved us over. We asked her what was going on, and she replied that there was a rumor spreading that President Gordon B. Hinckley (1995–2008) was in route to the center and was due to arrive at any moment. Reflecting back on the directions my research had taken me, I had no way to anticipate that on one of my trips to the Polynesian

Cultural Center I would be in the presence of the prophet. But there I was, jockeying for a good position along the path that leads from the main entrance to the village gate. News spread that the prophet would indeed arrive at any moment, but he would not stop. Instead, he would proceed directly to the Aliʻi Lūʻau where he would address the congregation. The anticipation of his pending arrival was growing with every second that ticked by. A low murmur spread through the crowd that confirmed the prophet's arrival, which was followed by silence as we all waited with bated breath to witness this momentous event—the prophet was at the Polynesian Cultural Center. With held breaths and cameras ready we waited in anticipation for his chauffeured golf cart to arrive. When it did arrive it was truly inspirational; we let out our collective breath and spontaneously began singing "We Thank Thee Oh God for the Prophet."

The scene of the prophet being chauffeured on a golf cart through the Polynesian Cultural Center punctuates the role that religion as a system of beliefs and as an institution plays in identity formation at the center and in the histories of conquest and settlement in Hawaiʻi and elsewhere in Oceania. On this Friday afternoon, there was no mistaking the spiritual and religious dimensions of the center. And although this experience was a unique one for me, similar scenes have played out in different times and in different places. In my research I came across many interviews where people shared the spiritually uplifting experience of being in the presence of a prophet. Indeed, the oral histories of old Lāʻie abound with visits by former prophets. Josephine Moeai was born in Kaluanui, just five miles outside of Lāʻie, but was raised in Lāʻie. As she remembers, "Many great men from Salt Lake City passed through here. My father as a young boy stood at the flag raising ceremony where President of the Church David O. McKay attended and he [her father] remembered it mentioned of a large institute of learning being established here in Lāʻie."[69]

I had ambivalent feelings about seeing the prophet at the center. On the one hand, I was excited to see this important leader. President Hinckley had been a visible figure in the church long before being called as the prophet. On the other hand, I was also curious about the meaning of his visit to the center on this day, the fortieth anniversary of its dedication. What did it mean to have the prophet of the church make an appearance at the anniversary celebration of this tourist facility? I think my ambivalence was, in part, connected to what I know now about the role religion plays at the Polynesian Cultural Center, in the larger Lāʻie community, and in the history of the church in Hawai'i. As I have demonstrated throughout this book, Lā'ie is a sacred place where people believe that great and miraculous things are destined to happen. But it seems that at the dawn of a new century old Lā'ie was being replaced by a new Lā'ie dominated by capitalism and individualism. The spiritual roots of the place seemed to be replaced by the secular world of tourism and commercialism. Cy Bridges and other cultural center workers longed for the old days when cultural performance and spirituality found a way to coexist.

Perhaps the prophet's visit to the center signaled an attempt to remind all of us of its religious foundation. Maybe the prophet was paraded through the center in order to reinforce the view that an ideology of faithfulness is an extension of one's faithfulness to the church. In this chapter I have been attentive to the ways in which faithfulness to church-run organizations is seen and experienced as faithfulness to the church. It is significant that at the center faithfulness to it intersects with faithfulness to the gospel under the auspices of the spirit of aloha. Von D. Orgill, president of the center, stated that he was committed to restoring the spirit of aloha to the institution. In his statement in the fortieth anniversary special edition of the center's newsletter, *Imua Polynesia*, Orgill writes: "May each of you and all of our guests constantly find themselves energized by the opportunity to interact with our young students, who are absolutely filled with a love for life, with boundless energy and unfailing optimism for the future. Such is the true spirit of aloha, which is the spirit of God. This spirit lives in the lives of these young people and everyone associated with the Polynesian Cultural Center."[70] Orgill explicitly makes the connection between tourists, young student workers, the spirit of aloha, and the spirit of God. He effectively brings all of these disparate forces into the same frame, a frame that is very familiar to those who would be reading his words at the reunion.

CONCLUSION

Within the context of industrialized society, spirituality is typically divorced from the work experience. At the Polynesian Cultural Center the workers, managers, and founders attempt to transcend the divide between work and religion, profane and sacred. The belief is that the center is the physical manifestation of prophecy, and the testimonies of the religious benefits that are gained by former workers demonstrate how faith and faithfulness are very much a part of the workers' experiences at the center. In this way work at the center is, presumably, less alienating because it reinforces a religious identity. I complicate this framework by demonstrating how an ideology of faithfulness is used to garner the consent of the community members to freely give their labor to this capitalistic project.

When I began this project I felt a certain amount of confusion when I read and heard people's descriptions of their time as employees at the Polynesian Cultural Center as being more than just a job. Through my research I came to see how the center was more than just a cultural tourist attraction that sells race. It also, intentionally or not, provided some Polynesian workers with access to cultural capital and religious advantage that they were able to use later in their lives. Despite their enthusiasm over these added benefits of working at the center, I always found myself stopping short of complete acceptance of this perspective because of the issue of the material consequences of the tourism industry in Hawai'i. The industry relies overwhelmingly on compliant locals to sell race to tourists, and in return these mid- and low-level workers are paid a salary that is not commensurate to the actual costs of living in Hawai'i. An ideology of faithfulness has been a useful tool for clarifying how workers might make sense of this contradictory situation. At the center this ideology has been used as a mechanism of power, but it has also been used by subalterns toward their own material ends. When they speak of faith they are expressing their own sense of spiritual faith; pride in their heritage, a way of life that is cooperative and not capitalistic; and old as well as new forms of trans-Pacific social cohesion. At the Polynesian Cultural Center faith is malleable. Faith is also used as a mechanism of control that obscures the structures of inequality and the capitalistic motivations of the church. As I have demonstrated, workers have engaged in a process of redefining what it means to sell race to tourists. Perhaps in addition to selling race to tourists, workers are also sold a bill of goods that through an ideology of faithfulness can be a gift or a curse. At the end of the day, however, something sacred has taken root there and continues to grow. Tourists and researchers may not be able to see it, but perhaps it is not for us to see. After all, certain knowledge within a Hawaiian worldview is not open and free to everyone; instead, one must demonstrate kuleana before being granted access to it.

5

Voyages of Faith: Contemporary Kanaka Maoli Struggles for Sustainable Self-Determination

IN THE PREVIOUS CHAPTER I DOCUMENTED THE TENSIONS THAT AROSE between members of the Polynesian Cultural Center management who approached culture as a material object for tourism and the Polynesian student workers who got more out of their jobs than just a paycheck. For some, working at the center provided them with a genuine opportunity to learn and develop an appreciation for their customs and practices while it also reinforced and strengthened their religious faith. In this chapter I return to the intersection of religious faith and cultural perpetuation by looking at the construction of a wa'a kaulua (double-hulled canoe) called the *Iosepa*. The wa'a kaulua 'o *Iosepa* is just one component of a vision put forth at Brigham Young University–Hawai'i by the Jonathan Nāpela Center for Hawaiian Language and Cultural Studies (home of the Hawaiian Studies program) to reestablish the familial relationship between Kanaka and the 'āina.[1] At the university Uncle Bill Wallace was the visionary leader who saw an alternative future for the Lā'ie community as well as for those people beyond the community who would be touched by the projects he initiated. I attended his funeral in spring 2009, and although it was a time of loss it was also a time of reflection on what is possible when there is mana (authority, power) and foresight. Uncle Bill left us with a strong foundation, a kahua, upon which we can continue to grow. This chapter is dedicated to Uncle Bill and the work he began, which will be pushed forward by those whose lives he touched and transformed.

The cultural restoration and regeneration projects initiated by Uncle Bill and carried forward at Brigham Young University–Hawai'i, in contrast to those perpetuated and performed at the Polynesian Cultural Center, form the basis upon which sustainable self-determination can be achieved.[2] In this chapter I peel back the layers of meaning, stories, and hopes embedded in the name Iosepa in order to reveal how the historical and spiritual relationships of Mormonism and Native Hawaiian self-determination have been imagined and how in turn they might be knotted and secured together. Additionally, the Hawaiian Studies program and the waʻa kaulua ʻo *Iosepa* provide students, community members, and others willing to learn and work with access to cultural and spiritual practices that in turn hold the potential to, according to the program's mission, "teach, nurture, and enhance the values of the Church of Jesus Christ of Latter-day Saints."[3]

Indigenous scholars disagree about the extent to which Christianity can be a part of cultural reclamation projects, given the role that missionaries and various religious ideologies have played in the colonization and racialization of indigenous peoples.[4] And as I have documented, the LDS church has been complicit in the colonization of Native Hawaiians while at times also providing a necessary refuge for its members. The events surrounding the construction and launching of the waʻa kaulua ʻo *Iosepa* offer a glimpse of how Mormonism and Hawaiian struggles for self-determination might coexist. The launch ceremony of the canoe appeared to successfully join two distinct ritual practices, with each remaining separate yet knotted together to produce a deeply spiritual experience. The religious foundation of the *Iosepa* makes it unique in the voyaging community. Keakaokalani Moʻikeha, a crew member of the *Makaliʻi* voyaging canoe built by the Kawaihae community on Hawaiʻi island, has worked on other community-based canoe projects, and at the time of his interview for the Native American Higher Education Initiative he was training students to crew for the *Iosepa*. As Moʻikeha notes, "It's very different. This community is very different. That's what makes it special, too. It has a lot of religious take on it, and a different type of religion, a different type, more Western. Not saying that it's not Hawaiian, but it's a little different in the sense of the spirituality of it but not—it's hard to explain."[5] Moʻikeha's inability to pin down the complex relationship between the religious foundation of the *Iosepa* and the spiritual qualities that are at once Western and Hawaiian is indicative of how complicated it is to understand how Hawaiianness and Mormonism come together in the waʻa project. How are Hawaiianness and Mormonism articulated and understood by the people affiliated with the project?

Despite the potential that the *Iosepa* project has to bring about substantive change in the Lāʻie community, there are still challenges ahead. I conclude this chapter with a brief discussion of the potential challenges associated with the construction of a hālau kālai waʻa (school for canoe instruction and training) at the Polynesian Cultural Center as a way to talk about the continued fight to prevent Polynesian cultural practices from being absorbed by tourism. In chapter 4, I described how the perpetuation of performative cultural practices served to depoliticize and decontextualize them, and how culture served as an aesthetic object that could be packaged and sold to tourists but could not sustain the community in substantive ways. As I describe below, Mormon tropes, values, emotions, and beliefs pervade many of the cultural practices of building and launching the *Iosepa*, a distinctive Hawaiian artifact. However, I contend that global tourism rather than Christian proselytizing appears to be the more immediate threat to our hopes for a future founded on sustainable self-determination.

Ceremony and Ritual: The *Iosepa* Is Born

On November 3, 2001, the waʻa kaulua ʻo *Iosepa* was born as thousands of hands pushed the fifty-seven-foot vessel across the sand and into the waters of Lāʻie Bay.[6] I attended the ceremony with my parents, who were part of a contingent from Utah representing the Board of Directors of the Iosepa Association. The festivities began in the morning with ceremonial gift giving in the Pacific tradition followed by speeches and prayers in the Mormon tradition. My father embodied this syncretic joining of Hawaiian and Mormon ritual practice: he was dressed in a white button-down shirt and dark dress slacks reflecting appropriate attire for religious occasions. Draped across his body, however, was a purple kīhei gathered and tied on his right shoulder. In contemporary Hawaiʻi, the kīhei, a rectangular piece of fabric draped across the body and tied at the shoulder, is worn to signal respect for and acknowledgment of Hawaiian protocol and ritual practice. When it was time for the Iosepa Association representatives to make their presentation, Uncle Cy Bridges introduced them with an oli (chant), then, speaking in Hawaiian, he asked permission for the group to approach.

Uncle Bill Wallace replied in Hawaiian welcoming them to the celebration and granting the group permission to approach the dignitaries. With the formal protocol completed, my father and the other representatives from Utah moved forward and presented their hoʻokupu (tributes) to the master carvers Sione Tuione Pulotu, a Tongan who immigrated to Lāʻie in the 1960s as a labor missionary, and Kāwika Eskaran, a Native Hawaiian who

Uncle Cy Bridges and my dad pose for a picture after their presentation at the ceremony celebrating the launching of the waʻa kaulua ʻo *Iosepa*. Photograph by Diana Merrick.

had worked as a master carver at the Polynesian Cultural Center, both of whom were responsible for bringing the waʻa to life. These same protocols were repeated as groups or individuals paid their respects by offering food, hula, mele, and lei. Once the hoʻokupu were given and received the program turned to speeches by representatives from the W. K. Kellogg Foundation, which provided the financial support for the project, and by former Brigham Young University–Hawaiʻi president Eric B. Shumway. The speech section culminated with a speech and dedication by Elder M. Russell Ballard of the Quorum of the Twelve Apostles of the Church of Jesus Christ of Latter-day Saints, who was also a great-grandson of the canoe's namesake Joseph F. Smith.

With the dedication completed the master carvers and crew took their places on the *Iosepa*. Everyone present was invited to join together to help carry the waʻa into the ocean. Surrounded by a sea of people, the *Iosepa* stood majestic over the crowd. The energy was electric as everyone pushed and pulled together as one. Slowly, inch by inch, the waves began to caress the hulls, and then all at once a large wave came just as the crowd pushed and the *Iosepa* left land and found the ocean. In that moment when the

Representatives from the Executive Board of the Iosepa Association from Utah thank Uncle Bill (second from right) after the completion of the protocols. Photograph by Diana Merrick.

A sea of people, working toward a single objective, completed the wa'a's journey to the sea. Photograph by Diana Merrick.

wa'a entered the kai, the voices of those present cried out in a chorus of pure joy. Many followed the *Iosepa* into the sea, including my mother. As she made her way back to shore she looked renewed by the spirit of the moment. Throughout the ceremony, I remember feeling an intimate connection with the people around me, many of whom were complete strangers. At that moment we embraced and shed tears of joy. Free from the tether of land, the crew sailed the *Iosepa* a few hundred yards off shore where it dropped anchor. The festivities ended with a lū'au, where those gathered shared food and fellowship. As the sun began to set, my family and I took one last look at the *Iosepa* before getting in our car and heading back to town.

Three months before the launching of the *Iosepa* I had an opportunity to sit down with Uncle Bill Wallace to talk about how his life experiences informed the work he had done at Brigham Young University–Hawai'i. Our interview was scheduled on the same day as the Hawaiian Studies program was preparing to host a lū'au for the Lā'ie Community Association. The interview started in his office, but we finished our discussion at the end of the day at the hale wa'a (canoe house) where the canoe was still under construction. At the time of our conversation, Uncle Bill recognized that the members of the Hawaiian Studies community at Brigham Young University–Hawai'i was just beginning their journey. But he articulated this journey as following a path laid out by his kūpuna. His reference to kūpuna was quite literal, as his maternal grandparents had a strong influence on his life and the choices and decisions he has made as an adult. Additionally, his grandfather played a direct role in guiding him during the process of building the wa'a kaulua. At the launching ceremony in November, he had this to say to those gathered, "In a dream, I was inspired by my grandfather to name the canoe *Iosepa*."[7]

Within a Hawaiian worldview names (inoa) are considered one's personal property; indeed, as Mary Kawena Pukui notes, they are "a kind of force in its own right." She notes further that, "once spoken, an *inoa* [takes] on an existence, invisible, intangible, but real."[8] The name *Iosepa* can be described as an inoa ho'omana'o, which is defined by Pukui as "a commemorative name given to honor a person or record an event."[9] In this context, the name is a mnemonic device that when uttered brings forth the memory of past events. When the inoa ho'omana'o is spoken, the memory of past events are brought into the present and made alive again. But names are also genealogies that demonstrate how different events, the past and the present, are all connected. In the era before Hawaiian was transcribed into a written

Hawaiian concept of names.

language, inoa hoʻomanaʻo and genealogies were the "verbal shorthand" that preserved stories, histories, and events for future generations.

The literal translation of Iosepa is Joseph. Although the waʻa was named for the former president and prophet Joseph F. Smith whose presence and vision greatly influenced the place and community of Lāʻie, it also references Joseph Smith Jr., the founder of the Mormon church. When we peel back another layer of meaning we learn about the story of the nineteenth-century Hawaiians who migrated to Utah where they built a thriving community in the desert called Iosepa, but then were forced to return to Lāʻie. For Uncle Bill, the history of the Iosepa community in Utah was literally a part of his genealogy. His grandparents grew up and later married in Iosepa, Utah, and they brought those experiences with them when they returned to Lāʻie. The place Iosepa is also signified by the street name where these families put down new roots and raised their families. Peel back another layer of meaning and the name is also a referent for a contemporary Hawaiian Mormon diaspora. When we utter the name Iosepa, we call to mind those Polynesian Latter-day Saints who, since the 1970s, have gathered each year at Iosepa, Utah, to commemorate the past while also practicing a contemporary articulation of a Polynesian Mormon identity within a disasporic community setting.[10] The very act of reclaiming a larger Polynesian legacy of open-ocean voyaging signals another layer of meaning that can be traced back to the peopling of the islands themselves. Through the name Iosepa, we are able to tack back and forth through time and space to trace a long legacy of voyaging and settlement and voyaging again.

The meanings evoked in the name Iosepa, and indeed in the tradition of star navigation and open-ocean voyaging, offer an important challenge to binaries between the rootedness of home and the routes that people follow away from the homeland.[11] Vicente Diaz uses the Carolinian voyaging concepts and techniques of *etak* and *pookof* to theorize an indigenous notion of space-time that challenges these binary conventions. The technology of etak describes the experience and epistemology of voyaging whereby the canoe appears to stand still while the stars and islands circle around it. The technology of pookof, Diaz notes, "is the inventory of creatures indigenous to a given island, as well as their travel habits and behavior." It was during Diaz's training in the art of Carolinian navigation, he recalls, that he "first learned about ikelap, the big fish. Pookof is part of a larger system of land finding by way of expanding an island, which can also be contracted if necessary. When you see a given species of bird or fish, and you know who belongs where and most especially, their travel habits—the pookof of an island—you also then know into whose island home you have sailed. Thus are islands known by dint of the furthest travels of their indigenous creatures."[12] Within this framework, the boundaries of an island are not defined by land but are reckoned according to the "indigenous creatures" associated with the place. The notion of pookof forces us to shift the relationship between indigeneity and diaspora from one of binary oppositions to that of thinking about the diaspora as an extension of the indigenous homeland.

Just as the *Hōkūleʻa*, the first waʻa kaulua built in contemporary Hawaiʻi, did in the 1970s, the *Iosepa* reminds us of the traveling habits of Polynesians, where we voyaged, settled, built relationships, and established and put down new roots. Whereas the *Hōkūleʻa* recalls moʻolelo (stories, histories, and epic tales) of Polynesian migrations from the western edges of the Pacific Rim to the eastern edges of the South American continent and north to the remote islands of Hawaiʻi, the *Iosepa* recalls moʻolelo of Hawaiian Mormons in Utah, a history that is also linked to other nineteenth-century Hawaiian migrations to the North American continent.[13] As Diaz and J. Kēhaulani Kauanui clarify in their introduction to the field of Native Pacific cultural studies, these kinds of stories of indigenous mobility challenge "the more common view, in popular mainstream academic discourses (both native and nonnative alike), [that regards] displaced Islanders as having forfeited their heritage."[14] In contrast to arguments that emphasize "distance from the island" as a moving away from home, tradition, and culture—moving away from indigeneity—the notion of pookof privileges travel, Diaz and Kauanui argue, as "journeys back and forth, which might be viewed as essential to [the] making of island traditions (or nationalist formation)."[15] One of the important contributions that the *Iosepa* and other voyaging canoes make to contemporary reckonings of indigenous struggles for self-determination is a view of indigeneity that is "understood in terms of native travel and movement" rather than native insularity, fixity, and remoteness.[16] Just as a canoe must be firmly and securely lashed if it is to make it through a long voyage or difficult seas, the knotting together of indigeneity and diaspora provides students with a secure and firm foundation.

The *Iosepa* provides students from Hawaiʻi as well as from the diaspora with an opportunity to connect with a Hawaiian identity that challenges binary thinking that automatically assumes that Hawaiians raised in the diaspora are culturally deficient compared to their island-raised counterparts. To be sure, maintaining cultural practices in the diaspora is difficult, but as I have documented in this book, cultural practices, values, and knowledge struggled to survive in the islands as well. Kanale Sadowski, a former student at Brigham Young University–Hawaiʻi and a crew member of the *Iosepa*, was born and raised in Utah where his mother tried to incorporate Hawaiian values into their lives. During his interview for the Native American Higher Education Initiative, he addresses this contrast quite clearly.

Why do you think it was important for you and others to learn more about the Hawaiian ancestry and culture?

KS: I think it's important because it helps you identify yourself and know who you are, I guess, to give you self-identity. I grew up on the mainland, and I think if you go by census figures, there's probably as many Hawaiians there as there are living here. And you see it for all Polynesians. There's big Tongan communities in New Zealand and Australia. As we're being taken away from the islands, I think it's more important for us to reach out to our identity or we start to lose it, especially in the world today. It's so commercialized and globalized, and it's hard to have an identity. You start to forget who you are and where you came from. Being a part of Hawaiian Studies gave me a better understanding of that and helped me understand the things that my ancestors did and the amazing things they did with what little resources they had. I think it really helped me today because just knowing what they got by on and how they survived and came together to do great things, it gives me hope that we can still do that today and overcome the many problems that face us.

Did you not have previous opportunities to learn about your culture? Did your parents talk to you a lot?

KS: I think I had less opportunities because I was growing up on the mainland, but I always loved coming back here to visit and I loved learning about the culture and just being in the water and going into the mountains, you know, doing a lot of things, fishing, exploring and just being here in Hawaiʻi. But a lot of the traditional cultural practices, like growing certain plants and different kinds of foods and how you gather them, a lot of that's lost today, and the Hawaiian Studies program gives us an opportunity just to continue those things.[17]

When asked the importance of learning about one's culture, Sadowski's answer reflects an understanding of identity that does not fall into a trap where the local is automatically associated with the authentic. Rather, his figuring recognizes the impact that migration, global capital, and tourism have on all Polynesian identity formations. Although he understands the significance of the homeland as a source for knowledge, he is also keenly aware of how traditional cultural practices have been lost and need to be revived.

The *Iosepa*: A Floating Classroom for Pono

The *Iosepa* was one of the many projects that Uncle Bill Wallace envisioned, and with a grant from the W. K. Kellogg Foundation he was able to purchase giant logs from Fiji, have them shipped to Hawai'i, and then transported by truck to Lā'ie. There, the master carver Sione Tuione Pulotu used a chainsaw to make the first cuts that would become the wa'a kaulua 'o *Iosepa*. The wa'a was a key component of the two-pronged curriculum of the Hawaiian Studies program, Mālama 'Āina (caring for the land) and Mālama Kai (caring for the sea). The Mālama 'Āina project, Uncle Bill explained during my interview with him, would include looking "at our different types of variety of taro that we are going to be planting, what are the good types, what do we need to do for taro, banana, sweet potatoes?" He stated further that there was a need to improve the water quality in the streams, and hopefully get "back into the streams a kind of streamlife like 'o'opu the fish, the snails, the urchins, the hīhīwai [a freshwater snail], the freshwater limu, the seaweeds, that used to fill this entire ahupua'a." Under the curriculum for Mālama Kai, he explained, "we are going to have projects . . . canoeing, surfing, canoe racing, and actually reef patrols by measuring the limu [saltwater seaweed] and charting the fish that come into our bay."[18] Both projects were created with the intention of educating students in cultural practices and values while also reinforcing, as noted in the program's mission statement, "gospel-centered principles as the piko or central force that connect all of our programs."[19] For Uncle Bill, teaching students how to be sensitive to the natural world around them and to care for the creatures and life forms of the land and sea is necessary in order to return pono to the land. As he told me, "Right now things are not balanced, they're not pono. And it's out of sync. What we are trying to do is see what we can do to try to balance it off. I think for our Hawaiian Studies program this is what we can try to do. It may take more than my lifetime, several lifetimes to see it happen, but at least we can start the journey."[20] Although Uncle Bill is no longer here to see all of the changes he envisioned, I believe he continues to keep watch over those whom he helped to start on their journeys.

In previous chapters, I describe the process by which Lāʻie came to lose its pono. As Uncle Bill's life experiences illustrate, the construction of the college contributed to this imbalance. "I was also here," he tells me, "when they cleared out this area and started building this campus. One of the things I remember about this place, before it was cleared out, I tell my students about this, this entire area was predominantly taro and watermelon fields." Prior to the construction of the college, the land where it was built was a source of food and a place where cultural knowledge was sustained. When the land was cleared and the stream that fed the loʻi was redirected underground, a new knowledge system and educational practices were introduced. To be sure, since the school was built it has given thousands of Pacific Islanders a four-year college education. But problems arise when indigenous knowledge is not integrated into Western development projects. For example, Uncle Bill tells me that since the church leaders, architects, and contractors responsible for planning for the college did not include the Native Hawaiian knowledge of how water flows through Lāʻie, "two major floods have already hit this community."[21]

As I document in earlier chapters, and share from the painful stories about my dad's college days, Brigham Young University–Hawaiʻi has not always been a place that nurtured let alone reproduced Hawaiian cultural practices and rituals. In fact, looking to public schools as a site for the regeneration of Hawaiian cultural practice and ritual is quite ironic in light of the history of the U.S. occupation of Hawaiʻi. Scholars of the history of schooling in Hawaiʻi have documented how various assimilation projects institutionalized in public schools beginning in 1898 brought about the near annihilation of the Hawaiian language and the suppression of Hawaiian practices and values.[22] In the 1980s, nearly a century later, the walls of this bastion of U.S. imperialism began to erode through initiatives such as Pūnana Leo, a Hawaiian-language immersion preschool program modeled after the language nests in Aotearoa, and Kula Kaiapuni, the Hawaiian-language immersion schools for kindergarten through twelfth grade.[23] Since 1978 Hawaiian has become the second official language of Hawaiʻi, and today most colleges and universities in Hawaiʻi offer classes in Hawaiian language and Hawaiian studies. In addition to the expansion of the Pūnana Leo and Kula Kaiapuni schools, the charter school movement in Hawaiʻi has produced over a dozen Hawaiian-focused charter schools that use Hawaiian values, practices, and rituals as the foundation of their curriculum.[24] The Hawaiian Studies program at Brigham Young University–Hawai'i, through the Mālama 'Āina and Mālama Kai curriculum, is part of this new movement for Hawaiians to take control of their schools by making their own decisions about what is important for haumāna (students) to learn and how it will be taught.[25]

The Hawaiian Studies program, then, is one attempt to try to make Brigham Young University–Hawai'i a more pono part of the larger community. This is done by the program's emphasis on Native Hawaiian protocols, values, and practices, which is intended to provide a cultural foundation that allows students to enhance their religious foundation. The discussion that I had with Uncle Bill about the kapu (verbally encoded rules) placed on the hale wa'a gets at some of the complexities of how religion and spirituality are both separate yet knotted together. Uncle Bill explained that some of the kapu that govern the site include a ban on smoking and alcohol and food consumption in the space reserved for the wa'a. My attention was piqued when Uncle Bill qualified himself by saying that these kapu were not established because Mormonism prohibits the use of alcohol and tobacco by its members but because the kapu reflected Hawaiian ritual practices that define the space as sacred, another meaning of the word kapu. He also tells me that everyone who visits, whether haumāna from Hawaiian-language immersion schools or tourists coming from the Polynesian Cultural Center, must respect the protocols of the space, which include asking permission to enter.

Uncle Bill's need to explicitly mark the site as spiritually significant, especially given the fact that Brigham Young University–Hawai'i is a college owned and operated by the LDS church and where religious instruction is part of the curriculum, is ironic and points to one of the tensions between Western religion and Native spirituality. Western religious traditions draw a clearly delineated line between the sacred and the profane such that religious practice is limited to sacred places such as churches, temples, and religion classes. In contrast, when Uncle Bill explicitly noted that the kapu placed on the hale wa'a are not Mormon, I think he was signaling a Native notion of the intrinsic sacredness of nature.

Within a Hawaiian worldview, the 'āina is sacred because of its familial relationship with the people, because it is a source of food, and because it can also be the kino lau (the physical manifestations) of many deities. Uncle Bill's hope is that by making students sensitive to the world around them they will understand the intrinsic sacredness of nature. Today, it appears that students have started to learn this lesson. Jude Sells, a crew member of the *Iosepa* and a Hawaiian Studies major, explicitly identifies in his interview for the Native American Higher Education Initiative the work he has done with the Mālama ʻĀina and Kai projects as key to finding his cultural roots: "What really kind of gets me in tune with the spirit of being Hawaiian or with my roots is this canoe project and also Kahuaola, our farm area above the campus and the [heiau] up there. I guess the Hawaiian thinking is they really thought a lot about their relationship to the land but also to the sea and these two projects kind of combine that within one program. I get the best of both worlds."[26]

As Sells's reflection illustrates, the Hawaiian Studies mission and curriculum provide a foundation for learning Hawaiian cultural knowledge and practice that is essential for instilling in him an indigenous spirituality. In part this resensitization to the sacred is important not only for restoring pono to Lāʻie and for connecting students to their roots but also for the church. For Vine Deloria Jr. the modern world and modern religions are incapable of providing people with "any valid religious experiences or knowledge whatsoever," in part because churches are institutions with complex bureaucracies where religious leaders are chosen based on their ability to navigate organizational structures and not on their spiritual character or charisma. As he prophesizes, "The religions that depend on the articulation of doctrinal propositions to maintain themselves are doomed to disappear beneath their own silliness. Those religious traditions that depend primarily upon invoking some kind of experience that is qualitatively distinct from everyday feelings will become the vehicles for religious expression in the future."[27] In chapter 3 I documented the ways in which the bureaucratization of the LDS church separated the laity from their leader. However, I also described how the Polynesian Latter-day Saints in Lāʻie found a syncretism between Mormonism and their customs and practices that people describe as enhancing community life. The spiritual connection people feel when they participate in the *Iosepa* is an example of a "qualitatively distinct" experience that stands in stark contrast to the routinization of everyday life. Reclaiming Hawaiian protocol, ritual practice, and spirituality offers one answer to the existentialist need to find meaning in the world. And within the political context of contemporary Hawaiʻi, this desire is also connected to a need to restore pono by returning the knowledge of our ancestors to the community so that the ahupuaʻa can be sustainable once again.

"Sailing in the Wake of the Ancestors"

For crew members of the *Iosepa,* the experience of open-ocean voyaging connects them to their ancestors as they literally follow ancient voyaging routes.[28] Within a Hawaiian thought world, kūpuna are our grandparents, both living and dead, those of our grandparents' generation, or the elders in the community. The term also refers to a broader category of ancestors, namely those people known and not known who came before us. According to Mary Kawena Pukui and Samuel Elbert, the term kupuna (the singular form of the word) also refers to the starting point, or source.[29] For the late Tongan scholar Epeli Hauʻofa, the very future of Oceania is dependent upon its young people understanding the vastness with which kūpuna approached their world. As he so eloquently proclaimed, the peoples of Oceania did not experience the vast sea as a barrier that kept them isolated and landlocked on little islands. Rather, "their universe comprised not only land surfaces, but the surrounding ocean as far as they could traverse and exploit it, the underworld with its fire-controlling and earth-shaking denizens, and the heavens above with their hierarchies of powerful gods and named stars and constellations that people could count on to guide their ways across the seas."[30] The regeneration of a Polynesian seafaring tradition is a journey that returned contemporary Native Hawaiians to the source of that knowledge, our kūpuna, our ancestors. How do notions of kūpuna inform the spiritual significance of voyaging and the meanings ascribed to the *Iosepa?*

Namealoha Curtis, who was born and raised in Utah and became involved with the *Iosepa* after transferring to Brigham Young University–Hawaiʻi from its sister school in Provo, describes the opportunity to sail on the *Iosepa* as marvelous: "It is amazing for me to think about going on long distance voyages, and to be like my ancestors and to be out on the open ocean sailing to other places."[31] For Mikilani Yuen, sailing on the ocean is a spiritual experience because in doing so she reenacts the actions of her ancestors: "These are things that our ancestors, our kūpuna, did in the past, you can feel this spirit as you sail. And it's really a calming and peaceful kind of feeling. It kind of brings balance to everything else going on."[32] Indeed, for Uncle Bill and others associated with the *Iosepa,* kūpuna were ever present throughout the process.

Kūpuna are important in the waʻa project because they are literally a source of knowledge for students. For Jude Sells, kūpuna have words of wisdom that can guide us through our lives: "I think one of our kupunas said it best when she said we can't know where we're going unless we know where we've been. And how we tie that in is we can't push on forward if we don't know what's already been done in the past. It brings us closer because we have our relationship with the canoe, which is a spiritual relationship. It's not our people [turned into] wood or some kind of crap; it's a living entity. It's something which we believe has a spirit, you know, that needs, I guess, reciprocity from us and also we need reciprocity from it."[33]

For Lono Logan who was born and raised in Lāʻie and whose grandfather was a well-known fisherman and community leader, the canoe project afforded him an opportunity to learn about himself by working with kūpuna: "So when I heard that the canoe was going to be built in our community I thought it was going to be awesome because there will be opportunities for us to learn about ourselves, about our extended families and our ancestors. It's just that kind of combination of working with our elders, the present, and then you see the little children coming up. And so that's the first thing and it sounds long but that's what I thought."[34] In addition to sharing a common feeling of appreciation for being able to learn from elders in the community, the impressions of these students also reflect a Hawaiian orientation to time that is reminiscent of the Carolinian navigational technology of etak. Diaz describes etak as follows:

First you steer towards the stars that mark the island of your destination. While doing so, you also back sight your island of departure until you can no longer see it. At the same time, you also calculate the rate at which a third island, off to the side, moves from beneath the stars where it sat when you left your island of departure, toward the stars under which it should sit if you were standing in the island of your destination. Let me simplify: you get on your canoe and you follow the stars in the direction where lies your destination island. As your island of departure recedes from view, you also pay attention to a third island, as it appears to move along another prescribed star course. Let me make it even simpler. The first modern scholars to seriously study this, and *get it*, described the sensation that the canoe remained stationary while the islands zipped by.[35]

Etak resonates with a Hawaiian reckoning of time-space insofar as moving forward requires us to keep track of where we came from, and at times it feels as though we are standing still while the past and future recede and approach. As Lono so clearly states, within a Hawaiian worldview we cannot move forward if we do not know where we came from. Thus the path ahead in many ways is dictated by how well we know the paths already traveled. For students and community members affiliated with the *Iosepa*, a critical aspect of the path already traveled includes the LDS church and its history in Hawai'i.

The integration of church history into a Hawaiian way of knowing is best illustrated by a kupuna of Lā'ie, Aunty Gladys Pualoa-Ahuna, who in June 2009 described the significance of the *Iosepa* to Kathleen Majdali, a student reporter for Brigham Young University–Hawai'i. For Aunty Gladys, one thing that makes the *Iosepa* important is that it connects the young people today to the ancestors. As the student reporter Majdali writes, "With a quiver in her voice and a tear welling in her eye, Aunty Gladys continued, 'It's so beautiful to see [the *Iosepa*] on the horizon. For me, it represents our kupuna, our ancestors. This wa'a was named after Joseph F. Smith who started the Church on Maui and brought the people to Lā'ie. When I see the boat, I think of George Q. Cannon, Jonathan Nāpela, [William] Uaua, and [K. H.] Kaleohano, who were some of the first members and leaders of the Church in the islands. I think of our ancestors who raised taro and lived on fish from the bay to survive.'"[36]

When I first read this article I was struck by Aunty Gladys's comments not because of her reference to the kūpuna but because of the kūpuna she includes. I was not startled to see Joseph F. Smith recognized in her list because he is the namesake of the canoe, but I was not expecting to see George Q. Cannon listed alongside prominent Hawaiian leaders such as Nāpela, Uaua, and Kaleohano. To be sure, my surprise says more about my personal relationship to my Hawaiian Mormon identity than it does to what Aunty Gladys actually stated. Today, I understand Aunty Gladys's comments as a rearticulation of kūpuna that does not rely on biology or lineage as measures for connectedness.[37] Rather, Cannon along with Nāpela and others made possible the voyages of faith that I document in this book. Cannon's vision provided the much needed rationale for establishing a mission among Kanaka, and Nāpela's faith in the potential of the LDS church to provide a viable alternative to other Christian denominations inspired other Kānaka to join the church.

Lilikalā Kame'eleihiwa, a Native Hawaiian historian and genealogist, explains that mo'okū'auhau (genealogies) "are perceived by Hawaiians as an unbroken chain that links those alive today to the primeval life forces—to the *mana* (spiritual power) that first emerged with the beginning of the world." She goes on to state that "Hawaiian genealogies are the history of the

Hawaiian people," as they teach us about the "exploits and identities of our ancestors—their great deeds, and their follies, their loves and their accomplishments, and their errors and defeats."[38] In this context, moʻokūʻauhau are histories, family lineage, and great epic tales that provide us with a link to the past and the mana of the natural world. Kameʻeleihiwa stresses that even when genealogy is limited to an accounting of one's ancestors, from a Hawaiian standpoint lineage is not limited to biological parentage within a heteronormative nuclear family context. Rather, lineage is inclusive of the vast array of sexual and parental relationships that are reflected in the notion of ʻohana.

The genealogy of the *Iosepa*, in addition to including the LDS missionaries and the first Native Latter-day Saints, can also be figured bilaterally from Polynesian and Micronesian. This dual genealogy has influenced the contemporary movement in explicitly gendered ways, as I will describe below. This genealogy can be traced back to the *Hōkūleʻa* built by the Polynesian Voyaging Society, the first waʻa kaulua built in the contemporary era. The *Hawaiʻiloa,* also built by the society, is part of this legacy as it was built from natural materials (although not indigenous koa logs) and traditional practices, rituals, and techniques (including modern chainsaws). The *Makaliʻi,* a voyaging canoe built by the Kawaihae community on Hawaiʻi island, is also part of the *Iosepa* genealogy as the *Makaliʻi* crew were trained on the *Hōkūleʻa* and *Hawaiʻiloa.* The crews of these vessels were trained by Mau Piailug, a Carolinian navigator from Satawal who restored star navigation to the Hawaiian people. Just as this moʻokūʻauhau illustrates, when we approach the concept of kūpuna as multiple threads that are pulled together to produce one kaula (rope), then questions of authenticity or a quest for a single origin become subordinate to the relationships that bind people, nature, and events together.

For the student crew of the *Iosepa*, the ʻaha (cordage) that knots their faith to their culture is not grounded in a teleological quest for a single origin. Through their work with the *Iosepa* and their religious instruction at Brigham Young University–Hawaiʻi, an ideology of faith rearticulates *The Book of Mormon* with nineteenth-century Polynesian origins to affirm their Hawaiian Mormon identities. Indeed, the restoration of voyaging customs and practices secures this relationship even as it elides its own internal contradictions. In chapter 1, I traced the various debates about Polynesian origins including those that locate the Americas as its source. One of the central objectives for building and then sailing the *Hōkūleʻa* to Tahiti was to disprove those theories.[39] *Hōkūleʻa*'s maiden voyage and every voyage since then has added new evidence that proves that Polynesians possessed the technological skills to navigate on the open ocean, that their double-hulled canoes were seaworthy enough to survive long ocean voyages, and that they used their canoes and navigational skills to purposefully travel widely across the Pacific Ocean. Given the symbolic and scientific importance of voyaging canoes in general, it does appear contradictory that people would still hold to Cannon's vision as truth. Once again, I suspect that people are able to bypass these contradictions because of the fluid nature of the notion of kūpuna and because of faith. Regardless of whether or not the connection between *The Book of Mormon* and Polynesia can be substantiated, the *Iosepa* and all that it signifies for people associated with it agree that it is a catalyst for cultural renewal and change.

"Carry Your Culture on Your Canoe"

Chadd Paishon, executive director of Nā Kālai Waʻa Moku ʻo Hawaiʻi and master navigator for the *Makaliʻi*, offers a vision of the canoe that connects the cultural importance of voyaging to the very future of the Hawaiian people.[40]

> The canoe is an island. All that you do on the canoe—how you interact with each other, care for each other and the responsibility that you take—contribute to the efforts to take care of the resources aboard. . . . What you learn on this floating island helps you understand your role in becoming responsible community members. The lessons and actions are no different when you come back home. It continues for not only you, but your children and your children's children, as well as honors our ancestors.[41]

The waʻa can be a model for rebuilding the lāhui (nation) and the Kanaka. On the canoe everyone must rely on each other for survival, and this interdependence makes each person responsible for taking care of the whole. Although every individual on the canoe has a specific job to do, the success of the voyage depends on each person committing to one shared vision and goal.

At a speech given at the Pacific Education Conference in Honolulu, Hawaiʻi in 2007, thirty-one years after the first voyage of the *Hōkūleʻa*, Nainoa Thompson, the renowned Hawaiian navigator of the *Hōkūleʻa* and a community leader, tells the audience a cautionary tale about the early years of the canoe. He acknowledges that the *Hōkūleʻa* should be remembered and celebrated as a great achievement and a symbol of the rebirth of a Kanaka consciousness. However, Thompson's speech was not a nostalgic celebration of this history but a deeply personal account of the tragedy that surrounded the early voyages. Thompson remembers, and asks the audience to be attentive to, two events that shook him to his core. First, was the circumstances that drove Mau Piailug, a master navigator who captained the *Hōkūleʻa* from Hawaiʻi to Tahiti in 1976, to abandon the project upon arrival in Papeʻete Harbor. The second tragedy took place in 1978 when a few short hours into *Hōkūleʻa*'s second voyage the waʻa capsized during a terrible storm. Eddie Aikau, famed lifeguard, big wave surfer, and my uncle, was lost at sea trying to paddle his surfboard in search of help. Looking back, Thompson attributes these crises to the fact that there was no shared vision and goal in the early years. Ben Finney agrees that the voyage was originally seen as a scientific experiment to prove his theory that Polynesians possessed the knowledge to sail the Pacific; the cultural aspects of the project were important but secondary. The lack of shared vision, Thompson notes, is what drove Piailug to walk away from the canoe in Tahiti and it was a contributing factor to the capsizing of the canoe in 1978.[42] By remembering the tragedy of these historic events Thompson asks us to remember a different aspect of the *Hōkūleʻa*, not the voyage itself but the process of training for the voyage, the commitment to a shared vision of what the waʻa can give to the community and how it can be a catalyst for change. The kind of change Thompson has in mind is not limited to Hawaiʻi but has to include all of the Pacific Islands, and it must also be about sustainability.

Two Hulls, One Nation

The waʻa kaulua can be seen as a contemporary expression of what Jeff Corntassel calls "sustainable self-determination." In his commitment to "move beyond the limitations of the existing rights discourse," Corntassel argues that indigenous peoples must move toward strategies that "meet contemporary challenges to indigenous nationhood." He offers "the concept of sustainable self-determination as a benchmark of restoration of indigenous livelihoods and territories for future indigenous political mobilization."[43] For Corntassel the regeneration of indigenous livelihoods and territories is a necessary precondition for political mobilization. Indeed, I would argue that the restoration of customs and practices related to mālama ʻāina and mālama kai, which are founded upon Kanaka's familial ties to place, are a necessary part of the contemporary Native Hawaiian sovereignty project. But interestingly, in his interview with me, Uncle Bill described the Mālama 'Āina and Kai programs as part of a cultural project to restore Hawaiian language, customs, and practices that is not directly tied to a political agenda of restoring the aupuni (government). Rather, his life's work appears to have been committed to the revitalization of the lāhui, the nation and its people.

Although Uncle Bill's vision for the *Iosepa* was not political, the wa'a kaulua offers a model for restoring the lāhui. The twin hulls of the wa'a kaulua are ideal for open-ocean voyaging because in combination they provide balance and raise the crew high enough above the ocean's surface to survive a long voyage. The duality of the hulls also represents the duality of masculinity and femininity, an indigenous Hawaiian notion of gender complementarity, which produces pono. When gender is approached from the perspective of pono, it is not tethered to any particular biologically sexed body. Rather, all life forces are comprised of masculine and feminine energies that combine to produce pono. In Hawai'i, the contemporary sovereignty struggle is mired in microbattles over which path is pono and who our leaders are or should be. Since the 1970s when Haunani-Kay Trask accused the men of Protect Kaho'olawe of being sexist, gender has been a part of this struggle. Recently, the Kanaka 'Ōiwi scholar Ty Kāwika Tengan made the case in his book *Native Men Remade* that it was time for Kanaka 'Ōiwi men to take their rightful place in the struggle. For some of the men he interviewed, the underlying assumption was that women such as Trask and other prominent women in the sovereignty movement needed to step aside so that men could take their "rightful" place as leaders. As Tengan notes, this articulation of how gender matters runs the risk of reproducing hegemonic, heterosexist, Western notions and practices. Whereas Tengan argues for a notion of Native Hawaiian masculinity that does not require the subordination of Native Hawaiian women, his framework does not actually get us there.

The doubling of the hulls and the way they are gendered can be a metaphor for how to move forward in restoring the lāhui while not reproducing oppressive sexual and gendered structures. Within a Hawaiian seafaring tradition, the left hull is considered wahine (female) and the right hull is kāne (male), mirroring the duality of gender reflected in the kino (body). The *Iosepa*'s twin hulls are also distinguished by gender: "the left hull of the canoe is considered the wahine, given the name, Kekaipahola. The right hull of the canoe is the kāne, named Anianikū."[44] Although it is accepted that each kino incorporates both femininity and masculinity, scholars continue to theorize, analyze, and interpret gender duality within a binary frame.[45] Rather than think about gender in binary ways, I want to think about the doubling of gender—in one body, one vessel, and one cosmogonic sphere. The canoe itself resembles this doubling. The two hulls are mirror images of each other, separated and yet tethered together and interdependent. Between the two hulls is a platform upon which the crew navigates.

Given this pono approach to thinking about gender, we would also expect to see a balanced representation of men and women in all aspects of seafaring. Although today women are represented in all of seafaring's facets, this has not always been the case. For example, women were not allowed to be part of the maiden voyage of the *Hōkūle'a* from Hawai'i to Tahiti in 1976. This decision was made in part because within Mau Piailug's Carolinian tradition, voyaging is men's domain and women's domain is the land.[46] I note this not to judge Carolinian traditions but to signal the problematics of cross-cultural borrowing. The *Iosepa* along with the other wa'a kaulua are potential models and metaphors for restoring gender balance and pono as we rebuild the lāhui and strive for sustainable self-determination. Additionally, the *Iosepa* has the possibility for challenging patriarchy within both Mormon and Hawaiian cultural practices. As Kanaka 'Ōiwi Hawai'i chart our journey forward we must do so on our own terms. My desire is for that journey to be liberating for everyone.

TOURISM AND CULTURAL REGENERATION

On June 28, 2008, the Hālau Wa'a 'o *Iosepa* exhibit at the Polynesian Cultural Center opened for visitors. At the groundbreaking ceremony for the exhibit, Uncle Cy Bridges had this to say: "The canoe takes me back to the days when my kūpuna, my ancestors, first came on waa kaulua [twin-hulled] canoes much like *Iosepa,* that came upon these fair shores and called it home. Almost everything that will be displayed in this place are a great legacy and a monument to our kūpuna and cultural traditions. For us, as island people, culture and tradition are very, very important."[47] Indeed, culture, tradition, and the kūpuna are very important to Hawaiian people. But one must wonder what the implications are of housing the canoe at the Polynesian Cultural Center.

In chapter 4 I documented the stories of former students who described how they considered working at the Polynesian Cultural Center as not only

Because of ocean conditions, the waʻa was not in the Hālau Waʻa ʻo *Iosepa* during the opening ceremony in June 2008. Since it made its way to the Hālau it has not returned to the sea. Photograph by author.

a job but also a site for cultural education, where they were able to learn cultural protocol, practices, and values within a loosely traditional setting. Given the degree to which Hawaiian language and practices were suppressed, it is no surprise that in the 1960s and 1970s a tourist facility such as the Polynesian Cultural Center appeared to be an appropriate site for the reproduction of culture because prior to the cultural renaissance, Hawaiian culture was either "extinct" or a commodity for tourists. The Hālau Waʻa opens up an opportunity to think about whether the Polynesian Cultural Center can or should serve as a site for cultural education today. During my interview with Uncle Bill, he made clear that the Polynesian Cultural Center and the Hawaiians Studies program have very different objectives and roles to play in the perpetuation of culture.

Within the current political climate and in light of the critique of the impact that a tourist economy has had in the islands, it is no surprise that Uncle Bill made the case that the Polynesian Cultural Center is no longer the appropriate site for haumāna to learn their culture. One could argue, moreover, that college isn't that site either. As noted above, one outcome of the Hawaiian cultural renaissance and sovereignty movement has been the strident critique of schooling in Hawai'i. Indeed, schools have become a site for cultural reclamation and renewal. What makes this entire discussion confusing is the decision to build the Hālau Wa'a at the Polynesian Cultural Center as a new exhibit in the Hawaiian village. As one former crew member wrote in his blog, housing the *Iosepa* at the Polynesian Cultural Center limits who can have access to the canoe and shifts the focus from a community-centered project to a tourist-driven one. As Uncle Bill explained, the space that surrounded the wa'a was intentionally made kapu to mark it as sacred, thus requiring Hawaiian cultural protocol and ritual practice. Siting the Hālau at the center shifts the meaning of the space from a Hawaiian cultural register to one determined by money and tourism. The former crew member raises important concerns and identifies a critical tension, noted by Uncle Bill, between the mission of the Polynesian Cultural Center as tourism and that of the Hawaiian Studies program as a service to students and the community.

dialectic — tourist [community] vs. project.

The Polynesian Cultural Center at one time was a site where cultural work could be done, but as I argue in chapter 4 the economic needs of the institution overtook the cultural imperatives of the community. This shift was also articulated by Uncle Bill. He recalled a time when the doors to the Polynesian Cultural Center were open to the community, and kūpuna were a visible part of the center: "The one thing that I really enjoyed at Polynesian Cultural Center in its early years and when I was there was being able to see the number of kūpuna and our elders in the villages. I mean now when you go around to the different villages you don't see too many of the old people there, you see the young students." Although he recognizes the importance of the Polynesian Cultural Center for these young people, he worries that the absence of kūpuna in the villages means cultural knowledge is not taught in a traditional way. He continued by stating, "I think Polynesian Cultural Center has gotten a little commercial in some areas, but again so has some other areas, so it has changed."[48] Uncle Bill emphasized that his critique should not be interpreted as a negative criticism of the center or of the management decisions made there but as a difference between the mission of the center and the mission of the Hawaiian Studies program. To be sure, the center provided him and others from his generation with a cultural opportunity that was not readily available to them in the 1960s and 1970s. But in the wake of the cultural renaissance taking place across the islands in the late 1970s and the political climate in the 1990s, the shift toward a commercial mission rather than a cultural one made the center no longer an appropriate place for the perpetuation of culture. Only time will tell how housing the Hālau Waʻa at Polynesian Cultural Center will impact community access to the *Iosepa*. I do not know whether there is a process for community people to gain access to the waʻa without paying admission to the facility.

The Mālama ʻĀina and Mālama Kai projects at Brigham Young University–Hawaiʻi provide students with an opportunity to be a part of much larger cultural regeneration projects. Today, communities across the pae ʻāina (archipelago) have initiated sustainability projects born out of a need to breathe life back into their families, communities, ahupuaʻa, and moku (districts). Uncle Bill envisioned the canoe and Kahuaola (the loʻi kalo sponsored by the Hawaiian Studies program) as a way to nurture the students who in turn could care for their families, the ʻāina, and the kai. As he stated to me, "We centered our program around nurturing, around taking [students] in, caring for them, caring for their physical well-being but more importantly their naʻau, their spiritual well-being." But his vision was never limited to just the students. "In everybody's way, in everything that they are doing, we are trying to accomplish the same thing. And that same thing is to make sure that our race, our people, our culture, our language never dies. And that's what the bottom line is. It's all coming to that same common purpose. The good of Kanaka Maoli. Yah, Kanaka Maoli Ka Pae ʻĀina nei o Hawaiʻi."[49]

CONCLUSION

This chapter examined the distinctly religious articulations of the *Iosepa* by looking at the meanings the participants bring to the project as well as looking at what they get out of their experiences working on or sailing the waʻa. I situated the Hawaiian Studies program and the *Iosepa* project within a broader context of schools as sites of political struggle and cultural regeneration in Hawaiʻi. And I focused on how these projects fit into the larger contemporary struggle for sustainable self-determination in Hawaiʻi that was ignited by various cultural revitalization projects in the 1970s.

In this chapter, I described how the Hawaiian Studies program and its projects offer a contemporary example of how a Hawaiian Mormon identity is expressed and practiced; namely, how it is expressed in the language used to describe the program as a place where faith and gospel teachings are sustained by Hawaiian history, language, and culture, and practiced through the

Mālama 'Āina and Kai projects. The *Iosepa*, as part of a larger mission of the Hawaiian Studies program at the university, is also an example of a new direction in the indigenous peoples' movement that focuses on indigenous reclamation and regeneration. Once again, this case is unique because of the explicitly religious aspect of it. As I have argued throughout this book, the link between an ethnic identity and a religious one is both strong and constantly being made and remade. At times this link has been strained, but it has also produced opportunities for resistance to colonial and capitalist forces.

Global tourism is a storm that wreaks havoc on our canoe. All members of the crew must work with a single vision and purpose in order to secure the 'aha and kaula that hold the two hulls together. These hulls, when tethered together, will provide balance, flexibility, and a foundation that will carry our culture and lāhui forward. The journey through the storm requires that we steer directly into the waves; if we go around them or approach them from the side then we will capsize. As I describe above, the construction of the Hālau Wa'a at the Polynesian Cultural Center will challenge the Mālama Kai project as its members journey through this storm. I am optimistic that they will see this storm through; however, it is only one leg of a longer journey.

Conclusion:
Holomua, Moving Forward

WHEN I SET OFF ON THE HUAKAʻI THAT BECAME THIS BOOK I WANTED to make sense of how Polynesian members of the Mormon church negotiate what appeared to me to be an irreconcilable tension between a (politicized) ethnic identity and a Christian-American-Mormon affiliation. I began this book with my childhood memories of growing up Hawaiian and Mormon in a small Polynesian community in Utah. The personal stories I share reflect my complex and at times painful relationship to these two identities. That relationship, in turn, became the central aim of this book; namely, to examine how the religious norms, ideologies, and expectations of Mormonism are negotiated by Native Hawaiian Latter-day Saints. Although I continue to have an ambivalent relationship with the church, I learned that many Polynesian Latter-day Saints have creative and inspiring relationships to the church that include opportunities for them to express, embody, and perpetuate cultural practices. I did not know that during the course of my work I would learn that cultural regeneration can happen in unexpected places and with unexpected alliances. My bias going into this project was that the Mormon church was a racist institution that played a role, even if a minor one, in the exploitation and dispossession of Hawaiians. What I found is that the story is not that simple. For example, although the church bene-fited from the privatization of land and continues to profit from the Māhele, Lāʻie has been a spiritual, educational, and cultural puʻuhonua for Hawaiian and other Polynesian Latter-day Saints. This is not to say that the commu-nity did not overcome significant problems and conflicts. In fact, what most interested me was encountering those moments when indigenous ways of knowing and being Mormon came into conflict with American-Mormon worldviews and practices and then seeing how the subsequent tensions were negotiated. What I learned is that the venerated status that came from being of the House of Israel played an important role in how Polynesian Latter-day Saints managed to weather these storms. As I document, the Polynesian-Israelite connection was a racial formation that reiterated existing racial hierarchies that could have turned Hawaiians against the church. However, rather than rejecting the connection they embraced it, and they were able to use their status as a chosen people to meet their own cultural, familial, and community needs. What I learned from reading the oral histories and listening to my aunties and uncles talk about their religious and ethnic identities is that they were not in conflict with each other but instead had been knotted together. Their relationship to the gospel of the church embodies what Thomas Tweed theorizes as the essence of religion: "Religions are confluences of organic-cultural flows that intensify joy and confront suffering by drawing on human and suprahuman forces to make homes and cross boundaries."[1]

The articulation of a Mormon identity with a Hawaiian one was embodied in a speech that Kamoaʻe Walk gave at Brigham Young University–Hawaiʻi after returning from a voyage to sail the waʻa *Maisu* to Mau Piailug in Satawal. The waʻa kaulua ʻo *Maisu* was built to show the Hawaiian people's aloha to Piailug. Walk is a professor of Hawaiian language at Brigham Young University–Hawaiʻi and a captain of the waʻa kaulua ʻo *Iosepa*. I quote below a lengthy portion of this speech where he draws an analogy between the spiritual journey that Mormons believe we are all on and the huakaʻi he just completed.

We are all a part of a spiritual voyage and we made preparations for this voyage before we came to this world. There were crews that were selected. We were put into watches just like we are on a canoe, those that we call ʻohana or family. We have our watch captains. And our captains . . . those are our fathers and our mothers that look after us and give us direction in this voyage. When we step onto the canoe we put our lives in each other's hands. And we have to trust each other that when the call is made and something needs to be done on the canoe that it will be done the way it needs to be done. There are many, many knots, thousands of knots on the canoe and when we make a knot we need to know that the proper knot is made and we need to know what knot it is so that if we need to untie it, it can be undone quickly and we can know what we need to do.

Kawika [Eskaran] and I have been preparing ourselves for Ku Holo Mau for six or seven years now. And that brought us to the point where we were physically, emotionally, and spiritually ready for this journey. We must know the purpose of our sail, our voyage. Knowing that purpose will give us direction, it will help us through those difficult times. Navigating, way finding, we've always been taught that when the Polynesian, and Micronesian, and Pacific Islanders sailed you always had to know where you came from in order to know where you're going. In our voyage here upon this earth, in our spiritual voyage it's the same. We must know where we came from in order to know where we're going and why we're trying to get there. We came from the presence of our father in heaven who created our spirits. Our voyage here is to go through and reach the other side, which is to return home to our father in heaven. There will be challenges along the way. There are going to be days when we are going to face storms. And on our voyage we had many different squalls. Squalls can bring many different things ... You cannot outrun a storm ... What do you do when you get caught in a storm when you make every preparation to avoid large storms? When you're there you have to weather the storms the best you can.[2]

The analogy Walk draws between the spiritual journey and the open-ocean voyage is a wonderful example of how Hawaiianness and Mormonism come together: the waʻa kaulua is comprised of two separate, distinct hulls that have been joined together through a complex network of thousands of knots. The stories I have shared in this book name some of those knots that bind these two disparate parts together. Not only must all crew-family members work together in a shared vision and purpose with each attending to his or her individual kuleana for the voyage to be successful, the waʻa must also be pono. This view can also serve as a cautionary tale; just as the two hulls of the canoe must be equally balanced, so too must Hawaiianness and Mormonism. When they are out of balance, the spiritual and cultural foundation becomes unsteady and threatens to capsize unless the balance is restored. Uncle Bill believed the Mālama ʻĀina and Kai projects were a step toward righting that canoe. As I speculated in chapter 5, the future of the waʻa kaulua ʻo *Iosepa* is uncertain. Will the community be able to continue to restore pono between Hawaiian culture and the Mormon church or will the balance shift one way or another? Too much in either direction could be devastating for this community. I am hopeful that the journey ahead will be a pono one, but as Walk reminded his audience, in order to know where you're going you have to know where you came from.

Walk's reference to this understanding was historical and cultural; however, I want to expand it to include the political. As I document in chapter 1, the church believes it has overcome its racist past by ending its blatantly discriminatory policy against blacks. I agree with Newell Bringhurst who states that the church has not fully come to terms with its racist past and the continued impact of racial ideologies that differentially affect black, Native, and Polynesian Latter-day Saints. I believe that for the church to move toward an alternative future that does not reproduce the same kinds of racial, gender, and sexual disparities it has promoted, members and nonmembers alike need to know how these racial ideologies came to be so that they can be disarticulated and rearticulated in new, liberating ways. I also believe that it is important for Polynesian members of the church to know this political history so that when we embrace our venerated status we do not inadvertently reproduce these racial ideologies. This is the alternative future I envision for Mormonism.

Finally, I am inspired by Walk's hopefulness that we have the provisions to weather squalls and the rough seas they bring. Indeed, the gospel and teachings of the church prepare its members well to weather a variety of storms. They teach that we approach these storms head on as faith building experiences that can strengthen our testimony of the gospel. But when out on the ocean we must also be prepared to weather the doldrums, when there is no wind or waves and we cannot move. In life, the doldrums are complacency, maintaining the status quo, apathy. The doldrums are when in the face of conflict we take the path of least resistance and don't push back, when we buy into an ideology of faithfulness of blind obedience. In the journey that is this book I was most inspired by the stories of people who pushed back and were not complacent. They did not follow their leaders blindly but challenged them to do better, be better, and to see it their way, and they did this not for the good of the individual but for the good of their families, communities, and ultimately their church. The stories of resistance to blind obedience should also be part of our journey forward. I have provisioned my canoe with these stories of aloha for family, community, lāhui, and the church.

Acknowledgments

I was not a solitary traveler on this journey but was aided in my pursuits by colleagues, friends, and family. I thank Russell C. Taylor at the L. Tom Perry Special Collections Library at Brigham Young University–Provo for his help in accessing missionary records and oral histories and Kris Nelson at the Charles Redd Center for Western Studies at Brigham Young University–Provo for her help transcribing many of the interviews I conducted for my work. At Brigham Young University–Hawai'i, mahalo to the former university archivist Greg Gublar and the current university archivist Matthew Kester at the Joseph F. Smith Library. I am indebted to the generosity of the late Dr. William K. Wallace, former director of the Jonathan Nāpela Center for Hawaiian Language and Cultural Studies; he shared his mana'o (thoughts) with me and gave me access to the Lā'ie Oral History Project archives. Mahalo to President Von D. Orgill of the Polynesian Cultural Center, who granted me access to the Polynesian Cultural Center Oral History Project. Financial support for this project came from a Ford Foundation Diversity Dissertation Fellowship and from postdoctoral fellowships and a course release from the Political Science Department at the University of Hawai'i at Mānoa.

Because this book began as a dissertation, I thank my mentors Jennifer L. Pierce, Jean O'Brien, David W. Noble, and Doug Hartmann, whose support got this project going. Jennifer's dissertation writing group, Piercing Insights, taught me that research and writing should not be done alone. The members of that group—Sara Dorrow, Karla Erickson, Peter Hennen, Wendy Leo, Debra Smith, and Amy Tyson—pushed me to be a better writer, thinker, and colleague. Noelani Goodyear-Ka'ōpua, Alice Te Punga Somerville, Ty Kāwika

Tengan, and Felicity Schaeffer-Grabiel also read many drafts of the dissertation as well as contributed much to its revision. Today, a decade later, Jennifer, Karla, and Noelani are still an active part of this journey.

Noenoe Silva, Jon Goldberg-Hiller, kuʻualoha hoʻomanawanui, Kapā Oliveira, Leilani Basham, Charles Lawrence III, Vernadette Gonzalez, Roderick Labrador, Pensri Ho, Ehito Kimura, Katharina Heyer, and John Charlot read chapters and shared their manaʻo. Mahalo nui loa to the two reviewers, Gregory Johnson and Vicente M. Diaz, whose enthusiasm and critical insights made this a better book. Jason Weidemann, my editor at the University of Minnesota Press, saw something germinating in the manuscript several years ago and nurtured it to completion: thank you for your patience and commitment.

During the writing of this book several important people who helped me understand the meaning of a Hawaiian Mormon identity have passed on. The loss has been significant, but their passing reminds me that their stories will live on in this book. Moreover, I want to make sure that when future generations read this volume they will see that Native Hawaiians and Polynesians have dignity and self-determination. Noenoe Silvaʻs research reminds us of the Native Hawaiians who in the nineteenth century embraced the written word to become "authors, agents, and practitioners." Whereas oral traditions kept alive the moʻolelo (stories) and the moʻokūʻauhau (genealogies) of our kūpuna, Hawaiian-language newspapers published by Native Hawaiians from the late nineteenth century to the early twentieth became a powerful repository for our moʻolelo and moʻokūʻauhau in the contemporary era. I present this book in the spirit of my kūpuna who embraced the written word as a strategy for survivance and as part of a legacy of struggle for self-determination. The stories I feature here are examples of a dogged determination for meaningful lives committed to service to church, communities, and families.

Stories and memories from my childhood were the inspiration for this project. I would be remiss if I did not thank my aunties and uncles in Utah and in Lāʻie who let me into their homes and their lives by sharing their stories with me. I left each interview with a greater understanding of how the pieces of our community fit together and an increased appreciation for the sacrifices that the interviewees and my parents made in order for their children to be able to pursue their dreams.

My book begins and ends with my ʻohana. To my parents, Ned Kalili and Sharon Lee Foote Aikau, I owe a deep gratitude for their encouragement even when it seemed as though the book would never be finished. To my mother, thank you for loving and feeding my children while I worked on final revisions. My parents too read early drafts (once even a draft I had thrown in the rubbish that my Mom found and read then passed on to my Dad); their feedback was a constant reminder that I should listen to my naʻau. While conducting research at Brigham Young University–Provo, my younger sister, Mapuana Aikau Weiss, and her family opened their home to me. Mahalo to my siblings, whose support has been unwavering. My research at Brigham Young University–Hawaiʻi would not have been possible without the generosity of Auntie Janice McArthur, a retired professor in the School of Education, who housed and fed me during my research trips to Lāʻie.

Finally, my deepest aloha goes to my partner Daniel Kaipo Dabin Sr. for his bottomless well of support. He has sacrificed much in order to see me achieve my goals, and he has done it with optimism, joy, and love. Our children, Sanoe Kamakaniokaulumamo, ʻĪmaikalani Kawaileleakeakuaokekua-lono, and Hiʻilei Kauakilihuneokamawailualani, are a constant reminder that labor brings forth new possibilities for love and spiritual contentment.

Notes

PREFACE

1. John Daniel Thompson McAllister and Lucile Cardon Reading, "The Hand Cart Song," 1989, http://www.lds.org/churchmusic/.

2. "The *stake* is the basic geographical unit of the Church" (Britsch, *Moramona*, 204). Within LDS imagery, the Church is likened to a tent which is tethered and kept secure by stakes. The Church provides shelter for its members while also providing an overarching ideology that allows diverse people to come together. Each stake is comprised of smaller units called wards. In areas where there are small numbers of members or in missionary contexts, smaller units called branches organized according to districts are formed.

3. The term haole, like other Hawaiian words, has many meanings including anything foreign or not native to Hawai'i nei (Hawai'i). However, over time its meaning has evolved to refer to white folks, specifically Americans and Europeans. The political meaning has changed and is sometimes seen as an epithet for white people. I use it as a racial designator and also to mark the difference between Kanaka Maoli, Native Hawaiians, and foreigners or settlers—that is, people not indigenous to this 'āina. For analysis of the racialized meaning of haole, see Rohrer, "Haole Girl."

4. "Inactive" is a phrase used to describe one's membership status in the church. Active members are those who attend weekly religious services, hold ecclesiastical callings in their congregation, pay their tithing, and are found worthy of attending sacred services in the temple by living the doctrine and covenants set forth by the church. In-active members are those who no longer live according to the full dictates of the church. Inactive members maintain their membership on the rolls of the church but often receive fellowship, a form of missionary work performed by active members to bring in-active members back into full participation in the church.

5. Aloha is a concept whose meaning has been hollowed out and commodified by the Hawai'i tourism industry. I use it here to mean the kind of affection and love that comes from mutual respect and understanding. Mary Kawena Pukui describes aloha as the fellowship between people who "are strengthened [by] mutual regard and love" (Pukui, Haertig, and Lee, *Nānā I Ke Kumu*, 3).

INTRODUCTION

1. The Church of Jesus Christ of Latter-day Saints, although the official name, is popularly referred to as the Mormon church. Mormon is the prophet who is believed to have inscribed the history of his peoples, the descendents of Lehi, onto plates of gold that his son Moroni buried. Later the plates were found and translated by Joseph Smith Jr. as *The Book of Mormon.* I use Mormon and LDS interchangeably to refer to the institution; Mormonism to refer to the doctrine and faith; and Mormons, Latter-day Saints, and Saints interchangeably to refer to members of the church.

2. Throughout this book I use several terms when referring to Native Hawaiians, the indigenous peoples of Hawai'i nei, including Kanaka, Kanaka Maoli, Kanaka 'Ōiwi Hawai'i, as well as Hawaiian. At several points throughout the book I make a distinction between Hawaiians and Polynesians. Finally, I use the term Polynesian recognizing fully well that the division of Oceania into three regions (Micronesia, Melanesia, and Polynesia) was and continues to serve a colonial, anthropological, and racial project. I continue to use it, however, because this is the term the people I interviewed used to describe themselves and their relationship to the LDS church.

3. See Tweed, *Crossing and Dwelling.*

4. Alexander, "Erotic Autonomy as a Politics of Decolonization," 91.

5. Hall, "The Problem of Ideology," 27.

6. "Who Are the Mormons?" *Newsroom,* January 1, 2008 (accessed July 4, 2011), http://newsroom.lds.org/.

7. See Bringhurst, *Saints, Slaves, and Blacks.*

8. See Coates, "Brigham Young and Mormon Indian Policies"; Lyman, *Out of Obscurity into the Light*; and Jorgensen, "Building the Kingdom of God."

9. William Mulder, quoted in Bringhurst, *Saints, Slaves, and Blacks,* 206.

10. See Britsch, *Moramona.*

11. Embry, *Asian American Mormons,* 15.

12. See Mauss, *All Abraham's Children.*

13. O'Dea, *The Mormons,* 1.

14. Ibid., 255.

15. Quoted in Britsch, *Moramona,* 176.

16. See Maffly-Kipp, *Proclamation to the People;* and Shipps, "Difference and Otherness."

17. See Maffly-Kipp, "A Mormon President?"

18. Heinerman and Shupe, *The Mormon Corporate Empire,* 4, 3.

19. The use of the monikers Uncle and Aunty here is part of the Hawaiian tradition to denote the author's relationship to people of her parents' generation.

20. Ronald Sing and Wendy Sing, interview by author, May 6, 2002. Tape recording, Orem, Utah.

21. See Prentiss, "'Loathsome unto Thy People.'"

22. In this example, I situate Hawai'i outside the boundaries of the United States because in 1850, the year the LDS church first turned its attention to the islands, Hawai'i was a sovereign kingdom. My understanding of race in the United States is influenced by Michael Omi and Howard Winant's *Racial Formation in the United States.*

23. The LDS church in Hawai'i has over sixty-six thousand members comprising approximately 5 percent of the population compared to nearly six million members nationwide comprising only 1.9 percent of the population. Data gathered from *Deseret News 2008 Church Almanac* (accessed March 19, 2008), www.mormonhaven.com/hawaii.htm/.

24. Edward L. Clissold, interview by R. Lanier Britsch, June 11, 1976. Transcript, Brigham Young University–Hawai'i Archives, 13.

25. Sterling and Summers, *Sites of Oahu*, 156.

26. According to Gerald Vizenor, "native survivance is an active sense of presence over absence, deracination, and oblivion; survivance is the continuance of stories, not mere reaction, however pertinent … Survivance stories are renunciations of dominance, detractions, obtrusions, the unbearable sentiment of tragedy and the legacy of victimry" (*Survivance*, 1).

27. Tweed, *Crossing and Dwelling*, 68.

28. I deliberately use the term colonialism in this context to challenge the notion that the United States did not have formal colonies. As I will demonstrate throughout this book, Lā'ie was described as a colony of the LDS church and literally functioned as such. The sugar produced by the Lā'ie plantation (1868–1931) was shipped to Salt Lake City, Utah, where the profits were used to support the growth of the church. As with European forms of colonialism, the LDS church appropriated material resources from Lā'ie, relied on the cheap labor of Hawaiian members of the church living in Lā'ie (including child labor), and played an influential role in the political and cultural structures of the community. Although I limit my discussion to the colonial actions of the LDS church, I also believe that Hawai'i functioned as a colony of the United States even before the country officially took over after the illegal overthrow and annexation of the kingdom. Mark Rifkin in his essay "Debt and the Transnationalization of Hawai'i" uses the debt relationship between U.S. merchants working in Hawai'i and the ali'i (chiefs) to argue that the United States has been in a "neocolonial" relationship with Hawai'i since the 1820s. See also Sally Engle Merry, *Colonizing Hawai'i*, for a discussion of how the adoption of American forms of law by the Kingdom of Hawai'i contributed to the colonial relationship between the United States and Hawai'i.

29. Burawoy, "Critical Sociology," 15.

30. Burawoy, "The Extended Case Method," 6.

31. See Kauanui, *Hawaiian Blood;* and Tengan, *Native Men Remade.*

32. Although a number of scholars have included a critique of Protestant missionaries in their historical accounts of colonization in Hawai'i, Juri Mykkanen in his *Inventing Politics* focuses exclusively on the role of Protestants in Hawai'i politics.

33. See Kame'eleihiwa, *Native Land and Foreign Desires;* and Osorio, *Dismembering Lāhui.*

34. My understanding of the tension between indigeneity and Christianity is informed by the work of Taiaiake Alfred and the late Vine Deloria Jr., who argue that Christianity is fundamentally incompatible with indigenous ways of life and spiritual practices and is a hindrance to claims for self-determination and expressions of sovereignty. They argue that one of the challenges to the process of returning to indigenous spiritual and religious practices is that Christianity has become so intertwined with indigenous identities that for some it is difficult to see where one begins and the other ends. See Alfred, *Wasáse;* and Deloria, *God Is Red.*

35. My research is in dialogue with scholars such as Vicente Diaz and Melani Anae who have taken on the task of exploring how it is that churches, namely the Catholic Church in Guam and the Newton Church in New Zealand, respectively, came to be sites of cultural reclamation for indigenous peoples. My findings are similar to Diaz and Anae, in that they are not oppositional or subversive as much as they reveal alternative

invocations of culture and faith that do not necessarily correspond to mainline Mormon teachings or ideologies. See Diaz, *Repositioning the Missionary*; and Anae, "Papalagi Redefined."

36. Treat, *Native and Christian*, 2.
37. Tweed, *Crossing and Dwelling*, 9, 11.
38. Ibid., 13.
39. Diaz and Kauanui, "Native Pacific Cultural Studies on the Edge," 317.
40. Tweed, *Crossing and Dwelling*, 59.
41. Hall, "The Problem of Ideology," 26.
42. Hall, quoted in Grossberg, "On Postmodernism and Articulation," 141.
43. Cannon, *My First Mission*, 14.
44. Hall, "The Problem of Ideology," 42.
45. Hall, quoted in Grossberg, "On Postmodernism and Articulation," 143.
46. Ibid., 142.
47. Peterson and Walhof, "Rethinking Religion," 13.
48. Kameʻeleihiwa, *Native Land and Foreign Desires*, 13.
49. Merry, *Colonizing Hawaiʻi*, 6.
50. Ibid., 31.
51. Mykkanen, *Inventing Politics*, 9.
52. Osorio, *Dismembering Lāhui*.
53. Shipps, "Difference and Otherness," 84.
54. I borrow the phrase "belated travelers" from the work of the postcolonial scholar Ali Behdad.
55. The missionaries from the American Board of Commissioners for Foreign Missions are referred to as Presbyterian missionaries, Calvinist missionaries (Kameʻeleihiwa), and Protestant missionaries (which I use). The board was formed by Congregationalists. Congregationalism is one of many Protestant churches. Protestantism is one of the five major divisions in Christianity and typically refers to denominations that grew out of the protest against the Roman Catholic Church. Presbyterianism describes those Christian denominations that adhere to Calvinist theology that also fall under the umbrella of Protestantism.
56. Behdad, *Belated Travelers*, 13.
57. Cannon, *My First Mission*, 8.
58. Behdad, *Belated Travelers*, 13.
59. Cannon, *My First Mission*, 9.
60. Cannon, "Journal of George Q. Cannon," 14.
61. Britsch, *Moramona*, 15.
62. Cannon, *My First Mission*, 14.
63. Shipps, "Difference and Otherness," 83.
64. The restoration of the true Church of Christ took place in the United States during the Second Great Awakening when many newly derived sects claimed to possess the knowledge of Christ's true church. According to the historian Dan Vogel, the early LDS church resembled other religious organizations that emerged at the same time such as Alexander Campbell's Disciples of Christ. See Vogel, *Religious Seekers and the Advent of Mormonism*.
65. A branch is a unit formed within a mission. It is smaller than a ward, a local congregation comprised of two hundred to five hundred members, and is marked by its small

size and, occasionally, distinctive population. Branches established within a mission fall under the leadership of the mission president.

66. Pukui and Elbert, *Hawaiian Dictionary,* 179.

67. My thinking about kuleana is informed by the work of the Native Hawaiian scholar and activist Noelani Goodyear-Ka'ōpua. See her dissertation, "Kū i ka Māna: Building Community and Nation through Contemporary Hawaiian Schooling," for a more extensive discussion of kuleana.

68. Diaz and Kauanui, "Native Pacific Cultural Studies on the Edge," 318.

69. Ibid.

70. Haraway, *Simians, Cyborgs, and Women,* 192.

71. Ibid., 191.

1. Mormonism, Race, and Lineage

1. Britsch, *Moramona,* 5. The ordinance of salvation to which he refers is the act of baptism. The LDS church shares this tenet with other Christian denominations. However, their paths depart on two points; the first is that as part of the restoration of the gospel to earth, only Joseph Smith Jr. and his successors were granted the authority of the priesthood as it existed during the time of Christ. Second, as stated above, the saving ordinance of baptism has the symbolic effect of establishing a genealogical link between the newly saved with the House of Israel.

2. See Mauss, *All Abraham's Children;* Bringhurst, *Saints, Slaves, and Blacks;* Prentiss, "'Loathsome unto Thy People'"; Cowan, "Theologizing Race"; Bushman, *Contemporary Mormonism;* and Embry, *Black Saints in a White Church.*

3. Armand Mauss in *All Abraham's Children* mentions Polynesians, but he frames his reference as a contemporary identity construction.

4. Kuper, *The Invention of Primitive Society,* 5.

5. For an extended critique of the temporal and spatial logics of anthropology and primitive societies, see Fabian, *Time and the Other.* For an extended discussion of how notions of the primitive played out in the colonial context, see McClintock, *Imperial Leather.*

6. Kuper, *The Invention of Primitive Society,* 194.

7. McClintock, *Imperial Leather,* 37.

8. Ibid., 38.

9. See Bringhurst, *Saints, Slaves, and Blacks;* and Mauss, *All Abraham's Children.*

10. Mauss, *All Abraham's Children,* 8, 9.

11. Bringhurst, *Saints, Slaves, and Blacks,* 10.

12. Ibid., 6.

13. Gordon, "Inventing Mormon Identity in Tonga," 87.

14. Shipps, "Difference and Otherness," 83.

15. 2 Nephi 5:20 (*The Book of Mormon*).

16. 2 Nephi 5:21–22 (*The Book of Mormon*).

17. I contend that although the racialization process underlying this narrative of Nephites and Lamanites appears to be mutable, in practice whiteness continues to have supremacy in the organizational structure of the church.

18. Prentiss, "'Loathsome unto Thy People,'" 128.

19. Newell Bringhurst in *Saints, Slaves, and Blacks* argues that in the 1830s missionaries who baptized American Indians and blacks expected their skin to change colors. When

their skin color did not become white, a figurative interpretation of the *Book of Mormon* began to take hold.

20. Cowan, "Theologizing Race," 114.

21. Douglas, "The Sons of Lehi and the Seed of Cain," 92.

22. Mauss, *All Abraham's Children,* 26.

23. Anne McClintock offers a very concise gender analysis of the family metaphor for the evolution of humanity and history: "The merging of the tree and family into family Tree of Man provided scientific racism with a *gendered* image for popularizing and disseminating the idea of *racial* progress. There is a problem here, however, for the family Tree represents evolutionary time as a *time without women.* The family image is an image of disavowal, for it contains only men [, and the notion of] . . . women as historical actors is disavowed and relegated to the realm of nature" (*Imperial Leather,* 39).

24. Bringhurst, *Saints, Slaves, and Blacks.*

25. Mauss, *All Abraham's Children.*

26. Abraham 3:22 (*The Pearl of Great Price*).

27. Abraham 3:24 (*The Pearl of Great Price*).

28. Abraham 3:27 (*The Pearl of Great Price*).

29. Moses 7:37–69 (*The Pearl of Great Price*).

30. Prentiss, "'Loathsome unto Thy People.'"

31. Harvey, "'A Servant of Servants Shall He Be.'"

32. Wolfe, "Land, Labor, and Difference."

33. Omi and Winant, *Racial Formation in the United States,* 55.

34. Howe, *The Quest for Origins,* 38.

35. Fornander, *An Account of the Polynesian Race,* 1: 26.

36. Interestingly, Bruce Sutton argues that the debate about the lineage of Native Americans has been put to rest; once a Native American is baptized they become adopted into the lineage of Nephi. What is presumed but unmarked by Sutton is the assumption that Native Americans are, originally, Laminates and have to become Nephites through the rejection of sin and the embrace of the gospel. Polynesians, he argues, were originally Nephite and their acceptance of the gospel is a restoration to their prior state. See Sutton, *Lehi, Father of Polynesia,* 3.

37. Bringhurst, *Saints, Slaves, and Blacks.*

38. Sutton, *Lehi, Father of Polynesia,* 3.

39. Ibid.

40. Ibid., 4.

41. See Cole and Jensen, *An Appendage to Israel in the Pacific.*

42. See Howe, *The Quest for Origins.*

43. Ibid., 25.

44. Cannon, "Journal of George Q. Cannon," 14.

45. See Douglas, "The Sons of Lehi and the Seed of Cain."

46. Kuper, *The Invention of Primitive Society,* 7.

47. McAllister, "Important Appeal to Native Hawaiians and Other Polynesians," 705.

48. Ibid., 710.

49. For a contemporary debate about whether Hawaiians believed Cook to be Lono, see Sahlins, *How "Natives" Think*; and Obeyesekere, *The Apotheosis of Captain Cook.*

50. Cole and Jensen, *An Appendage to Israel in the Pacific,* 22.

51. Tengan, *Native Men Remade,* 35.

52. Cole and Jensen, *An Appendage to Israel in the Pacific*, 64.
53. Ibid., 63.
54. Loveland, "Hagoth and the Polynesian Tradition," 63.
55. Ibid., 70.
56. Omi and Winant, *Racial Formation in the United States*, 117.
57. Bringhurst, "An Unintended and Difficult Odyssey," 27.

2. LĀʻIE, A PROMISED LAND, AND PUʻUHONUA

1. Frymer-Kensky, "Biblical Voices on Chosenness," 27.
2. Farred, "The Unsettler," 796.
3. Jacobs, *Edge of Empire*, 5.
4. Kameʻeleihiwa notes that the mating of Papa and Wākea produced Hawaiʻi island, their first born, followed by Maui island and Hoʻohōkūkalani (the maker of stars), a daughter. Wākea mated with Hoʻohōkūkalani and had two male offspring. The first was Hāloanakalaukapalili, who was stillborn and was buried beside their home. The first kalo plant grew from that place. Their second child was male and also named Hāloa. It is said that Wākea's desire for his daughter angered Papa, who then left him. According to Samuel Kamakau, in *Tales and Traditions of the People of Old*, during this time Papa gave birth to Oʻahu island, whose father was Lua. Wākea also had other children: "Molokaʻi and Lānaʻi were the children of Wākea by different wives. Hina was the mother of Molokaʻi and the child was called Molokaʻi a Hina. The mother of Lānaʻi was Kaʻulawahine. They became the ancestors of the people of those islands" (129). Papa and Wākea would have four more island children: Kauaʻi, Niʻihau, Lehua, and Kaʻula. See Kameʻeleihiwa, *Native Land and Foreign Desires*, 24.
5. Andrade, *Hāʻena*, 25.
6. Trask, *From a Native Daughter*, 189.
7. Andrade, *Hāʻena*, 29, 30.
8. Ibid., 94.
9. Ibid., 30.
10. According to Jonathan Osorio, *Dismembering Lāhui*, the first laws of the kingdom were meant to "deal with the naturalization of foreigners through the taking of the oath of allegiance." The first documents on record regarding citizenship appeared in 1838 and were known as the "Alien Law," "which . . . was 'never promulgated into law' but formed the basis for the eventual definition of citizenship in the kingdom. The first two articles of the law described who proper subjects of the realm were. Those who were not born in the Islands, born to Natives living abroad, or born aboard a ship belonging to the Sandwich Islands were aliens unless they took the oath of allegiance" (57). After the passing of the Residency Laws of 1850, foreigners were allowed to maintain dual citizenship as well as the right to own land, to vote, and to hold office in the government.
11. According to Preza, fee simple title could not be granted until the passage of the Kuleana Act of 1850. Until that time only rights were granted, not title. See Preza, "The Empirical Writes Back."
12. Kameʻeleihiwa, *Native Land and Foreign Desires*, 212.
13. See Perkins, "Teaching Land and Sovereignty," for a discussion of the horizontal division that, he argues, preserves native tenants' one-third dominium rights to land.
14. See Osorio, *Dismembering Lāhui*; Kameʻeleihiwa, *Native Land and Foreign Desires*; and Chinen, *The Great Mahele*.

15. See Preza, "The Empirical Writes Back."
16. See Beamer, "Na wai ka mana?"
17. *An Act Confirming Certain Resolutions of the King in Privy Council, passed on the 21st day of December, A.D., 1849, Granting to the Common People Allodial Titles for Their Land and House Lots, and Certain Other Privileges,* act of August 6, 1850 [1850] Hawaiian Kingdom Laws, 203.
18. Preza, "The Empirical Writes Back," 138.
19. Despite the new research conducted by Preza that clearly demonstrates that a larger percentage of land stayed in Kanaka hands, the Māhele process still benefited the haole more than it did the common Kanaka. Furthermore, this new research does not shed any additional light as to why so few maka'āinana applied for claims and why less than 50 percent were awarded.
20. See Stover, "The Legacy of the 1848 Mahele and Kuleana Act of 1850."
21. Stanton, "A Gathering of Saints," 23.
22. Mulder, *Homeward to Zion,* 18.
23. Ibid., 19.
24. Noall, *To My Children,* 28.
25. Britsch, *Moramona,* 35
26. See Blackhawk, *Violence Over the Land.*
27. Kame'eleihiwa, *Native Land and Foreign Desires,* 243
28. According to Kame'eleihiwa's extensive research on the process of Māhele, Lāna'i poses an interesting case. As a smaller island, it was not divided into regions or moku as was customary on other islands. Therefore, the charts that relate to the Māhele of Lāna'i indicate that five parcels were set aside for the government while one parcel, previously part of Liholiho's land holdings, was relinquished to the Mō'ī and one parcel was retained by Kekau'ōnohi, the sister-cousin of Leleiōhoku for whom Ha'alelea was the primary konohiki. See Kame'eleihiwa, *Native Land and Foreign Desires,* 243.
29. Ha'alelea and Kekau'ōnohi were married shortly after the death of Leleiōhoku in 1848. Kame'eleihiwa, *Native Land and Foreign Desires,* 284.
30. Ibid., 243.
31. Beck, "Iosepa," ii.
32. Britsch, *Moramona,* 40.
33. Farred, "The Unsettler," 797.
34. Britsch, *Moramona,* 74.
35. Ibid., 73.
36. Spurrier, *Great Are the Promises unto the Isles of the Sea,* 17.
37. Cummings, *Centennial History of Laie, 1865–1965,* 14.
38. Spurrier, *Great Are the Promises unto the Isles of the Sea,* 15.
39. Ibid., 16.
40. Quoted in Britsch, *Moramona,* 63.
41. Britsch *Moramona,* 75.
42. Ibid., 103.
43. For examples of how other Native communities have resisted colonization, expropriation, and dispossession on the continent, see O'Brien, *Dispossession by Degrees;* and Silverman, *Faith and Boundaries.* For a discussion of how the Chamorros in the Mariana Islands engaged with Catholicism, see Diaz, *Repositioning the Missionary.*
44. Stover, "The Legacy of the 1848 Mahele and Kuleana Act of 1850," 70.

45. Compton, "The Making of the Ahupua'a of Lā'ie into a Gathering Place and Plantation," 83.

46. Quoted in Ibid., 83.

47. According to scholars of nineteenth-century Hawai'i history, Native Hawaiians lost the majority of their land between 1888 and 1903 due to a law passed in 1874 that allowed foreclosure on land without going through any formal judicial process. Scholars disagree about the extent to which Native Hawaiians were dispossessed of land prior to the passing of the 1874 law, but there appears to be agreement that massive foreclosures due to unpaid debts and taxes contributed to large-scale land alienation. Stover's research found that the LDS church was able to acquire land titles from Native church members due to the 1874 law; however, the church purchased these foreclosed properties only after the fact. The church was not the lender who foreclosed on and then assumed ownership of these parcels. See Stover, "The Legacy of the 1848 Mahele and Kuleana Act of 1850."

48. See Stauffer, *Kahana.* See also Andrade, *Hā'ena.*

49. Quoted in Compton, "The Making of the Ahupua'a of Lā'ie into a Gathering Place and Plantation," 179n65.

50. See Andrade, *Hā'ena;* and Stover, "The Legacy of the 1848 Mahele and Kuleana Act of 1850."

51. See Compton, "The Making of the Ahupua'a of Lā'ie into a Gathering Place and Plantation."

52. Quoted in ibid., 105.

53. Andrade, *Hā'ena,* 89.

54. Chase, "The Hawaiian Mission Crisis of 1874," 61.

55. The Word of Wisdom is a set of doctrines or guidelines for healthy living that focus on abstinence from any substance that can cause harm to the body, including smoking and drinking alcohol and caffeinated beverages, as well as directives against overeating. As Lance Chase states in "The Hawaiian Mission Crisis of 1874": "Church members voluntarily complied with the Word of Wisdom until the 1920s, when strict adherence became a requirement for temple recommend" (65). In his footnotes, he mentions the names of various church leaders who were known to have a glass of wine for special occasions in order to emphasize how in the 1870s Mitchell's strict adherence to the Word of Wisdom was excessive for the time.

56. Harvey Cluff, *Autobiography,* quoted in Compton, "The Making of the Ahupua'a of Lā'ie into a Gathering Place and Plantation," 107.

57. Stover, "The Legacy of the 1848 Mahele and Kuleana Act of 1850," 78.

58. Britsch, *Moramona,* 108.

59. Stover, "The Legacy of the 1848 Mahele and Kuleana Act of 1850," 87.

60. See Noall, *To My Children;* and Britsch, *Moramona.*

61. Britsch, *Moramona,* 110.

62. Cowan, "Temples in the Pacific," 131.

63. Ibid., 132.

64. Ibid., 130.

65. Vailine Leota Niko, interview by William Wallace, January 16, 1972. Transcript, Lā'ie Oral History Program, Brigham Young University–Hawai'i Archives, 5.

66. Britsch, *Moramona,* 151.

67. Amoe Meyer, interview by Palota Purcell, February 19, 1985. Transcript, Lā'ie Oral History Program, Brigham Young University–Hawai'i Archives, 5.

68. Edward L. Clissold, interview by R. Lanier Britsch, June 11, 1976. Transcript, Brigham Young University–Hawai'i Archives, 13.

69. Lucas, "E Ola Mau Kākou I Ka 'Ōlelo Makuahine," 8.

70. Ibid., 9.

71. Viola Kawahigashi, interview by Kenneth W. Baldridge, June 7, 1978. Transcript, Lā'ie Oral History Program, Brigham Young University–Hawai'i Archives, 5.

72. Ibid., 3.

73. Ibid.

74. Thomas H. Au, interview by Faith Wrathall, July 18, 1980. Transcript, Lā'ie Oral History Program, Brigham Young University–Hawai'i Archives, 10, 2.

75. Ibid., 6.

76. Ibid., 8.

77. Ibid., 20.

78. I recognize the methodological limitation of my interpretation of how critique operated in this community. Oral histories can only tell us part of a much larger, complex story. Admittedly, my approach to an ideology of faithfulness is based on what individual people chose to share in their interviews, and I also recognize that resistance, critique, and dissent could have, and I assume did, take place in other forms and in other contexts. I want to stress that just because explicit criticism is not present in the majority of interviews does not mean that it did not exist. I want to thank Rose Ram for reminding me of this important distinction.

79. Tom Fanene, interview by Kalili Hunt, October 18, 1982. Transcript, Polynesian Cultural Center Oral History Program, Brigham Young University–Hawai'i Archives.

3. Called to Serve

1. Habermas, *The Philosophical Discourse of Modernity*, 1.

2. Weber, *Wirtschaft and Gesellschaft*, 1: 227, quoted in Bendix, *Max Weber*, 93.

3. Thomas H. Au, interview by Faith Wrathall, July 18, 1980. Transcript, Lā'ie Oral History Program, Brigham Young University–Hawai'i Archives, 6.

4. See McClintock, *Imperial Leather*; and Fabian, *Time and the Other*.

5. Weber is also relevant because he was a contemporary of Joseph Smith, who appears to inform his thinking about authority and charisma. In the essay "Religious Rejections of the World and Their Directions," Weber's description of how the charisma of a leader draws upon "magic"—in the case of Smith his visitation by heavenly personages—and is maintained through "certain very regularly recurrent conditions" could be applied verbatim to the historical evolution of the LDS church.

6. See Shipps, "Difference and Otherness."

7. Heinerman and Shupe, *The Mormon Corporate Empire*, 102.

8. Prince and Wright, *David O. McKay and the Rise of Modern Mormonism*, 30.

9. Heinerman and Shupe go on to explain that the triadic model of the First Presidency and the organizational structure of the church hierarchy are modeled after LDS beliefs about, as they state, the "spiritual realm: that is, the Church of Jesus Christ of Heavenly Saints. For Mormons the Celestial Kingdom (or Heavenly Zion) parallels earthly Zion in both organization and function" (*The Mormon Corporate Empire*, 86).

10. Ibid., 87.

11. See Aikau, "Indigeneity in the Diaspora."

12. See Edward L. Clissold, interview by R. Lanier Britsch, June 11, 1976. Transcript, Brigham Young University–Hawai'i Archives.

13. According to Owen J. Cook, the church had three elementary schools and one high school in Western Sāmoa, one high school in Mapusaga in American Sāmoa, an elementary school (closed temporarily) and Liahona High School in Tonga, the Church College of New Zealand in Temple View, New Zealand, and a school in Tahiti (although it is unclear where the school was and whether it was an elementary or high school). Owen J. Cook, interview by Kenneth W. Baldridge, March 8, 1980. Transcript, Lāʻie Oral History Collection, Brigham Young University–Hawaiʻi Archives, 7–8.

14. Britsch, *Moramona*, 180.

15. Cook, interview, 20

16. Ibid., 18.

17. Polynesian Latter-day Saints who immigrated to Hawaiʻi in the late 1950s and 1960s saw it as part of the United States because since 1898 it was a U.S. territory, and it became a state in 1959. Although scholars demonstrate the illegality of these two events—annexation and statehood—the geopolitical status of Hawaiʻi did change.

18. Bendix, *Max Weber*, 289.

19. Ibid., 89

20. Weber, *The Protestant Ethic and the Spirit of Capitalism*, 54, 62.

21. Giddens, introduction to Weber, *The Protestant Ethic and the Spirit of Capitalism*, 5.

22. Britsch, *Moramona*, 180.

23. Ibid., 181.

24. Cowan, "Temples in the Pacific," 137.

25. Louise Gallacher Robinson, interview by Dalisay A. Garcia, October 27, 1980. Transcript, Lāʻie Oral History Collection, Brigham Young University–Hawaiʻi Archives.

26. Ibid., 11.

27. Ibid., 5.

28. Ibid., 6.

29. Ibid., 9.

30. Ibid., 11.

31. See Ty Kāwika Tengan, *Native Men Remade*, for extended discussion of the stereotypes about Native Hawaiian men and Native masculinity in general. The domestication of the native man, Tengan argues, perpetuates a broader imperial project that effectively emasculates Native men. See also Anne McClintock, *Imperial Leather*, for the cult of domesticity as a central trope in imperial projects, and see Amy Kaplan, "Manifest Domesticity."

32. Robinson, interview, 10.

33. Ibid., 16.

34. Cook, interview, 31.

35. Kent, *Hawaii*, 122.

36. Sione Feinga, interview by Kalili Hunt, November 1, 1982. Transcript, Polynesian Cultural Center Oral History Program, Brigham Young University–Hawaiʻi Archives, 3.

37. See Stanton, "A Gathering of Saints."

38. See Small, *Voyages*.

39. Feinga, interview, 1.

40. Small, *Voyages*, 51.

41. Feinga, interview, 2.

42. Robinson, interview, 11.

43. Feinga, interview, 2.

44. Britsch, *Moramona,* 193.
45. Feinga, interview, 3.
46. Charles Barenaba, interview by Kalili Hunt, December 22, 1982. Transcript, Polynesian Cultural Center Oral History Program, Brigham Young University–Hawaiʻi Archives, 11.
47. Feinga, interview, 5.
48. Max Bean and Patricia Bean, interview by Anne Marie Corburn and Kenneth W. Baldridge, May 26, 1989. Transcript, Lāʻie Oral History Program, Brigham Young University–Hawaiʻi Archives, 25.
49. Rita H. Stone, interview by Kenneth W. Baldridge, April 23, 1983. Transcript, Polynesian Cultural Center Oral History Program, Brigham Young University–Hawaiʻi Archives.
50. Ibid., 16.
51. Ibid., 17.
52. Au, interview, 8–9.
53. Vailine Leota Niko, interview by William Wallace, January 16, 1972. Transcript, Lāʻie Oral History Program, Brigham Young University–Hawaiʻi Archives, 5.
54. Barenaba, interview, 12.
55. Ibid., 13.
56. Stanton, "A Gathering of Saints," 29.
57. See Stanton, "The Polynesian Cultural Center."
58. Tom Fanene, interview by Kalili Hunt, October 18, 1982. Transcript, Polynesian Cultural Center Oral History Program, Brigham Young University–Hawaiʻi Archives, 4.
59. The Hukilau, an event involving a type of fishing where a net lined with ti leaves is cast from the shore and a small group of people pull together to bring in the catch, was a community initiative to draw tourists to Lāʻie where they could watch a "traditional" means of fishing and then feast on what was caught. The Lāʻie community began using the Hukilau as a fundraising effort in 1947, and it continued until 1971 when it was discontinued because it could no longer compete with the Polynesian Cultural Center.
60. George Q. Cannon Jr., interview by Kalili Hunt, October 19, 1982. Transcript, Polynesian Cultural Center Oral History Program, Brigham Young University–Hawaiʻi Archives, 7.
61. Agnes Lua, interview by Peter Birati, April 11, 1985. Transcript, Lāʻie Oral History Program, Brigham Young University–Hawaiʻi Archives.
62. Ruby Enos, interview by Kalili Hunt, October 20, 1982. Transcript, Polynesian Cultural Center Oral History Program, Brigham Young University–Hawaiʻi Archives.
63. Barenaba, interview, 15.
64. Fanene, interview, 15.
65. Stanton, "Samoan Saints," 19.
66. William Kanahele, interview by Kalili Hunt, June 23, 1982. Transcript, Polynesian Cultural Center Oral History Program, Brigham Young University–Hawaiʻi Archives, 19.
67. For a discussion of Western education in the South Pacific context, see Bray "Education and the Vestiges of Colonialism."

4. In the Service of the Lord

1. Emosi Damuni, interview by Kalili Hunt, August 5, 1983. Transcript, Polynesian Cultural Center Oral History Program, Brigham Young University–Hawaiʻi Archives, 1.
2. Isireli Racule, interview by Kalili Hunt, July 17, 1983. Transcript, Polynesian Cultural Center Oral History Program, Brigham Young University–Hawaiʻi Archives.

3. Damuni, interview, 1.

4. Ibid., 2.

5. The term camouflage carries two meanings; the first literally refers to the need to disguise the internal framing of the structure used to meet the building standards for a tourist facility as well as the sprinkler system needed to meet fire regulations. The second meaning is more metaphorical. From his interview, it is clear that Damuni was committed to a type of disguise that was intended to deceive visitors into believing that they were no longer on the island of Oʻahu but in a real village in Fiji.

6. Damuni, interview, 5.

7. Ibid., 15.

8. Williams, "Althusser on Ideology."

9. Ibid., 51.

10. Susan James, quoted in ibid.

11. Trask, *From a Native Daughter*, 192.

12. Desmond, *Staging Tourism*, 56.

13. Ibid., 49.

14. In 1973, the Church College of Hawaiʻi became a four-year accredited university and the name was changed to Brigham Young University, Hawaiʻi Campus. I use Church College of Hawaiʻi when referring to the college prior to 1973 and Brigham Young University–Hawaiʻi after that time.

15. See Kent, *Hawaii*.

16. See Wineera, "Selves and Others."

17. Polynesian Cultural Center (accessed August 23, 2006), http://www.polynesia.com/pcc_mission_statement.html/.

18. Wineera, "Selves and Others," 97.

19. Ross, *The Chicago Gangster Theory of Life*, 42–43.

20. Ibid., 87.

21. See Urry, *Consuming Places*; and Kirshenblatt-Gimblett, *Destination Culture*, 131.

22. MacCannell, *Empty Meeting Grounds*, 18.

23. Approximately seventy-one oral histories were completed for the Polynesian Cultural Center Oral History Program as part of the twenty-year anniversary celebration. Despite the vast amount of knowledge that is shared by the oral history participants, there are two methodological concerns that have informed my analysis and conclusions. First, the majority of all interviews were conducted with men who had worked at the center; in addition, a small number of women (approximately eleven) were interviewed alone, and seven couples, both men and women, were interviewed together. One explanation for this gender disparity can be attributed to the gender bias inherent in the church, where men are expected to hold the highest leadership positions because they hold the priesthood, with the authority given to men who prove their worthiness to act in the name of God. This is not to say that women, who are also deemed worthy, do not hold high-ranking leadership positions in the church, but rather is to suggest that there is a kind of glass ceiling above which women cannot rise in leadership positions. The magnitude of building and sustaining a project such as the Polynesian Cultural Center required a buy-in at the highest levels in the church and those participants were men. In addition, gender also appears to be a factor in how jobs were allocated; for example, although it was common practice to hire men as village "chiefs," women were often hired as cultural experts. Given these gendered practices, it is no surprise that more men than women are represented in

the oral histories. Rather than see this as a limitation, I analyze the interviews with a gender-conscious lens by asking how participants articulate a racial and gendered identity at the center. The second concern is that the majority of the participants were at the time of the interviews still active in the church. One of the arguments I make in this chapter is that an ideology of faithfulness garners the consent of workers. One could argue that my conclusions are flawed because my sources only reflect those people who have bought into the religious ideology, and thus buying into an ideology of faithfulness at work is not a very big stretch. I admit that perhaps my theoretical reach is not as far as I would like, yet even among "believers" a direct or indirect challenge to an ideology of faithfulness takes place—producing what I contend are acts of resistance.

24. See Carroll and Noble, *The Free and the Unfree.*

25. Richard Poulson and Noe Poulson, interview by author, June 8, 2003. Tape recording, Salt Lake City, Utah.

26. Ibid.

27. García Canclini, *Transforming Modernity,* 17.

28. See Wineera, "Selves and Others."

29. Ibid., 105.

30. Damuni, interview, 7.

31. Ibid., 9.

32. Epanaia Whaanga (Barney) Christy, interview by Kalili Hunt, June 18, 1982. Transcript, Polynesian Cultural Center Oral History Program, Brigham Young University–Hawai'i Archives, 22–23.

33. See Melani Anae's "Papalagi Redefined: Toward a New Zealand–Born Samoan Identity" for an example of how indigenized Christian churches have become spaces through which cultural identities are made and remade. Anae contends that "the institution of the PIC [Pacific Island Congregational] church gives the N.Z.-born [Sāmoans] the most viable way to maintain a Pacific Island identity" (161). I do not intend to suggest that the LDS church has become significantly indigenized, but rather I contend that through its various institutions and at different historical moments the church has provided some Polynesians with an opportunity to learn cultural practices that might not have been available to them otherwise.

34. Christy, interview, 23.

35. Patoa Benioni, interview by Kalili Hunt, June 18, 1982. Transcript, Polynesian Cultural Center Oral History Program, Brigham Young University–Hawai'i Archives.

36. Appadurai, *Modernity at Large,* 12.

37. Ibid., 12.

38. Ibid., 13.

39. Wineera, "Selves and Others," 13.

40. See Edward Bruner's *Culture on Tour* for a discussion of how the divisions within ethnic theme parks in Kenya, Indonesia, and China are intended to present "a revivalist essentialism" (212).

41. Appadurai, *Modernity at Large,* 15.

42. See Paul Nahoa Lucas's "E Ola Mau Kākou I Ka 'Ōlelo Makuahine: Hawaiian Language Policy and the Courts" for an extensive discussion of the process by which English-only language policies were institutionalized and their subsequent detrimental effect on Native Hawaiians.

43. See Limerick, *The Legacy of Conquest.*

44. See Hau'ofa, "Our Sea of Islands."

45. Cornell and Hartmann, "Conceptual Confusions and Divides," 28.

46. For additional perspectives on the Mormon-Pacific connection, see Britsch, *Moramona*; Gordon, "Inventing Mormon Identity in Tonga"; Loveland, "Hagoth and the Polynesian Tradition"; Ramstad, *Conversion in the Pacific;* and Underwood, *Voyages of Faith.* See also Prentiss, "'Loathsome unto Thy People,'" for a discussion of how the racial formation of Native Americans in LDS discourse contrasts with that of Polynesians.

47. Cornell and Hartmann, "Conceptual Confusions and Divides," 28.

48. Ezekiel Kamai and Merehau Kamai, interview by author, May 16, 2002. Tape recording, Orem, Utah.

49. I borrow the term "abstract native" from Halualani, *In the Name of Hawaiians.*

50. Barney, interview, 13.

51. Tommy Taurima, interview by Kalili Hunt, June 21, 1982. Transcript, Polynesian Cultural Center Oral History Program, Brigham Young University–Hawai'i Archives.

52. Nāpua Stevens Poire, interview by Pam Su'a and Anna Kaanga, March 14, 1983. Transcript, Polynesian Cultural Center Oral History Program. Brigham Young University–Hawai'i Archives.

53. Wineera, "Selves and Others," 13, 11.

54. Elliot Cameron, interview by Kalili Hunt, June 12, 1983. Transcript, Polynesian Cultural Center Oral History Program, Brigham Young University–Hawai'i Archives.

55. Webb, "Mormonism and Tourist Art in Hawai'i."

56. Damuni, interview, 6.

57. Ibid., 4.

58. Cy Bridges, interview by author, July 30, 2001. Tape recording, Lā'ie, Hawai'i.

59. The concept of ornamental culture and ornamental masculinity comes from Susan Faludi's work on post–World War II masculinity in *Stiffed: The Betrayal of the American Man.* She argues that in the era preceding the war, masculinity was defined by service to community, family, and nation, and then during the war it was defined through service to one's fellow soldiers. In contrast, the post–World War II era did not deliver on the promise of economic stability and a clearly articulated masculinity for the baby boom generation of men. In the media-saturated society after the war, masculinity was no longer defined by one's service to the community, the military, the church, or the household. Rather, Faludi states, "the culture we live in today pretends that media can nurture society, but our new public spaces,... are disembodied barrens, a dismal substitute for the real thing" (34). She calls this new sphere "ornamental culture" and "its essence is not just the selling act but the act of selling the self, and in this quest every man is essentially on his own, a lone sales rep marketing his own image with no paternal Captain Waskows to guide him" (35). The cultural tourism industry encapsulates ornamental culture, and I argue that at the Polynesian Cultural Center the Native male worker is expected to sell himself as well as his cultural traditions for a paycheck.

60. Ferre, "A History of the Polynesian Cultural Center's Night Show: 1963–1983," 25.

61. Ralph Barney, interview by Pam Su'a, October 1983. Transcript, Polynesian Cultural Center Oral History Program, Brigham Young University–Hawai'i Archives, 1.

62. Ibid., 12.

63. Bridges, interview.

64. Jay Akoi, interview by author, July 30, 2001. Tape recording, Lā'ie, Hawai'i.

65. Sione Feinga, interview by Kalili Hunt, November 1, 1982. Transcript, Polynesian Cultural Center Oral History Program, Brigham Young University–Hawai'i Archives, 5.
66. Bridges, interview.
67. Charles Barenaba, interview by Kalili Hunt, December 22, 1982. Transcript, Polynesian Cultural Center Oral History Program, Brigham Young University–Hawai'i Archives, 12.
68. Feinga, interview, 11.
69. Josephine Moeai, interview by Kalili Hunt, June 3, 1983. Transcript, Polynesian Cultural Center Oral History Program, Brigham Young University–Hawai'i Archives, 4.
70. Orgill, "President Orgill Welcomes PCC Alumni and Special Guests," 1.

5. Voyages of Faith

1. The wa'a project was funded by a grant by the W. K. Kellogg Foundation.
2. See Corntassel, "Toward Sustainable Self-Determination."
3. Brigham Young University–Hawai'i, Hawaiian Studies home page, (accessed June 16, 2009), http://academics.byuh.edu/hawaiian_studies/.
4. See Alfred, *Wasáse;* and Deloria, *God Is Red,* for arguments about the incompatibility of Christianity and indigenous struggles for self-determination.
5. Keakaokalani Mo'ikeha, interview, June 1, 2003. Native American Higher Education Initiative, W. K. Kellogg Foundation, Hukilau Beach, Lā'ie, O'ahu, Hawai'i (accessed July 28, 2009), http://wkkf.org/.
6. The moment when a voyaging canoe enters the ocean for the first time is considered its birth.
7. Rob Wakefield, "*Iosepa* Launched in Hawai'i," November 10, 2001 (accessed June 23, 2009), http://www.ldschurchnews.com/articles/40861/Iosepa-launched-in-Hawaii.html/.
8. Pukui, Haertig, and Lee, *Nānā I Ke Kumu,* 1: 94.
9. Ibid., 95.
10. See Aikau, "Indigeneity in the Diaspora."
11. See Teaiwa, "Lo(o)sing the Edge"; Clifford, *Routes.*
12. Diaz, "Moving Islands," 14.
13. See Barman and Watson, *Leaving Paradise.*
14. Diaz and Kauanui, "Native Pacific Cultural Studies on the Edge," 325.
15. Ibid., 325.
16. Ibid. My thinking here is also greatly influenced by the work of the late Tongan scholar Epeli Hau'ofa in "Our Sea of Islands," 7.
17. Kanale Sadowski, interview, June 1, 2003. Native American Higher Education Initiative, W. K. Kellogg Foundation, Hukilau Beach, Lā'ie, O'ahu, Hawai'i (accessed July 30, 2009), http://wkkf.org/.
18. William K. Wallace, interview by author, August 7, 2001. Tape recording. Lā'ie, Hawai'i.
19. Mission statement, Hawaiian Studies home page, accessed July 8, 2009. http://w2.byuh.edu/academics/hwnstudies/index.htm.
20. Wallace, interview.
21. Ibid.
22. See Benham, "The Voice 'Less' Hawaiian"; Lucas, "E Ola Mau Kākou I Ka 'Ōlelo Makuahine"; and Goodyear-Ka'ōpua, "Kū i ka mana."
23. See Warner, "*Kuleana*," and "The Movement to Revitalize Hawaiian Language."

24. See Nā Lei Naʻauao, "Education with Aloha."
25. See Goodyear-Kaʻōpua, "Rebuilding the ʻAuwai: Connecting Ecology, Economy, and Education in Hawaiian Schools," for an example of how this happens in a Hawaiian-focused charter school in urban Honolulu.
26. Jude Sells, interview, June 1, 2003. Native American Higher Education Initiative, W. K. Kellogg Foundation, Hukilau Beach, Lāʻie, Oʻahu, Hawaiʻi (accessed July 31, 2009), http://wkkf.org/.
27. Deloria, *God Is Red*, 234, 235.
28. The title for this section comes from Ben Finney's book of the same name. In his book Finney documents the events surrounding the construction and voyage of the waʻa kaulua ʻo *Hawaiʻiloa* and examines the re-creation of "the arts and crafts that went into building, launching, and sailing [the] ancestral vessel" (14).
29. Pukui and Elbert, *Hawaiian Dictionary*, 186.
30. Hauʻofa, "Our Sea of Islands," 7.
31. "Iosepa" (accessed July 6, 2009), http://www.youtube.com/watch?v=lyaitZSffhQ/.
32. Ibid.
33. Sells, interview.
34. Lono Logan, interview, June 1, 2003. Native American Higher Education Initiative, W. K. Kellogg Foundation, Hukilau Beach, Lāʻie, Oʻahu, Hawaiʻi (accessed July 30, 2009), http://ww2.wkkf.org/.
35. Diaz, "Moving Islands," 12.
36. Kathleen Majdali, "Lāʻie Community ʻOhana Turns Out for *Iosepa*'s Return," Nā Leo Hoʻomaluhia: Voices for Peace, BYU–Hawaiʻi, June 16, 2009 (accessed July 30, 2009), http://newsroom.byuh.edu/node/2220/.
37. Mahalo to the reviewer for helping me think through this.
38. Kameʻeleihiwa, *Native Land and Foreign Desires*, 19–21.
39. According to K. R. Howe, the theory of the American origins of Polynesia was first postulated in 1803 by Joaquin Martínez de Zuñiga. He speculated, first, that Polynesian voyaging canoes were so crude in construction that they could not withstand the challenges of open-ocean voyaging, and second, that the Polynesians did not posses the technological skills to purposefully navigate the vast Pacific but rather were at the mercy of the easterly winds. Thus his theory postulated that Polynesians had to come from South America where they could travel no more than "600 leagues" at a time from one island to another until they happened upon one that was habitable. Martínez de Zuñiga's theory also presumes that this was a one-way trip. What is intriguing about Martínez de Zuñiga's theory is that it went against the dominant understandings of the time that identified Southeast Asia as the original homeland of Pacific Islanders. In 1830 the missionary William Ellis put forward the theory that Polynesians were ancestrally connected to the Malays in Southeast Asia but made their way to the Pacific via a circuitous migratory path that took them across the Bering Strait south along the Pacific Northwest coastline to Mexico and South America where they then used easterly winds to make their way across the Pacific Ocean. The most notable American origins theorist, however, was Thor Heyerdahl whose famous *Kon-Tiki* raft appeared to confirm his thesis that American Indians used balsa-wood rafts, the winds, and the currents to settle the Pacific Islands. Finney notes that the *Kon-Tiki* demonstration had several flaws, including the fact that Heyerdahl had to be towed beyond the break to the westerly current in order to "float" to the nearest Pacific Island. See Howe, *The Quest for Origins*; and Finney, *Voyages of Rediscovery*, for a more extensive review of the literature on Pacific origins.

40. The quote on the subheading for this section is from Thompson, "E Hoʻi Mau," 23.
41. Lucas, "Makaliʻi to Sail Ocean Once More," *West Hawaiʻi Today,* January 27, 2008 (accessed June 18, 2009), http://namoolelookaaina.com/category/kawaihae/waa-hawaiian-canoe-kawaihae/.
42. Thompson, "E Hoʻi Mau."
43. Corntassel, "Toward Sustainable Self-Determination," 108, 109.
44. Hawaiian Studies, *Iosepa,* History (accessed June 29, 2009), http://academics/byuh.edu/hawaiian_studies/iosepa/history/.
45. Tengan's research accepts gender duality engendered in kino as central to his vision for Native Hawaiian masculinity; however, at times his analysis reiterates binary frames that construct masculinity and femininity as tethered to particular bodies, which I disrupt.
46. Women have been a part of every voyage since that momentous journey from Hawaiʻi to Tahiti.
47. Mike Foley, "BYUH, Polynesian Cultural Center Leaders, Others Break Ground for *Iosepa*'s Hālau Waʻa," *Nā Leo Hoʻomaluhia: Voice for Peace,* November 10, 2007 (accessed August 1, 2009), http://newsroom.byuh.edu/node/1477/.
48. Wallace, interview.
49. Ibid.

CONCLUSION

1. Tweed, *Crossing and Dwelling,* 54.
2. Walk and Eskaran, "Ku Holo Mau."

Glossary

Definitions in quotation marks are from Mary Kawena Pukui and Samuel H. Elbert, *Hawaiian Dictionary.* Others reflect my own understanding of the concepts and how I use them in this book.

ʻaha	"sennit; cord braided of coconut husk, human hair, intestines of animals"
āholehole	a young stage of the Hawaiian flagtail fish found in fresh and salt water
ahupuaʻa	a pie-shaped land division that typically followed natural geographical markers (such as ridges and streams) stretching from inland mountains to the foreshore
ʻāina	land, earth; "that which feeds"
akua	god, deity, gods, the Christian God
aliʻi	general term referring to the ruling class under the indigenous governance structure
aloha	"love, affection, compassion, mercy, sympathy, pity, kindness, sentiment, grace, charity . . . loving . . . charitable"
ʻauwai	an irrigation system that carries water from a stream or river to the loʻi kalo
ʻawa	kava plant *(Piper methysticum).* The root is dried and ground to produce a mild narcotic used in ceremonies and social gatherings
hālau kālai waʻa	a long house used for canoe instruction and training
hale pili	house thatched with pili grass
hale waʻa	canoe house
haole	"white person, American, Englishman, Caucasian; . . . formerly, any foreigner; foreign, introduced, of foreign origin"
haumāna	student
Hawaiʻi nei	here in Hawaiʻi

he'e	octopus
heiau	temple
hele mai	to come toward the direction of the speaker
hihiawai	"the swamp fern *(Ceratopteris thalictroides)*, an edible, somewhat succulent fern . . . it grows in mud or water, as around taro patches"
ho'okupu	"ceremonial gift giving to a chief as a sign of honor and respect"
huaka'i	trip, visit, tour, voyage, journey
hui	association, organization; cooperatives established to buy ahupua'a
hukilau	a type of net fishing; literally, to pull rope. The Lā'ie community staged a hukilau for tourists to raise money to rebuild their chapel and later as a fundraiser for individual wards
hula	a general term related to dance and dancers
hula kahiko	ancient dance style (as contrasted with more contemporary styles)
inoa	"name, term, title"
inoa ho'omana'o	a name to commemorate an event or honor a person
kahiko	"old, ancient, antique . . . long ago, beforehand; to age; old person"
kahua	foundation, base
kahuna (kāhuna)	a priest, of the priestly class (priests); any kind of contemporary Christian priest
kahuna pule	a priest who can use prayer to take life
kai	sea, ocean
kalo	taro *(Colocasia esculenta);* a plant found throughout the Pacific and a staple food of the Hawaiian people. The kalo is believed to be the elder sibling of the Hawaiian people
kanaka (kānaka)	person (people); Hawaiian
Kanaka Maoli	real or true people; Hawaiian
Kanaka 'Ōiwi	people of the bone; Hawaiian
kāne	man, male, masculine
kapu	sacred; verbally encoded rules
kaula	rope
kīhei	a cloak; rectangular piece of fabric worn over one shoulder and tied in a knot, a ceremonial garment
kino lau	physical manifestations and embodiment of the akua
konohiki	a low-ranking ali'i who managed the resources of an ahupua'a and mediated the relationship between high-ranking ali'i and maka'āinana
kua'ana	elder sibling–younger sibling relationship
kūkū kane	grandfather
kula	school; plains or pastures between the mountains and the shore

kuleana	responsibility, accountability, authority. The Kuleana Act established the procedures by which maka'āinana could secure fee simple title to land
kumu hula	a source of knowledge about hula
kupuna (kūpuna)	"grandparent, ancestor, relative, or close friend of the grandparent's generation"; elder
lāhui	people, nation
lānai	porch, veranda, patio, balcony
lauhala	the leaf of a pandanus tree *(Panadanus odoratissimus)*; used for weaving
limu	"a general name for all kinds of plants living under water, both fresh and salt"
lo'i kalo	water garden for taro cultivation
lū'au	a feast; named for the leafy tops of the taro plant
mahalo	a statement of gratitude and thanks
māhele	to divide. The Māhele established a process by which the collective interests of the ali'i, government, and people would be divided and the principle of private property ownership would be instituted
maka'āinana	commoners; those who are the land's eyes
mālama	to care for
mālama 'āina	to care for the land as one would care for an older sibling
mālama kai	to care for the sea
mana	spiritual power and authority
mana'o	thoughts, idea, belief, theory, meaning, suggestions
marae	the buildings associated with a Māori community or tribe that serve as the spiritual and cultural center of the community
mele	song
mō'ī	highest-ranking ali'i
moku	a district of an island
mokupuni	island
mo'okū'auhau	genealogy
mo'olelo	story, history, account
na'au	the gut; the source of knowledge in the human body
noa	open, free from kapu
oli	chant
'ōpae	shrimp
'o'opu	"general name for fish included in the families Eleotridae, Gobiidae, and Blennidae. Some are in salt water near the shore, others in fresh water, and some said to be in either fresh or salt"

pae ʻāina	the chain of islands that comprise the Hawaiian archipelago
Papahānaumoku	She who births islands
piko	the navel or umbilical cord. There are three piko on the human body: the fontanel, which connects a person to the ancestors who came before; the navel, which connects a person to the living; and the reproductive organs, which connect a person to future generations
poi	made from cooked and pounded taro root, it served as a primary source of starch
pono	balance; appropriate behaviors or codes intended to create balance
puʻuhonua	place of refuge
tūtū wahine	grandmother (alternative spelling of kūkū)
waʻa	canoe
waʻa kaulua	double-hulled canoe used for open-ocean voyaging
wahine (wāhine)	woman (women); female; feminine
Wākea	Sky father

Bibliography

Aikau, Hokulani K. "Indigeneity in the Diaspora: The Case of Native Hawaiians at Iosepa, Utah." *American Quarterly* 62, no. 3 (September 2010): 477–500.

Alexander, M. Jacqui. "Erotic Autonomy as a Politics of Decolonization: An Anatomy of Feminist and State Practices in the Bahamas Tourist Economy." In *Feminist Genealogies, Colonial Legacies, Democratic Futures,* edited by M. Jacqui Alexander and Chandra Talpade Mohanty, 63–100. New York: Routledge, 1997.

Alfred, Taiaiake. *Wasáse: Indigenous Pathways of Action and Freedom.* Peterborough, Ontario: Broadview Press, 2005.

Anae, Melani. "Papalagi Redefined: Toward a New Zealand–Born Samoan Identity." In *Pacific Diaspora: Island Peoples in the United States and Across the Pacific,* edited by Paul Spickard, Joanne L. Rondilla, and Debbie Hippolite Wright, 150–68. Honolulu: University of Hawai'i Press, 2002.

Andrade, Carlos. *Hā'ena: Through the Eyes of the Ancestors.* Honolulu: University of Hawai'i Press, 2008.

Appadurai, Arjun. *Modernity at Large: Cultural Dimensions of Globalization.* Minneapolis: University of Minnesota Press, 1996.

Barman, Jean, and Bruce McIntyre Watson. *Leaving Paradise: Indigenous Hawaiians in the Pacific Northwest, 1787–1898.* Honolulu: University of Hawai'i Press, 2006.

Beamer, B. Kamanamaikalani. "Na Wai ka Mana? 'Ōiwi Agency and European Imperialism in the Hawaiian Kingdom." PhD dissertation, University of Hawai'i at Mānoa, 2008.

Beck, Raymond Clyde. "Iosepa: Hawaii's Zion." Photocopy of Typescript, n.d. Special Collection. Harold B. Lee Library, Brigham Young University, Provo, Utah.

Behdad, Ali. *Belated Travelers: Orientalism in the Age of Colonial Dissolution.* Durham, N.C.: Duke University Press, 1994.

Bendix, Reinhard. *Max Weber: An Intellectual Portrait.* Berkeley: University of California Press, 1977.

Benham, Maenette K. "The Voice 'Less' Hawaiian: An Analysis of Education Policy from 1820–1960." *Hawaiian Journal of History* 32 (1991): 121–40.

Blackhawk, Ned. *Violence over the Land: Indians and Empire in the Early American West.* Cambridge, Mass.: Harvard University Press, 2006.

Bray, Mark. "Education and the Vestiges of Colonialism: Self-Determination, Neo-colonialism, and Dependency in the South Pacific." *Comparative Education* 29, no. 3 (1993): 333–48.

Bringhurst, Newell G. *Saints, Slaves, and Blacks: The Changing Place of Black People within Mormonism.* Westport, Conn.: Greenwood Press, 1981.

———. "An Unintended and Difficult Odyssey." *Sunstone*, March 2003, 23–27.

Britsch, R. Lanier. *Moramona: The Mormons in Hawaii.* Lāʻie, Hawaiʻi: Institute for Polynesian Studies, Brigham Young University, 1989.

Bruner, Edward M. *Culture on Tour: Ethnologies of Travel.* Chicago: University of Chicago Press, 2005.

Burawoy, Michael. "Critical Sociology: A Dialogue between Two Sciences." *Contemporary Sociology* 27, no. 1 (January 1998): 12–20.

———. "The Extended Case Method." *Sociological Theory* 16, no. 1 (March 1998): 4–33.

Bushman, Claudia. *Contemporary Mormonism: Latter-day Saints in Modern America.* Westport, Conn.: Praeger Publishers, 2006.

Cannon, George Q. *My First Mission.* Faith Promoting Series. Salt Lake City, Utah: Juvenile Instructor Office, 1879.

———. "Journal of George Q. Cannon: Dictated by him to his son Clawson Y. Cannon while on his trip to Honolulu, Hawaii on the Fiftieth Anniversary of the Founding of the Hawaiian Mission," January 29, 1900. Pacific Islands Special Collection. Brigham Young University–Hawaiʻi Library.

Carroll, Peter N., and David W. Noble. *The Free and the Unfree: A Progressive History of the United States.* 3rd ed. New York: Penguin, 2001.

Chase, Lance D. "The Hawaiian Mission Crisis of 1874: The ʻAwa Rebellion Story." In *Voyages of Faith: Explorations in Mormon Pacific History,* edited by Grant Underwood, 71–88. Provo, Utah: Brigham Young University Press, 2000.

Chinen, Jon J. *The Great Mahele: Hawaii's Land Division of 1848.* Honolulu: University of Hawaiʻi Press, 1958.

Clifford, James. *Routes: Travel and Translation in the Late Twentieth Century.* Cambridge, Mass.: Harvard University Press, 1997.

Coates, Lawrence G. "Brigham Young and Mormon Indian Policies: The Formative Period, 1836–1850." *Brigham Young University Studies* 18, no. 3 (1978): 428–52.

Cole, William, and Elwin E. Jensen. *An Appendage to Israel in the Pacific: A Genealogical Text for Polynesia.* Salt Lake City, Utah: Church of Jesus Christ of Latter-day Saints Genealogical Society, 1961.

Compton, Cynthia D. Woolley. "The Making of the Ahupuaʻa of Lāʻie into a Gathering Place and Plantation: The Creation of an Alternative Space to Capitalism." PhD dissertation, Brigham Young University, 2005.

Cornell, Stephen, and Douglas Hartmann. "Conceptual Confusions and Divides: Race, Ethnicity, and the Study of Immigration." In *Not Just Black and White: Historical and Contemporary Perspectives on Immigration, Race, and Ethnicity in the United States,* edited by Nancy Foner and George M. Fredrickson, 23–41. New York: Russell Sage Foundation, 2004.

Corntassel, Jeff. "Toward Sustainable Self-Determination: Rethinking the Contemporary Indigenous-Rights Discourse." *Alternatives: Global, Local, Political* 33, no. 1 (2008): 105–32.

Cowan, Douglas E. "Theologizing Race: The Construction of 'Christian Identity.'" In *Religion and the Creation of Race and Ethnicity: An Introduction*, edited by Craig R. Prentiss, 112–23. New York: New York University Press, 2003.

Cowan, Richard O. "Temples in the Pacific: A Reflection of Twentieth-Century Mormon History." In *Voyages of Faith: Explorations in Mormon Pacific History*, edited by Grant Underwood, 129–46. Provo, Utah: Brigham Young University Press, 2000.

Cummings, David. W. *Centennial History of Laie, 1865–1965*. Lāʻie, Hawaiʻi: Lāʻie Centennial Committee, 1965.

Deloria, Vine Jr. *God Is Red: A Native View of Religion*. 30th Anniversary Edition. Golden, Colo.: Fulcrum Publishing, 2003.

Desmond, Jane C. *Staging Tourism: Bodies on Display from Waikīkī to Sea World*. Chicago: University of Chicago Press, 1999.

Diaz, Vicente M. "Moving Islands." In *Sovereign Acts*, edited by Frances Negrón-Muntaner. Boston: South End Press, 2011.

———. *Repositioning the Missionary: Rewriting the Histories of Colonialism, Native Catholicism, and Indigeneity in Guam*. Honolulu: University of Hawaiʻi Press, 2010.

Diaz, Vicente M., and J. Kēhaulani Kauanui. "Native Pacific Cultural Studies on the Edge." *Contemporary Pacific* 13, no. 2 (2001): 315–42.

Douglas, Norman. "The Sons of Lehi and the Seed of Cain: Racial Myths in Mormon Scripture and Their Relevance to the Pacific Islands." *Journal of Religious History* 8, no. 1 (1974): 99–104.

Embry, Jessie L. *Asian American Mormons: Bridging Cultures*. Provo, Utah: Charles Redd Center for Western Studies, Brigham Young University, 1999.

———. *Black Saints in a White Church: Contemporary African American Mormons*. Salt Lake City, Utah: Signature Books, 1994.

Fabian, Johannes. *Time and the Other: How Anthropology Makes Its Object*. New York: Columbia University Press, 1983.

Faludi, Susan. *Stiffed: The Betrayal of the American Man*. New York: William Morrow, 1999.

Farred, Grant. "The Unsettler." In "Settler Colonialism," special issue, *South Atlantic Quarterly* 107, no. 4 (2008): 791–808.

Ferre, Craig. "A History of the Polynesian Cultural Center's Night Show: 1963–1983." PhD dissertation, Brigham Young University, 1988.

Finney, Ben. *Sailing in the Wake of the Ancestors: Reviving Polynesian Voyaging*. Honolulu: Bishop Museum Press, 2003.

———. *Voyages of Rediscovery: A Cultural Odyssey through Polynesia*. Berkeley: University of California Press, 1994.

Fornander, Abraham. *An Account of the Polynesian Race: Its Origins and Migrations and the Ancient History of the Hawaiian People to the Times of Kamehameha I*. Vol. 1. London: Trubner and Co., 1878. Reprint, Whitefish, Mont.: Kessinger Publishing, 2007.

Frymer-Kensky, Tikva. "Biblical Voices on Chosenness." In *Covenant and Chosenness in Judaism and Mormonism*, edited by Raphael Jospe, Truman G. Madesen, and Seth Ward, 23–32. Madison, N.J.: Fairleigh Dickinson University Press, 2001.

García Canclini, Néstor. *Transforming Modernity: Popular Culture in Mexico*. Austin: University of Texas Press, 1993.

218   *Bibliography*

Goodyear-Ka'ōpua, Noelani. "Kū i ka māna: Building Community and Nation through Contemporary Hawaiian Schooling." PhD dissertation, University of California, Santa Cruz, 2005.

———. "Rebuilding the 'Auwai: Connecting Ecology, Economy, and Education in Hawaiian Schools." *AlterNatives* 5, no. 2 (2009): 46–77.

Gordon, Tamar G. "Inventing Mormon Identity in Tonga." PhD dissertation, University of California, Berkeley, 1988.

Grossberg, Lawrence. "On Postmodernism and Articulation: An Interview with Stuart Hall." In *Stuart Hall: Critical Dialogues in Cultural Studies,* edited by David Morley and Kuan-Hsing Chen, 131–50. New York: Routledge, 1996.

Habermas, Jürgen. *The Philosophical Discourse of Modernity: Twelve Lectures.* Cambridge, Mass.: MIT Press, 1990.

Hall, Stuart. "The Problem of Ideology: Marxism and Cultural Studies." In *Stuart Hall: Critical Dialogues in Cultural Studies,* edited by David Morley and Kuan-Hsing Chen, 25–46. New York: Routledge, 1996.

Halualani, Rona Tamiko. *In the Name of Hawaiians: Native Identities and Cultural Politics.* Minneapolis: University of Minnesota Press, 2002.

Haraway, Donna. *Simians, Cyborgs, and Women: The Reinvention of Nature.* New York: Routledge, 1991.

Harvey, Paul. "'A Servant of Servants Shall He Be': The Construction of Race in American Religious Mythologies." In *Religion and the Creation of Race and Ethnicity: An Introduction,* edited by Craig R. Prentiss, 13–27. New York: New York University Press, 2003.

Hau'ofa, Epeli. "Our Sea of Islands." In *A New Oceania: Rediscovering Our Sea of Islands,* edited by Eric Waddell, Vijay Naidu, and Epeli Hau'ofa, 2–16. Suva, Fiji: University of the South Pacific, 1993.

Heinerman, John, and Anson Shupe. *The Mormon Corporate Empire.* Boston: Beacon Press, 1985.

Howe, K. R. *The Quest for Origins: Who First Discovered and Settled the Pacific Islands?* Honolulu: University of Hawai'i Press, 2003.

Jacobs, Jane M. *Edge of Empire: Postcolonialism and the City.* New York: Routledge, 1996.

Jorgensen, Danny L. "Building the Kingdom of God: Alpheus Cutler and the Second Mormon Mission to the Indians." *Kansas History* 15, no. 2 (1992): 192–209.

Kamakau, Samuel. *Tales and Traditions of the People of Old: Na Mo'olelo a ka Po'e Kahiko.* Translated by Mary Kawena Pukui. Honolulu: Bishop Museum Press, 1991.

Kame'eleihiwa, Lilikalā. *Native Land and Foreign Desires: Pehea Lā E Pono Ai?* Honolulu: Bishop Museum Press, 1992.

Kaplan, Amy. "Manifest Domesticity." *American Literature* 70, no. 3 (1998): 581–606.

Kauanui, J. Kēhaulani. *Hawaiian Blood: Colonialism and the Politics of Sovereignty and Indigeneity.* Durham, N.C.: Duke University Press, 2008.

Kent, Noel J. *Hawaii: Islands under the Influence.* New York: Monthly Review Press, 1983.

Kirshenblatt-Gimblett, Barbara. *Destination Culture: Tourism, Museums, and Heritage.* Berkeley: University of California Press, 1998.

Kuper, Adam. *The Invention of Primitive Society: Transformation of an Illusion.* New York: Routledge, 1988.

Limerick, Patricia Nelson. *The Legacy of Conquest: The Unbroken Past of the American West.* New York: Norton, 1987.

Loveland, Jerry K. "Hagoth and the Polynesian Tradition." *BYU Studies* 17 (1976): 59–73.

Lucas, Paul F. Nahoa. "E Ola Mau Kākou I Ka ʻŌlelo Makuahine: Hawaiian Language Policy and the Courts." *Hawaiian Journal of History* 24 (2000): 1–28.

Lyman, Melvin A. *Out of Obscurity into the Light.* Salt Lake City, Utah: Albany Book, 1985.

MacCannell, Dean. *Empty Meeting Grounds: The Tourist Papers.* New York: Routledge, 1992.

Maffly-Kipp, Laurie F. "A Mormon President?" *Christian Century* 124, no. 17 (2007): 20–25.

Maffly-Kipp, Laurie F., and Reid Larkin Neilson, eds. *Proclamation to the People: Nineteenth-Century Mormonism and the Pacific Basin Frontier.* Salt Lake City: University of Utah Press, 2008.

Mauss, Armand L. *All Abraham's Children: Changing Mormon Conceptions of Race and Lineage.* Urbana: University of Illinois Press, 2003.

McAllister, Duncan. "Important Appeal to Native Hawaiians and Other Polynesians." *Improvement Era* 24 (April/June 1921): 703–12.

McClintock, Anne. *Imperial Leather: Race, Gender, and Sexuality in the Colonial Contest.* New York: Routledge, 1995.

Merry, Sally Engle. *Colonizing Hawaiʻi: The Cultural Power of Law.* Princeton, N.J.: Princeton University Press, 2000.

Mulder, William. *Homeward to Zion: The Mormon Migration from Scandinavia.* Minneapolis: University of Minnesota Press, 2000.

Mykkanen, Juri. *Inventing Politics: A New Political Anthropology of the Hawaiian Kingdom.* Honolulu: University of Hawaiʻi Press, 2003.

Nā Lei Naʻauao. "Education with Aloha." White paper by the Native Hawaiian Charter School Alliance. Accessed January 3, 2011. http://www.halaulokahi.com/images/stories/nln_white_paper_pdf8.pdf.

Noall, Matthew. *To My Children: An Autobiographical Sketch.* Salt Lake City, Utah: Matthew Noall, 1947. Pacific Islands Special Collection. Brigham Young University–Hawaiʻi Library.

Obeyesekere, Gananath. *The Apotheosis of Captain Cook: European Mythmaking in the Pacific.* Princeton, N.J.: Princeton University Press; Honolulu, Hawaiʻi: Bishop Museum Press, 1992.

O'Brien, Jean M. *Dispossession by Degrees: Indian Land and Identity in Natick, Massachusetts, 1650–1790.* Cambridge: Cambridge University Press, 1997.

O'Dea, Thomas. *The Mormons.* Chicago: University of Chicago Press, 1963.

Omi, Michael, and Howard Winant. *Racial Formation in the United States: From the 1960s to the 1990s.* 2nd ed. New York: Routledge, 1994.

Orgill, Von D. "President Orgill Welcomes PCC Alumni and Special Guests." *Imua Polynesia,* 40th Anniversary Edition, October 2003.

Osorio, Jon Kamakawiwoʻole. *Dismembering Lāhui: A History of the Hawaiian Nation to 1887.* Honolulu: University of Hawaiʻi Press, 2002.

Perkins, ʻUmi. "Teaching Land and Sovereignty: A Revised View." *Hawaiian Journal of Law and Politics* 2 (Summer 2006): 97–111.

Peterson, Derek R., and Darren Walhof. "Rethinking Religion." In *The Invention of Religion: Rethinking Belief in Politics and History,* edited by Derek R. Peterson and Darren Walhof. 1–18. New Brunswick, N.J.: Rutgers University Press, 2002.

Pratt, Mary Louise. *Imperial Eyes: Travel Writing and Transculturation.* New York: Routledge, 1992.

Prentiss, Craig R. "'Loathsome unto Thy People': The Latter-day Saints and Racial Categorization." In *Religion and the Creation of Race and Ethnicity: An Introduction,* 124–39. New York: New York University Press, 2003.

Preza, Donovan C. "The Empirical Writes Back: Re-examining Hawaiian Dispossession Resulting from the Mahele of 1848." MA thesis, University of Hawai'i at Mānoa, 2010.

Prince, Gregory A., and William Robert Wright. *David O. McKay and the Rise of Modern Mormonism.* Salt Lake City: University of Utah Press, 2005.

Pukui, Mary Kawena, and Samuel H. Elbert. *Hawaiian Dictionary: Hawaiian-English/ English-Hawaiian.* Rev. ed. Honolulu: University of Hawai'i Press, 1986.

Pukui, Mary Kawena, E. W. Haertig, and Catherine A. Lee. *Nānā I Ke Kumu: Look to the Source.* Vol. 1. Honolulu: Hui Hānai, 1972.

Ramstad, Mette. *Conversion in the Pacific: Eastern Polynesian Latter-day Saints' Conversion Accounts and Their Development of a LDS Identity.* Kristiansand, Norway: Norwegian Academic Press, 2003.

Rifkin, Mark. "Debt and the Transnationalization of Hawai'i." *American Quarterly* 60, no. 1 (March 2008): 43–66.

Rohrer, Judy. "Haole Girl: Identity and White Privilege in Hawai'i." *Social Process in Hawai'i* 38 (1997): 140–61.

Ross, Andrew. *The Chicago Gangster Theory of Life: Nature's Debt to Society.* New York: Verso, 1994.

Sahlins, Marshall. *How "Natives" Think: About Captain Cook, for Example.* Chicago: University of Chicago Press, 1995.

Shipps, Jan. "Difference and Otherness: Mormonism and the American Religious Mainstream." In *Minority Faiths and the American Protestant Mainstream,* edited by Jonathan D. Sarna, 81–109. Urbana: University of Illinois Press, 1998.

Silva, Noenoe K. *Aloha Betrayed: Native Hawaiian Resistance to American Colonialism.* Durham, N.C.: Duke University Press, 2004.

Silverman, David J. *Faith and Boundaries: Colonists, Christianity, and Community among the Wampanoag Indians of Martha's Vineyard, 1600–1871.* Cambridge: Cambridge University Press, 2005.

Small, Cathy A. *Voyages: From Tongan Villages to American Suburbs.* Ithaca, N.Y.: Cornell University Press, 1997.

Smith, Joseph Jr. *The Pearl of Great Price.* Salt Lake City, Utah: The Church of Jesus Christ of Latter-day Saints, 1981.

Spurrier, Joseph H. *Great Are the Promises unto the Isles of the Sea: The Church of Jesus Christ of Latter-day Saints in the Hawaiian Islands.* Honolulu: Hawai'i Honolulu Mission, 1978.

Stanton, Max. E. "A Gathering of Saints: The Role of the Church of Jesus Christ of Latter-day Saints in Pacific Islander Migration." In *A World Perspective on Pacific Islander Migration: Australia, New Zealand, and the USA.* Kensington: Center for South Pacific Studies, University of New South Wales, 1993.

———. "The Polynesian Cultural Center: A Multi-ethnic Model of Seven Pacific Cultures." In *Hosts and Guests: The Anthropology of Tourism*, edited by Valene L. Smith. 247–62. Philadelphia: University of Pennsylvania Press, 1989.

———. "Samoan Saints: Socio-cultural Change among the Samoan Immigrants in the Mormon Community of Laʻie, Hawaii." Unpublished paper, 1999.

Stauffer, Robert H. *Kahana: How the Land Was Lost*. Honolulu: University of Hawaiʻi Press, 2004.

Sterling, Elspeth P., and Catherine C. Summers, eds. *Sites of Oahu*. Honolulu: Bishop Museum Press, 1978.

Stover, Jeffrey S. "The Legacy of the 1848 Mahele and Kuleana Act of 1850: A Case Study of the Lāʻie Wai and Lāʻie Maloʻo Ahupuaʻa, 1846–1930." MA thesis, University of Hawaiʻi at Mānoa, 1997.

Sutton, Bruce S. *Lehi, Father of Polynesia: Polynesians Are Nephites*. Orem, Utah: Hawaiki Publishing, 2001.

Teaiwa, Teresia K. "Lo(o)sing the Edge." *Contemporary Pacific* 13, no. 2 (2001): 343–58.

Tengan, Ty Kāwika. *Native Men Remade: Gender and Nation in Contemporary Hawaiʻi*. Durham, N.C.: Duke University Press, 2008.

Thompson, Nainoa. "E Hoʻi Mau: Honoring the Past, Caring for the Present, Journeying to the Future." *Hūlili: Multidisciplinary Research on Hawaiian Well-Being* 4, no. 1 (2007): 9–34.

Trask, Haunani-Kay. *From a Native Daughter: Colonialism and Sovereignty in Hawaiʻi*. Rev. ed. Honolulu: University of Hawaiʻi Press, 1999.

Treat, James. *Native and Christian: Indigenous Voices on Religious Identity in the United States and Canada*. New York: Routledge, 1996.

Tweed, Thomas A. *Crossing and Dwelling: A Theory of Religion*. Cambridge, Mass.: Harvard University Press, 2006.

Underwood, Grant, ed. *Voyages of Faith: Explorations in Mormon Pacific History*. Provo, Utah: Brigham Young University Press, 2000.

Urry, John. *Consuming Places*. New York: Routledge, 1995.

Vizenor, Gerald. *Survivance: Narratives of Native Presence*. Lincoln: University of Nebraska Press, 2008.

Vogel, Dan. *Religious Seekers and the Advent of Mormonism*. Salt Lake City, Utah: Signature Books, 1988.

Waddoups, William M. "The Gospel of Jesus Christ in Polynesia." Radio transcript. Originally broadcast on KSL, Salt Lake City, Utah, October 3, 1937. Special Collection. Harold B. Lee Library, Brigham Young University, Provo, Utah.

Walk, Kamoaʻe, and Kawika Eskaran. "Ku Holo Mau." Devotional, Brigham Young University–Hawaiʻi, April 12, 2007. http://devotional.byuh.edu/video0070412.

Warner, Sam L. [Noʻeau] "The Movement to Revitalize Hawaiian Language and Culture." In *The Green Book of Language Revitalization in Practice*, edited by Leanne Hinton and Ken Hale, 133–44. San Diego, Calif.: Academic Press, 2001.

———. "Kuleana: The Right, Responsibility and Authority of Indigenous Peoples to Speak and Make Decisions for Themselves in Language and Cultural Revitalization." *Anthropology and Education Quarterly* 30, no. 1, (1999): 68–93.

Webb, Terry D. "Mormonism and Tourist Art in Hawaii." PhD dissertation, Arizona State University, 1990.

Weber, Max. *The Protestant Ethic and the Spirit of Capitalism.* New York: Charles Scribner's Sons, 1958.

———. "Religious Rejections of the World and Their Directions." In *From Max Weber: Essays in Sociology,* edited by H. H. Gerth and C. Wright Mills, 327–28. New York: Oxford University Press, 1946.

White, Geoffrey, and Ty Kāwika Tengan. "Disappearing Worlds: Anthropology and Cultural Studies in Hawai'i and the Pacific." *Contemporary Pacific* 13, no. 2 (2001): 381–416.

Williams, Leonard. "Althusser on Ideology: A Reassessment." *New Political Science* 27 (Winter 1993): 47–66.

Wineera, Vernice. "Selves and Others: A Study of Reflexivity and the Representation of Culture in Touristic Display at the Polynesian Cultural Center, Lā'ie, Hawai'i." PhD dissertation, University of Hawai'i at Mānoa, 2000.

Wolfe, Patrick. "Land, Labor, and Difference: Elementary Structures of Race," *American Historical Review* 106, no. 3 (2001): 866–905. Accessed May 7, 2009. http://www.historycooperative.org/journals/ahr/106.3/ah000866.html.

Index

Abel, 40
Abraham, 24, 31, 40, 46; book of, 39, 46
African American. *See* black people
ahupuaʻa, 55, 58, 60, 66, 71–72, 75–78, 84,
    168, 171, 182
Ahupuaʻa Hui, 76
ʻaikapu, 50
Aikau, Eddie, 177
Aikau, Ned, x, 150, 153, 159, 160
ʻāina, 3, 27, 56–60, 71, 75, 77, 87–89, 144,
    157, 182, 193n3
Akoi, Jay, 151–52
Alexander, M. Jacqui, 2
aliʻi, 50, 58–60, 75–76, 195n28; aliʻi nui,
    62–63
Aliʻi Lūʻau, 153, 154
Alma, 51; book in *Book of Mormon*, 42
Althusser, Louis, 126
Amaka, 119
Amana, 119
Amelale, 119
American Board of Commissioners for
    Foreign Missions, 12, 19, 21, 196n55
American culture, 11
American frontier, 6
anachronistic, 33, 94, 135; anachronistic
    space, 34
Andrade, Carlos, 57–58, 75
anthropology, 33, 47, 135, 197n5
Appadurai, Arjun, 139–41
Apuakehau family, 81

articulation, xi–xii, 1, 7, 28–29, 42, 171,
    178, 186; of Hawaiian, 55; of
    modernity, 27; Polynesian Mormon,
    xi, 165; rearticulations, 174; religious
    articulations, 182; theory of, 15–18
assimilation, 11, 29, 44, 88, 129, 141;
    projects, 169
Au, Thomas, 86–87, 93–94, 115–16
Aumua family, 117–18
ʻawa, 72, 76

Baldridge, Kenneth, 135
Ballard, Russell M., 161
baptism, 5, 26, 31, 37, 43–44, 46, 53, 61,
    197n1, 197n19, 198n36
Barenaba, Charles, 112–13, 115–17, 119,
    152
Barney, Ralph, 143, 148–49, 152
Bean, Max, 113–14
Beck, Raymond, 63
Behdad, Ali, 21
Beirstedt, Robert, 101
Bendix, Reinhard, 101
Benioni, Patoa, 138–39
Bigler, Henry William, 20, 23–24, 26
Blackhawk, Ned, 62
black people, xi, 32–34, 39–41, 52, 188,
    197n19; black Africans, 6, 35; black
    labor, 41; black members, 32, 35; black
    men, 39, 52; blackness, 33, 36–38, 41,
    43; black skin, 31, 37, 44. *See also*

lineage; priesthood; race; Wolfe, Patrick

Blackwell, Hiram, 20, 23

blood, 7, 34, 45, 50; bloodline, 33–34; tests, 45; ties, 142. *See also* Lost Tribe of Israel; Native Americans

Board of Commissioners to Quiet Land Titles (Land Commission), 58–60, 77

Book of Mormon, xi, 1, 4, 16–17, 24, 33, 35–44, 48–52, 66, 175–76, 194n1; translation of, 26

Bridges, Cy, 146–47, 149–50, 152, 155, 159, 160, 179

Brigham Young University, 121

Brigham Young University–Hawai'i, 13, 27, 146, 164, 167, 172, 174, 186; development of, 87; effects on migration, 4; former Brigham Young University–Hawai'i president, 161; Hawaiian studies at, 164, 167, 169–70, 182; mural at, 7; relationship to Polynesian Cultural Center, 125, 129–30, 132, 157–58. *See also* wa'a kaulua o *Iosepa*

Bringhurst, Newell G., 5, 35, 40, 43, 52, 188

British Israelism, 37–38

Britsch, R. Lanier, 24, 45, 63–66, 69, 71, 79, 82, 99, 102, 112

Buroway, Michael, 11

call, 151; called, 57, 81, 100, 103–4, 112–13, 120, 154; called to serve, 20, 37, 97, 100–101, 104, 109, 111, 148; calling, 52, 91–93, 97, 100–101, 104–5, 110–13, 148, 152, 193n4; to gather, 61. *See also* Labor Missionary Program; missionaries and missionary work

Cameron, Elliot, 144

Cannon, George Q., x, 1, 3, 14, 20–26, 28, 46, 174; obligation to stay in Hawai'i, 16–17; proselytize to Hawaiians, 32, 45, 53, 92. *See also* visions

Cannon, George Q., Jr., 118

capitalism, 12, 93–95, 101, 126, 134, 155; capitalist force, 183; capitalist modernity, 94–95; LDS church and, 57, 78, 156; plantation economy, 75;

society, 138; system, 21. *See also* ideology of faithfulness; Labor Missionary Program

Carolinian Navigation, 15, 165–66, 173

chosen: chosenness, 31–32, 34, 101; by God, 40–41, 123; people, x–xii, 2–3, 16, 31, 33, 43, 46, 48, 53, 55, 57, 64, 71, 81, 88, 89, 92, 125, 186; race, 35. *See also* Abraham; call; lineage

Church Building Committee, 98–100, 148

Church College of Hawai'i, 11, 205n14; construction of, 27, 79, 89, 97–98, 102, 104, 108, 115, 120, 148; effects on migration, 4; former president of, 144; site divinely chosen, 88; students and employment, 114, 129, 145. *See also* Labor Missionary Program

Church of Jesus Christ of Latter-day Saints (LDS Church), ix, 1, 4, 31, 129, 158, 194n1; history of, 2–3

citizenship, 2, 34, 41, 199n10

Clissold, Edward L., 83, 98, 109, 114, 118, 123, 129, 136, 147–48

Cluff, Benjamin, 73

Cluff, Harvey, 72, 76–77

Cluff, William W., 80

Cole, William, 45, 49–50

colonialism, 11–13, 195n28; anticolonial struggle, 28; colonial agent, 13; impositions, 59; legacy, 12, 88; outpost, 70; overtones, 56; project, 18, 41, 127, 194n2; relationships, 13, 195n28; religious traditions, xii; structures, 30, 141. *See also* capitalism; race

colonization, xii, 9, 71, 88, 129, 158, 200n43; decolonization, 28, 29. *See also* assimilation; racialization

colonized, 55, 107, 114

colony, 53, 64, 67, 195n28

color-blind approach to equality, 52

Compton, Cynthia, 72, 74, 77

Cook, James (Captain), 49, 58

Cook, Owen J., 99–100, 108

Cornell, Stephen, 141–42

Corntassel, Jeff, 177

covenant, 3, 31, 43, 46, 53, 55, 61, 193n4; of the priesthood, 47. *See also* chosen

Cowan, Douglas, 37–38
Cowan, Richard O., 80, 103
cultural preservation, 124, 144
culturalism, 140–41
culture: commodifying, 121; Hawai'i
culture, 12; performance of, 131;
perpetuation of, 137, 180, 182;
preservation of, 125, 144; profane
culture, 133; and race, 140; religion
and, 44; representation of, 144;
reproduction of, 134, 180; sacred
culture, 133; secular culture, 91;
transmission of, 133, 135
Cummings, David W., 66
Curtis, Namealoha, 172

Damuni, Emosi, 123–25, 132, 136–37,
145–46
Damuni, Sereima, 123
Darwin, Charles, 33–34; theory of, 39.
See also evolution
Daughtery, Thomas, 60, 65
Deloria, Vine, Jr., 171
Desmond, Jane, 127
Diaz, Vicente, 15, 29–30, 165–66, 173
dispossession, 18, 27, 59–60, 71, 145, 185.
See also Kuelana Act; Māhele
Dixon, John, 20, 23, 25–26
Douglas, Norman, 38, 47

education: college, 169; cultural, 28,
135–38, 144, 180; higher, 102;
religious, ix
Elbert, Samuel, 172
Embry, Jessie, 5
Enos, Ruby, 118. See also Polynesian
Cultural Center; Relief Society
Ephraim, tribe of, 35, 38
Eskaran, Kāwika, 159, 187
etak, 15, 165, 173
evolution: evolutionary paradigm, 127;
of humanity, 198n23; social evolutionists, 34, 38, 42; theory of, 33–34
expropriation, 18, 41, 164, 200n43

family Tree of Man, 34, 42, 198n23
Fanene, Ailama, 88
Fanene, Ann, 117

Fanene, Tom, 88, 117–18
Farred, Grant, 55, 64
Farrer, William, 20, 23, 26
Feinga, Sione, 108–12, 151–52, 153
Ferre, Craig, 148
Fiji, 42, 123, 137, 168; dances of, 138
Fijian Village, 123–24, 137
Finney, Ben, 177, 209n28, 209n39
Fornander, Abraham, 42
Frymer-Kensky, Tikva, 55

García Canclini, Néstor, 134, 138
gathering, 49; of all God's spirit children, 40; fervor of, 61; principle of,
20, 53, 56–57; purpose for, 57; of
Saints, 56, 61, 66; spirit of, 62; of Zion,
61, 65
gathering place, 56, 61–62; Iosepa, 56;
Lā'ie as, 4, 27, 64–67, 73; Mormon, 68;
for Native Hawaiian Latter-day Saints,
55, 63, 77. See also Zion
genealogy, 49, 51, 82, 165, 175; ancestry
and, 33; and anthropology, 47; and
The Book of Mormon, 48, 51; of the
Iosepa, 175; and lineage, 44; Māori,
47; of power, 34; story, x; venerated,
74
Gentile, 41, 61; nations, 35. See also
gathering place; Kingdom of God
Gibson, Walter Murray, 64
globalization, 133
Goo's store, 86
Grant, Heber J., 81

Ha'alelea, 62–63
Habermas, Jürgen, 81
Hagoth, 42–43, 52
Hālau kalai wa'a, 159
Hālau wa'a o Iosepa, 179, 180
Hall, Stuart, 2, 15–18
Ham, 40
Hammond, Francis A., 65–66, 68, 80
happy native, 124, 127, 129
Haraway, Donna, 30
Hartmann, Douglas, 141–42
Harvey, Paul, 41
Hau'ofa, Epeli, 172
Hawai'i Loa, 51

Hawaiian Mormon identity, 1, 13, 15, 55, 174, 182; consolidated, 3; manifestations of, xiii; naturalness of, 28
Hawkins, James, 20, 23, 26
Heinerman, John, 8, 95, 97
Hinckley, Gordon B., 153–54
Hōkūleʻa, 175–77, 179
House of Israel, 24, 43–44, 46–47, 53, 55, 80, 88, 186, 197n1
Howe, K. R., 42, 45, 209n39
Howland, Henry S., 60
huakaʻi, 14, 27–29, 185–86
Hukilau, 118, 129, 204n59

ideology of faithfulness, 2–3, 87–89, 113, 114, 118, 119, 121, 126, 136, 138, 146, 147, 152, 156, 188, 202n78, 206n23
ideology of universalism, 31–32, 43, 51; universalistic message, 5
inactive, xi, 145, 146, 193n4
indigenous: colonization and racialization, 156; creatures, 166; cultural rejuvenation, xii; customs and practices, 129; discourses, 75; intersection with Christianity, 13, 195n34, 195n35; knowledge, 169; land tenure system, 21, 57, 75; land use practices, 3; nationhood, 177; notions of gender, 178; people(s), 28, 158, 183; relationships to place, 11, 88; scholars, 158; self-determination, 13, 94, 166; space-time, 165; spirituality, 171; understandings of land, 77, 87; ways of knowing, 185. *See also* kapu
Institute for Polynesian Studies, 139
invention of religion, 19, 65; religious invention, 1
Iosepa (name), 158, 164–65; community in Utah, 165; place on island of Lānaʻi, 56, 62, 64, 67, 69; street, 81; translated as Joseph, 165
Iosepa Association, Board of Directors, 159, 161

Jacob, book of, 37
Jacobs, Jane, 56

James, Susan, 126
Jensen, Elwin, 45, 49–50
Jews, 42
Joseph, Tribe of, 35

Kahiki, 47, 49
kahua, 157
Kahuaola, 171, 182
Kailikea family, 81
Kakau, 60
Kaleohano, K. H., 174
Kalili, 119
kalo, 2, 13, 71–75, 77; familial relationship to, 57, 199n4; and gathering, 74; production, 3; and spirituality, 3. *See also* loʻi kalo
Kamai, Ezekial, 142–43
Kameʻeleihiwa, Lilikalā, 12, 19, 59, 63, 174–75
Kamehameha I, 9, 59
Kamehameha V, 47, 68
Kanahele, Clinton, 88
Kanahele, William, 107, 119–20
Kanaloa, 50
Kāne (akua), 49, 50; kāne (male), 178. *See also* waʻa kaulua o Iosepa
kapu, 58, 75, 170, 181; system, 19
Kauanui, J. Kēhaulani, 12, 15, 29–30, 166
Kauikeaouli (Kamehameha III), 58–59. *See also* Māhele
Kawahigashi, Viola, 84–86
Keeler, James, 20, 24, 26
Kekauoha family, 81
Kekauʻōnohi, 63
Kent, Noel, 108
Kimball, Heber C., 66
Kimball, Spencer W., 35, 40
Kingdom of God, ix, 7, 43, 61
konohiki, 58–63, 75, 200n28
Kū, 49, 50
kuaʻana, 58, 86
kuleana (responsibility), 10, 14, 29–30, 58–60, 62–63, 75, 156, 187
Kuleana Act, 58–59; awards, 59–60, 63; claims, 60; parcels, 73. *See also* Māhele
Kumuhonua, 49. *See also* Waddoups, William M.

Kuper, Adam, 33–34, 47
kupuna, 12, 13, 28, 132, 135, 164, 172–76, 181
Lāʻie: community, 67–68, 82–84, 101, 104, 118, 129, 148–49, 151, 153, 154, 157; Lāʻie Bay, 74, 159; Lāʻie Community Association, 164; Lāʻie Elementary School, 7, 82; new Lāʻie, 71, 115–16, 155; old Lāʻie, 57, 71, 82, 86–87, 115–16, 154–55; plantation, 20, 66, 68, 70, 84–85, 195n28; puʻuhonua, 11, 66; sacred place, 155; temple, 47, 81, 89; tram tour of, 130. *See also* ahupuaʻa; Hukilau; Promised Land
labor missionaries, 20, 27, 91, 99–100, 103; building the Polynesian Cultural Center, 120, 150–51; immigration, 114; mission home, 105–9; parents to, 104; Polynesian, 28, 93, 100, 109–13, 110, 116–17
Labor Missionary Program, 91–92, 97–102, 104, 108–9, 112–14, 120. *See also* Church Building Committee; Mendenhall, Wendell B.
lāhui, 59, 176, 178–79, 183, 188
Laman, 36, 43; Lamanites, 36–37, 43–44, 197n17. *See also* baptism; ideology of universalism
Land Commission. *See* Board of Commissioners to Quiet Land Titles
land tenure. *See* indigenous: land tenure system
LDS theology. *See* Mormon theology
Lehi, 24, 36, 38, 50
Leleiōhoku, 62–63
Lemuel, 36
Liahona High School, 99, 109, 121, 203n13. *See also* Church Building Committee; Labor Missionary Program; Pacific Board of Education
lineage, 27, 31, 33, 43, 45, 174–75, 198n36; discourses of, 3, 32–34; Hawaiian-Israelite, 17; hierarchy of, 39, 46; Israelite, 31, 36, 41; Mormon, 35; Nephite, 51; Polynesian, 1, 42;

racialization of, 40. *See also* genealogy
loʻi kalo, 3, 13, 60, 75, 84, 86–87, 121, 126, 182; and water, 72
loathsome people, 10, 36–37. *See also* race
Logan, Lono, 173
Logan family, 81
Lomu, Mosese, 110
Lono, 49, 50
Lost Tribe of Israel, 16, 38, 42. *See also* British Israelism; covenant; genealogy; House of Israel; lineage
Loveland, Jerry, 50–51
Lua, Agnes, 118
lūʻau, 124, 129, 131, 164; Aliʻi Lūʻau, 153–54; Germaine's Luau, 131. *See also* Hukilau
Lucas, Paul F. Nahoa, 83–84
Lunalilo, 60. *See also* Kuleana Act: awards; Lāʻie

MacCannell, Dean, 131–32
Maffley-Kipp, Laurie, 7
Māhele, 55–60, 63, 73, 185, 200n19; pre-Māhele, 75. *See also* indigenous: land tenure system
Maiava, 119
Majdali, Kathleen, 174
makaʻāinana, 50, 58–59, 75, 77, 87. *See also* Māhele
Makaliʻi, 158, 175–76
mālama, 58
mālama ʻāina, 87, 177
Mālama ʻĀina program, 168, 170–71, 178, 182–83, 187
mālama kai, 171, 178
Mālama Kai program, 168, 170, 182–83, 187
mana, 157, 174–75
Marsden, Samuel, 42
Matsuda's service station, 86
Mauss, Armand, 6, 34–35, 37–38
McAllister, Duncan, 47, 49
McClintock, Anne, 34, 197n5, 198n23, 203n31
McKay, David O., 7, 9, 96–98, 100–102, 154

Meha, Stuart, 80
Mendenhall, Wendell B., 98, 100, 109–10, 114, 118–19, 129, 135–37, 147–48. *See also* Church Building Committee
Merry, Sally Engle, 19
Meyer, Amoe, 82
militarization, 28
missionaries and missionary work: acquire land for settlement, 63–64, 65; Catholic, 12; civilizing discourses, 56–57, 62, 68, 93, 105–7; families, 69–70, 73, 82; as fellowship, 193n4; first ten missionaries to Hawai'i, 14, 16–17, 20–27, 22; to Hawai'i, x, 9, 10, 32; Hawaiian, 107, 111; history of, 5–6, 9; *Iosepa*, 175; Israelite lineage rationale for, 48, 52, 55, 65; journals of, 11; King Kamehameha V limits influence of, 68; as laborers, 74, 99, 102–3; migration, 98; operated the plantation, 84; proselytizing, 1, 99, 112, 116, 130; Protestant, 12, 21, 119–20, 196n55; at the Punalu'u home, 104; relationship to colonization and racialization, 158; return to Utah, 64, 67; separate schools, 69; and settlers, xii; and spatial struggles in Lā'ie, 56, 75, 115; success in Hawai'i, 5, 45, 62; superiority, 38; from Tonga and Sāmoa, 106, 108–9; universal message of, 3, 5, 7–8, 10, 32; and visions, xi; volunteer labor, 105, 150. *See also* baptism; British Israelism; Cannon, George Q.; labor missionaries; Labor Missionary Program; Polynesian Cultural Center
Mitchell, Fredrick A., 76
modern capitalism, 93, 95
modernity, 92, 131–32; articulation of, 27, 79; and capitalism, 93–95; fate of, 93–94; Mormonism and, 95; out of time in, 106, 127, 140; and rationality, 91; spiritual and material effects of, 92; and tradition, 94, 121. *See also* Habermas, Jürgen; Weber, Max
modernization, 79, 94–95, 99, 120–21; impact of, 115–16; and tradition, 91. *See also* modernity; Weber, Max
Moeai, Josephine, 154

mō'ī, 58–59, 200n28. *See also* Māhele
Mo'ikeha, Keakaokalani, 158. *See also* Makali'i
Mormon theology, 8; and Cannon's vision, 47; and Lamanites, 43; LDS theology and race, 32–34; and Polynesian Cultural Center, 145; and Polynesian lineage, 1. *See also* Laman: Lamanites; lineage; race
Mormonism, xii, 5, 17, 31, 36, 95, 194n1; alcohol and tobacco, 170; alternative future for, 188; American nationalism, 18; and American patriotism, 7; blacks and, 52; contemporary, 5, 52; faithful to, 2; Hawaiianness and, 1, 3, 16, 29, 55, 67, 187; image of, 4; and indigenous culture, xii, 47; narrative map of, 35; Native Hawaiian self-determination, 158; persecution of, 8; religious tradition, xii, 24, 40; universalism, 51. *See also* British Israelism; lineage; racial ideology
Morris, Thomas, 20, 25
Moses, book of, 39–40. *See also Pearl of Great Price*
Mulder, William, 61
Mykkanen, Juri, 19

Nainoa family, 81
Nakayama store, 85
Nālimanui, 23–24, 45
Nāpela, Jonathan H (Jonatana), 26, 69, 174; Center for Hawaiian Language and Cultural Studies, 27, 157. *See also* Wallace, William K.
Native Americans: blacks and, 32, 34; curse of blackness, 38; descendants of Lamanites, 37; the fallen, 41; lineage of, 198n36; missionary work and, 5; Polynesians and, 33, 42; and race, 10, 33, 39. *See also* Laman: Lamanites; lineage; loathsome people; Nephites; race
Nawahine, 119
Nebeker, George, 65, 69, 76
Nephi, 36, 43, 47, 51
Nephites, 36–7, 42–44, 197n17, 198n36
Nibley, Charles W., 80

Niko, Vailine Leota, 81–83, 87, 116
Noall, Matthew, 61, 78–79, 99

Oceania, 17, 42, 142, 154; division of,
    194n2; future of, 173; racial classifi-
    cations, 45
O'Dea, Thomas F., 6, 10
Omi, Michael, 52
Orgill, Von D., 155
Osorio, Jonathan Kay Kamakawiwoʻole,
    12, 20

Pacific Board of Education, 98–99, 148
Paishon, Chadd, 176
panoptical time, 34
Papahānaumoku, 51, 57
paradise: Hawaiʻi as, 127
Paradise Cove, 131
Partridge, Edward, 74–75
Pearl of Great Price, 33, 35, 39–40
persecution, ix; of Mormons and
    Mormonism, 8, 71; in Palestine, 48;
    refuge from, 61–63. *See also* gathering;
    Kingdom of God
Peterson, Derek, 19
Piailug, Mau, 175, 177, 179, 186
pioneer(s), ix, 6, 63–63
plantation: Asian immigrant workers,
    82; company town, 84–87; economic
    support of the mission, 57, 72, 74–75,
    78; economy to tourism, 108–29;
    house, 73; Kahuku Plantation, 70, 79,
    84; labor, 74, 99; Lāʻie Plantation, 65–
    66, 68, 70, 195n28; Lāʻie plantation
    manager, 20, 77, 79, 114; moderniza-
    tion, 79; sugar plantation, 23, 74, 77,
    104. *See also* Lāʻie: old Lāʻie
Poire, Nāpua Stevens, 143–44
Polk, James K. (president of United
    States), 6
Polynesian Cultural Center, 98, 123, 128;
    authentic replica, 126; blurred bound-
    aries between work and religion, 149,
    153, 155; commercial enterprise, 181;
    cultural education, 134–35, 137–39,
    142, 180; cultural experts, 117, 133,
    147; cultural preservation, 124, 143–
    44; culture object for tourism, 157;

159; development project, 27, 97;
    doors open, 11; ethnographic tourism,
    130; family atmosphere, 124; financial
    support to students, 139; fortieth
    anniversary, 153; ideology of faithful-
    ness, 125; *Iosepa* exhibit, 179, 181, 183;
    labor missionaries, 109–13, 151;
    meaning of culture, 140; more than
    a job, 28, 30, 128, 133, 150–51, 153,
    156; Oral History Program, 132,
    205n23; power struggles, 114–16, 118,
    149, 152; President Hinckley, 154–55;
    quality of performance, 144; replaced
    loʻi, 13, 86–87, 115, 121; sells race to
    tourists, 127; spiritual and cultural
    significance, 136, 147; symbol of
    progress, 91; tourist facility, 4. *See also*
    call; happy native; race: sell(ing); spirit
    of aloha; tourists and tourism
Polynesian culture: competing meanings
    of, 125; educate workers about, 135;
    embrace, 142–43; material objects of,
    131; preservation, 13, 117, 124, 139,
    144; representation of, 127–28, 130,
    143. *See also* Polynesian Cultural
    Center; tourists and tourism
Polynesian Voyaging Society, 175. *See
    also* Hōkūleʻa
pookof, 165–66
Poulson, Noe, 142
Poulson, Richard, 133–35, 138–39,
    141–42
Pratt, Addison, 47
Pratt, Louise, 47
Pratt, Mary Louise, 107, 114
Prentiss, Craig, 10, 3. *See also* loathsome
    people; Native Americans
Preza, Donovan, 60, 200n19. *See also*
    Māhele
priesthood, 2, 20, 24, 35, 39, 205n23;
    authority of, 32, 197n1; and black
    men, 6, 51–52; covenant of, 47; power
    of, 67. *See also* black people: black
    members; race
primitive: and anthropology, 33, 197n5;
    and evolution, 39; ex-primitive, 131,
    133; fossilized, 137, 142; ideal primi-
    tive, 127; versus modern, 131–32; and

Native Americans, 38; native as, 140; Polynesian as, 128; primitivistic performance, 132; societies, 33–34; village, 66

Prince, Gregory, 96

private property, 18, 34, 59, 62; land as, 87; ownership, 21, 69, 77; tenure system, 75. *See also* Māhele

Promised Land, 4, 67, 79, 87; for a chosen people, 81; in the Pacific, 56, 62, 88; Polynesian Cultural Center as, 136. *See also* Lā'ie temple; pu'uhonua

Pualoa-Ahuna, Gladys, 174

Pukui, Mary Kawena, 164, 172, 193n5

Pulotu, Sione Tuione, 159, 168

pu'uhonua (place of refuge), 11, 55, 66–67, 68, 72, 88, 92, 185. *See also* Lā'ie

race, 194n22; British, 37–38; categories of, 10, 37, 140–42; chosen, 35; culture and, 140; and gender, 103–4, 127, 188, 205–6n23; in LDS theology, 32, 34, 37; lens of, 143; in Oceania, 45, 50; performing, 125, 127–28; politics of, 10; problem of, 52; sell(ing), 127–29, 140, 143, 156; universalistic message and, 5. *See also* color-blind approach to equality; haole; ideology of universalism; lineage; loathsome people; Omi, Michael; Winant, Howard

racial and religious boundaries, 1, 32–33, 35

racial assumptions, 32, 43, 45

racial binaries, 37, 44

racial bodies, 127

racial classifications, 45

racial discourse, 3, 6, 18, 31, 33, 42, 52, 128, 140–41

racial diversity, 5

racial dynamics, xi, 10

racial exclusion, 31, 39

racial formation, 16, 43, 186

racial hierarchy(ies), 4–5, 16, 35, 52–53, 103, 186

racial ideology, 6, 10, 51, 188

racialization, 10, 11, 28, 31–32, 35, 40–41, 126, 128, 193n3; of indigenous people, 158; of the Native, 140; process, 197n17; religious, 33. *See also* Omi, Michael; Winant, Howard

racial lexicon, 10

racial meanings, 41

racial minority, xi

racial policies, xi, 33, 35, 41, 105

racial politics, xii

racial project, 10, 124, 127, 194n2

racial social imaginary, 16

racial superiority, 5, 35, 38–39

racial tensions and contradictions, 2

racial triangulation, 41

Racule, Isireli, 123

Raymond, George, 70

regeneration, 13, 157, 182–83; cultural, 179, 182, 185; of Hawaiian cultural practice, 169; of indigenous livelihoods, 177; of Polynesian seafaring traditions, 172

Relief Society, 118–19. *See also* Hukilau; Polynesian Cultural Center

religious innovation, 32–33

religious rationalization, 92

Robinson, Louise, 104, 106–8, 111

Robinson, Owen, 105–7, 111

Ross, Andrew, 130–32

Sadowski, Kanale, 167

Salt Lake City temple, 80, 96, 147

salvation, 2, 7, 32, 37, 53, 65, 68, 197n1; blessing of, 39, 43, 46; eternal, xii, 40, 46; of Hawaiian members, 69; ineligible for, 41; plan of, 3, 40. *See also* baptism

Sāmoan(s), 71, 82, 87–88, 119, 127, 129; build the Polynesian Cultural Center, 117; fale, 124; imitate Fijians, 143; laborers, 104, 114; language, 84; migration, 10, 81, 83; section of night show, 151

Samuel, son of Lehi, 36

Sandwich Islands Mission, 20–27. *See also* missionaries and missionary work

savage, 6; noble, 41; staged savagery, 131

scientific racism, 34, 41, 127, 198n23
Sells, Jude, 171, 172–73
service of the Lord, 3, 21, 26, 61, 126
service to the Lord, 21, 32, 101, 121, 125, 148
Shipps, Jan, 20, 36
Shumway, Eric B., 161
Shupe, Anson, 8, 95, 96–97
Silva, Noenoe K., 12
Sing, Ron, 9
Sing, Wendy, 9
skin color, 31, 40, 43–45, 141, 198n19; white-skinned, 37. *See also* black people; lineage; race
Small, Cathy, 109, 111
Smith, Joseph. *See* Smith, Joseph, Jr.
Smith, Joseph, Jr., ix, 4, 9, 25, 32, 33, 35, 38–39, 41, 56, 61, 95–96, 165, 194n1, 197n1, 202n5
Smith, Joseph F., xii, 28, 80, 161, 165, 174
Smoot, Reed, 80
Snow, Lorenzo, 67, 78
Solomon, biblical king, 37
spirit of aloha, 132, 155
Spurrier, Joseph F., 66–67, 69
Stanton, Max, 10, 61, 109, 117, 119
Stauffer, Robert H., 72, 73
Stone, Howard, 115
Stone, Rita, 115
Stover, Jeffrey, 60, 71, 77, 201n47
sustainable self-determination, 18, 29, 158–59, 177, 179, 182
Sutton, Bruce S., 44–45, 51, 198n36

Tahitian(s), 47–48, 127, 139; section of night show, 142
Taurima, Tommy, 143
Taylor, John, 74
temple: and building projects, 112–14; dedication of, 81; and employment, 84; Hawai'i, 80–81, 120; LDS, 147; of God, 80; records, 51; visitors' center, 130; work, 80–81. *See also* ideology of faithfulness; Lā'ie; Smith, Joseph F.; Salt Lake City Temple
Tengan, Ty Kāwika, 12, 50, 178
Thompson, Nainoa, 176–77

Tongan(s), 109, 111, 159, 167
tourists and tourism, xii, 108, 144, 170, 181; the church and, 117–18, 147; cultural, 124, 137; desire, 140; economy, 2, 28, 93, 105, 108, 129, 180; enticement of, 150; ethnographic, 130–31, 140; facilities, 3–4, 128–30, 143, 152–54, 180; global, 11, 159, 168, 183; in Hawai'i, 5, 127–32, 140; Polynesian Cultural Center and, 123–33, 137, 155–57; religion and, 124–26, 145, 153; seduced by, 130. *See also* Hukilau; Mormon theology; race
Trask, Haunani-Kay, 12, 58, 126–27, 178
Treat, James, 13
Tweed, Thomas, 11, 14, 15, 186

Uaua, William, 174
Uelu, 119
Utah: *Iosepa* crew members from, 167, 172; migration to, 134, 153, 165; Polynesian community in, 185. *See also* Iosepa

visions, xi, 56; of angels, 14; associated with the Church College of Hawai'i, 88; associated with the temple, 80; Cannon's vision, x, 1, 3, 16–17, 24–26, 32–33, 42–43, 45–47, 64, 92, 174, 176; and innovation, 24, 32, 43; as rationale for Lā'ie, 66–67
voyaging canoe, xii, 27, 158, 166, 175–76, 208n6, 209n39. *See also* Hōkūle'a; Makali'i; wa'a kaulua o Iosepa

wa'a kaulua o Iosepa, xii, 27–28, 157–59, 162–63, 168, 179, 186–87. *See also* Iosepa
Waddoups, William M., 48–49
Wākea, 51, 57
Walhof, Darren, 19
Walk, Kamoa'e, 186–88
Wallace, William K. (Uncle Bill), 157, 159, 161, 164–65, 168–70, 172, 178, 187
Webb, Terry, 145, 147

Weber, Max, 91–95, 101
whiteness, 9–10, 33, 37–38, 41, 197n17;
   and Nephites, 43. *See also* race; skin
   color
Whittle, Thomas, 20, 24
Williams, Leonard, 126
Winant, Howard, 52
Wineera, Vernice, 135, 140, 144
Wolfe, Patrick, 41
Woodbury, John Stillman, 80
Woodruff, Wilford W., 78

Woolley, Samuel Edwin, 78–79
Wright, William, 96

Young, Brigham, ix, 6, 20, 35, 39, 41, 47,
   61, 65–66, 68–69, 80, 96
Yuen, Mikilani, 172

Zion, 20, 53, 66, 99; gathering of, 51;
   New Zion, 62; in the United States, 9.
   See also gathering; Lā'ie
Zion's Security Corporation, 115, 147

HOKULANI K. AIKAU is associate professor of political science at the University of Hawaiʻi at Mānoa. She is coeditor of *Feminist Waves, Feminist Generations: Life Stories from the Academy* (Minnesota, 2007).